Contents

Haltwhistle and Beyond

John Parker

ISBN   1 901237 24 9

Published by TUPS Books, 30, Lime Street,
Newcastle upon Tyne, NE1 2PQ
Tel No: 0191 233 0990 Fax: 0191 233 0578

Preface

To most strangers travelling these days between Newcastle and Carlisle, Haltwhistle might hardly exist any more. The by-pass has been a boon in some ways of course, keeping fast traffic out, but in the other balance must be weighed not only the losses to local tradespeople, but also the virtual burying of a large chunk of colourful history. Not only the story of Roman times and the Border Troubles, but of a fascinating era of industrial life.

Fortunately the wealth of its recent past has now been unearthed, as surely as the coal the area once lived upon, by John Parker. Sadly he did not long outlive his century, but what a century it was, and how well the man knew and loved it!

To say that John Parker was acquainted with everyone in the Haltwhistle district is hardly an exaggeration: certainly he knew everyone worth knowing. He also seems to have known every nut, bolt, wheel and engine ever employed round about in mining, transport, farming and engineering. For John's great passion was for things mechanical. To some this can be a dry subject, but he had the wonderful gift of telling with humour the story of the men who made, worked and loved these machines almost as much as he did himself. Men like the late Jake Johnson of Coanwood, who I'm sure would have invented the wheel as well as the internal combustion engine and the flying machine if he had been around that far back, and if he had had John Parker to help him.

I had the privilege of knowing both Jake and John Parker. Both were most kind and helpful to me, and patient and understanding of someone who can hardly even yet tell a nut from a bolt.

John in particular gave me a great deal of assistance when, back in the seventies, I was making a BBC film about coal-mining in the area, based on (and down) the Wrytree Colliery. In this book he reveals not only a truly wonderful recall of his fascination with the mining way of life, but of his deep love for his native area and its folk, and his gift for writing it. Haltwhistle now has a record unsurpassed by places far better known, by-passed or not. And just in time...

David Bean

Acknowledgements

We would like to thank the following people for their help, advice, photographs and patience:

Derek Armstrong, Gerald Armstrong, Ross Bainbridge, Alan Banks, Gordon Banks, Jean Banks, David Bean, Jonty Bell, Pedro Bell, Sam Blackburn, Julie Brooks, Alan & Anne Burns, Heidi Burns, Ethel Burns, John Caldwell, John Carrick, Elaine Coates, Peter Cowan, Thelma & Clive Dixon, Mr Dodd of Langley, Freda Gents, Marlene Henderson, Mark Henderson, Ted Heslop, Alan Hewitson, Pat Howe, Ian Hunter, Margaret Hunter, Robert Hunter, Colin Keen, Joe Keen, Eric & Heather Laidlow, John Lattimer, Kenneth & Peggy Lattimer, Cathy Parker, John Parker (jnr.), Barry & June Reed, Ken Rickerby, Clive Seal, Ivan Seymour, Susan & Richard Sim, Billy Treloar, David & Ruth Watson, Eric & Shirley Watson, Isobelle West, Anna Williams, Eleanor & Richard Wilson.

We are extremely grateful for the generosity and trust shown by the people who have lent us their precious photographs. We have by no means exhausted the supply and intend to compile another book, which will be a photographic record of Haltwhistle. If anyone has photographs that they think may be of interest, we would be pleased to hear from you.

Introduction

The author in his 20s. (T Dixon)

This is an account of my life in and about Haltwhistle and Redpath; it is also a tribute to the industrious inhabitants of the West Northumbrian town known locally as Hodissel, its ancient pronunciation. Within 20 miles of the Scottish border and on the east side of the watershed between east and west coasts, the town is situated on the north bank of the South Tyne, where this river changes course from a northerly direction to flow east to the North Sea. Two miles to the north the Great Whin Sill breaks the surface in the form of a north-facing cliff across the country in an east-west direction; these whinstone crags were utilised by Emperor Hadrian's builders as a good foundation for the central part of their Roman Wall.

I was born just before the large mines closed so unfortunately saw none of these earlier pits in full production. The working population reached a peak in the 1920s, followed by pit closures in the early 1930s, the cause of much hardship and unemployment which forced many miners to move away to other, expanding coalfields.

However, some were employed in building the new Smith and Walton paint works; coincidentally, a few of the men had previously worked in that same factory area, but 600 feet below in the South Tyne Colliery workings. For a short time coal was mined in that area underground at the same time that the factory building was taking place on the surface.

From the early 1930s I have kept my eyes and ears open to local developments and as a result, this book is based mostly on my own experience, but also on many a gud crack with local folk skilled in the Haltwhistle tradition of talking the night away.

I am most grateful to my wife Dorothy, who managed to put in order my accumulation of notes, some faded with age and invariably scribbled in my native language; we hope that readers will enjoy looking through this book as much as I did 'ratching' things out over the years.

Chapter One

John Parker, the author's father, stands at the front of the now demolished Bastle house at Redpath. According to the door-head date, the windows and the door had been added to the solid walls in the 1700s. The basement, or byre, floor was seven feet lower than the stone paving shown on the yard surface. Inside a 'modern' Yorkshire cooking range was fitted and the roof renewed with blue Welsh slates in about 1900.

The most important event in the late 1920s, from my point of view, was my first appearance in the district at Redpath, over a mile to the west of Haltwhistle, in an old Bastle house with a cow byre underneath, all now unfortunately demolished. The midwife was either district nurse Riddle, Battle or Schollick, with neighbours Mrs Edgar and Mrs Hall doing their bit.

All drinking water was carried in buckets a long distance from Jackson's Well in the middle of a pasture field, so my coming into the world during a February snow-storm must have caused a lot of extra work.

Farmer Hugh Edgar, who lived nearby, was on maternity duty that night to attend one of his Shorthorn cows which was about to calve. He walked from the farmhouse to the byre periodically to check on Daisy's progress and on one trip he heard through the snow-storm the first cries from our house and thought: 'By Goy, yon's a grand pair o' lungs.'

I sometimes wonder how the district nurse managed to get home the mile and a half to Haltwhistle on that snowy night; the last bus to Haltwhistle - the ten o'clock - would be long gone.

Redpath hamlet was then, and is now, quiet and peaceful: an idyllic place for children, although according to history books, it wasn't always so, but that was before my time. A new house was built in about 1940, attached to one of the original cottages to make one farmhouse. By that time, the number of habitable dwellings had been reduced to four; our old house which stood empty for some years, was demolished in the 1960s; the only one to have any significant historical value and they had to knock it down. Mother, who died in 1942, would have thought of it as a blessing, getting rid of the draughty old place.

Father regarded the proposed knocking down of his ancestral home as an act of vandalism but he died in 1948, so never saw it happen, although if he could have seen how it was carried out, his 'tash' would have twitched. Hugh Edgar reckoned the landlord's estate workmen dismantled the two upper storeys, but when it came to the lower byre walls, a certain council worker from Bank Foot removed the stonework, piece by piece, even sorting through the lime mortar. This was a slow process and after the walls were cleared away, he dug up the cobbled byre floors and stalls. Presumably, he handled every stone in the lower half of the building and as some of them were massive - as heavy as two or three hundredweights each - he must have put in a lot of hard work.

Hugh's brother Harry asked in passing, if he had lost something but the council worker just grunted and carried on. Apparently this worker had heard that Father had built a box of gold sovereigns into the inside wall of the byre, then had suffered a lapse of memory. Harry and Hugh knew about this tale and guessed what was going on, so they let him get on with it.

The Edgars had one advantage over the digger: they knew how much of the story was true and how much Father had 'leaked' for a bit of fun. Father had indeed hidden the money in the byre walls before he went into hospital for an operation - this was before he married - but he changed his mind in hospital and thought it wasn't a good idea to bury his money, so he gave a friend precise instructions on how to retrieve the box and keep it safe. The friend, with the help of the Edgars, did this and Father got it back when he came out of hospital.

Eventually the story about hiding the money spread round the district - but not the part about recovering it. This is what they called making their own amusement, although the council man was far from amused.

For some reason, the houses at Redpath were spread out over a long distance to the top of Currys Hill, just as if none of the occupants liked to be near their neighbours and preferred to be on their own. Ours and Edgars' farmhouse stood on opposite sides of the road, but the others, apart from Halls' house which had a basement used as a flat under it, were well spaced out over more than a quarter mile.

Our bastle house would have had a preservation order applied had it stood a few more years but, like Haltwhistle's Musgrave Tower, the Melkridge village green house and others, it was demolished before the public realised what they were losing.

Growing up in the 1930s, I never dreamed that one day our house would be gone; it was built like a fortress, with stone walls three feet thick. The lower part, built as a cow byre, supposedly to protect the cattle from marauding Scots, had a stone-cobbled floor and stalls for ten cows of slimline proportions; the two-feet-wide doorway on the north side, must have restricted the size of cows that could be housed. I used to wonder what happened if the cows fattened up during their stay in the byre: did they have to be starved to get them out?

Musgrave Tower shortly before demolition. (E Coates)

Another two-feet-wide doorway in the East gable was built up prior to my explorations and was thought to be there for access to the stackyard or field, in what eventually became our large garden. A third and wider most mysterious doorway was built up in the rear byre wall which was directly below the windows and door of the house above. When we bairns first saw this rear doorway, we imagined that it led to another dungeon under Currys Hill - all kinds of treasure might be hidden there.

This secret tunnel would have been under our yard, which was about seven feet above the byre floor level but as later events proved, it appears it was only in our imagination. Many years later we reckoned that the ground surface originally had been almost level round all four sides of the building and the yard had been filled up to a new house doorstep level, with a sloping road down the west gable end; perhaps fattened cows came out of the wider south side door before this was built-up.

Above the byre, the supports for the living room floor were fifteen-feet-long oak trees, roughly chopped out by adze or axe to an eight-inch-square section. These were spaced out at two-feet centres over the twenty feet or so inside length of the building and two-feet wide stone flags laid over the oak beams to form the floor surface. Lime mortar was used to bed down the flag stones on the beams; the spanning joints between the stones were a plain butt contact, no jointing material appeared to have been used; the aroma seeping through from ten or twelve cows down below can only be imagined.

It was thought that the first people to live above the byre, before the south side windows and door were added in the 1700s, probably used the byre door, which still had brackets and holes in the walls for slotting in strong iron bars, then climbed a step-ladder, which would allow far more smells to come up but the place would be quite secure and warm.

The cows had long departed before I started crawling and the byre was used mainly as a firewood store but I now realise that it also held many relics of the past, kept because they might 'come in handy some day'. Most of the wooden cow-stall divisions were gone and some of the timber had been used as supports under the oak beams, which helped to steady the floor, although as we grew older, and heavier, we could still make the ornaments rattle on the sideboard by jumping about on the floor. This was very entertaining while it lasted but a display of pewter plates decided to crash down one day and I got the blame for it.

The pewter plates were set up on edge in what Father called a Welsh dresser and what I remember as a rather unstable wobbly plate rack, fitted atop of the long oak sideboard, and it took very little vibration to send the contents flying. There were in the house over twenty of these sixteen-inch-diameter pewter plates, but only twelve could be displayed in the racks; even so, the glorious clatter that they made when they came down was unbelievable. The two grandfather clocks in opposite corners of the room

The author and big sister Anne Parker.

never worked properly and no wonder, they would always be shifting 'off balance' with all the jumping about.

A disadvantage of the flagged floor was its ability to 'swallow up' our marbles when we played indoors. The marbles often disappeared through a small gap under the sideboard and we had to borrow Mother's long, hooked fire poker to retrieve them.

We were not always successful and it was some time before we discovered that one of the flagstones under the sideboard had a corner broken off and this allowed the marbles to roll down into the byre below. An expedition was organised. Out of the house door we went, each clutching a candle; down the yard, round the gable end, opened the creaking door and crept into the dark byre where we gathered up most of the lost marbles from among the heaps of firewood near the door. After a quick sortie up to Currys Hill field to scoop a handful of clarty clay to stem the hole in the floor under the sideboard, play was resumed.

A grand pantry, or larder, was formed inside the three-feet-thick east gable end wall and being about two feet deep left about a foot thickness of wall at the back. Most of the shelves were two-inch-thick stone slabs built into the walls; neither windows nor ventilators were fitted but everything seemed to keep well enough. On one occasion Mother unintentionally burst a new bag of flour as it dropped into the metal flour bin - and gave us a bit of a fright when she emerged from the dark pantry, all white-faced and ghost-like.

The black iron oven range in the west gable wall heated the sizeable room, cooked our food and heated the washing water in the set-pot. There was no date on the range to indicate when it had been manufactured, but remembering how it was constructed, I would say about 1900, a much more modern addition than anything else about the house apart from the slate roof.

It was thought that the wide living room window, with the bedroom window above, was formed facing south on to the higher yard, at the same time as the doorway with its stone jambs and dressed stone lintel, marked 1786, had been added. If the wide window sill had been cleared of aspidistras etc., a body could quite easily have stretched out flat and slept on it. We youngsters played on it more than once with disastrous results for the odd geranium and pots. None of these south-facing openings could

Fire-irons and cauldron hook support as used in the Redpath house.

be seen from the road and most people thought this building with only a single door on the road side was a barn belonging to the nearby farm.

Originally there would have been an open hearth fire with a 'bak steean' for baking bread, barley bannocks, oatcakes, etc.; I remember that when the range fire was out, I could lean into the fire opening to look up the massive chimney and see clouds moving across the sky. The daylight on sunny days, coming down the chimney, always lightened up the coal shelf on the back of the fire, and heavy rain often hissed and steamed in the flames.

I never knew the dimensions of the chimney but I could have climbed up had there been anything to hold on to. There was only one bar fitted across the flue, to carry the cauldron creuck, which was used when cooking the sheep's head broth or soup. I can still remember the smell of that broth and Tommy Hall often had a sniff of it as it wafted up to his house on the hill.

The fire range was sometimes fired with wood, which might be fallen branches, old fence posts or the trimmings off the tree tops when felling was in progress, but it was a never-ending job, keeping the fire up to heat, whereas coal was slower-burning and could be stored on the brick shelf at the back of the fire, to be drawn forward when necessary, using what we called the collar, or coal rake, and what the Edgars, who came originally from the North Tyne area, called the caul ree-ak.

Unfortunately, coal was expensive and if we ran short it could be a few days before a fresh supply was delivered, whereas wood could usually be gathered under the trees for nowt, especially after a high wind. I enjoyed pretending to be a chain horse, dragging branches back home with a short length of clothes line. Sometimes the timber was too big for me to saw into fire-sized logs, so we took them into the kitchen as they were, stuck one end into the oven flue and propped the other end up with the back of a chair; as the log burnt away the supporting chair was moved up closer until the branch was short enough to be stood up on end in the fire and eventually laid down to burn away.

Logs up to three feet long could be skewered into the flue under the oven and the other end dropped into the fire; this really moved the oven into life but the log obstructed the slots in the flue mouth and if the oven overheated, the fire person could not get the metal nigget dropped in to block the flue. There could be some difficulty clamping the burning log with the long tongs, pulling it out from under the oven and standing it upright in the fire and then fitting the nigget.

The nigget was made by the blacksmith from thick metal plate and was quite heavy to lift with the long hooked poker, the same poker often used by marble players under the sideboard. Oven overheat or underheat usually happened when somebody, not acquainted with its peculiarities, attempted to bake without instructions from the expert: Mother.

Mother mastered it, having had some things altered about the fire range. For full oven heat the damper above the oven was pulled out to its limit; the nigget removed between the fire and the oven bottom; the two air inlets closed, one under and one above the oven door; a metal cover hung on hooks to restrict the main chimney, forcing the draught through the oven flue, with plenty of fire going. For a further boost, another metal sheet with a handle fitted, known as the bleezer, or blazer, could be stood on the front firebar top and up to the main chimney restricter; this forced all the air through the fire and the oven flue but it could not be left for long before the fire went very bright and was liable to melt the metal parts round the grate when burning coal. Nowadays people like Mother are called - by some - 'only housewives'.

Once boosted up and the bleezer removed, the oven temperature was controlled by the damper and one of the two niggets that Mother had; one was a solid piece of metal that could blank off the direct heat to the oven; pulled up half-way and tilted in the slots provided some restricted heat; out completely gave full heat the other had about twelve holes drilled through it and fully fitted it gave a relatively lower direct heat; half-way and tilted gave slightly more heat than the solid nigget tilted. Stoking was a highly skilled job, not appreciated by those who only press knobs and switches.

The air inlets under and over the oven were used to vary the heat between top and bottom inside the oven and could be completely removed for cleaning soot from the flues. The two knobs in the top corners above the oven door were not there for decoration as might be thought but were fitted to the ends of long rods attached to a scraper bar shaped to fit round the outside and top of the oven.

The oven was made in two parts, the inside baking oven being fitted inside a larger metal enclosure, with about a one-and-a-half-inch heating space between them; this space was kept clear of soot by pulling the scraper knobs back and forth. As a young schoolboy I often used these knobs as make-believe gear levers and throttle in an imaginary vehicle; no

Greta Parker, the author's mother.

need for an engine, revving noises were easily provided by tight-together lips and plenty of puff. Unfortunately, the two scraper knobs were liable to stick with one knob well out and the other knob right in. When Mother came along, she knocked the delinquent knob in with the large fire tongs. In some older ranges the inner oven was built into a brick chamber with the same heating space and scraper.

Wood made for a cleaner chimney whereas coal made black soot which clung to everything - a menace if the wind blew the smoke back down the chimney. Soot often showered over loaves of bread, set out along the fireside fender to prove, or rise, in the gentle heat. Many are the loaves of bread that went through that oven, whatever the fuel, and how it disappeared; I doubt if there was ever a stale loaf in our house. By comparison, modern bread-making in a coal-fired Rayburn, as performed by my wife, is pretty dull, although the end result is the same.

An earthenware crock manufactured by Reays of Bardon Mill stood in the wall pantry and was used to store the loaves, but not for long; it was soon emptied, although not always by our family. We often had visitors - strangers - tramping the roads and Mother never saw them go by without 'a bite to eat'. Mother was often blessed and thanked by these roadsters as they went on their way. When we asked them where they were going they usually said they never knew until they got there. Young though we were, my sisters and I were disturbed to think that those men slept behind walls and hedges and not in cosy beds like ours.

Because our house was on a minor road, we didn't see many of the long-distance tramps; our visitors were often on their way up Redpath bank to the 'Black Jack' past Midgeholme. Years later I discovered that Black Jack was the spelter works, which meant nothing much to us young'uns but Hugh explained that when tramps - most of them ex-servicemen - got there they often left the job after only an hour or so, as they were too weak to work and were moved on without any pay because they had not been there long enough to earn any.

When a contractor began converting a pasture into the Haltwhistle cricket field, passing tramps would ask - beg - for work. They were given a barrow and shovel and told what to do but if they straightened up to ease their aching backs, the foreman whistled and pointed to the road: "No slackers here," and they had to go without being paid.

The same often happened at Bank Foot coke ovens but there the foreman never needed to chase anybody away as the men were usually set on to draw the coke out of the ovens, a job a very fit man could barely manage, so in their weakened state most of the tramps went off in a very short time, again without pay. These unscrupulous firms used a lot of free labour from half-starved men.

The Hungry Thirties never affected us; we always seemed to have plenty for ourselves and any callers. I remember seeing one of Father's pay packets and by what I knew of other peoples' wages, he had a very good pay; was never on the dole, did very little drinking or smoking and grew most of our own vegetables and fruit. Nothing was wasted and Father had the idea that good quality clothes were cheaper in the long run, although some of his quarry clothes did get in a state owing to the rough stone he worked with. One night Father was walking from the quarry on his way home down the main road when he passed a tramp going the other way who looked him up and down and asked: "You on the roads, mate?" to which Father replied: "No...but not damned far off", and walked on. Being partly deaf, Father picked up only half of the tramp's response but he wouldn't tell us what was said.

The bedroom above our living room was always well warmed up after a baking day because of the free circulation of heat up the short stairs and through the gaps between the plain butt-jointed wood boards, there being no ceiling fitted in the living room and very few floor mats upstairs. As in the stone-flagged floor, the bedroom was supported on oak trees squared out to about six inches then boarding fixed across with what I clearly remember were almost-square-headed, hand-cut nails.

There was no bedroom ceiling either and I can remember lying in bed, seeing frost sparkling on the underside of the slates. The worst thing about this unlined roof was when some of the lime mortar parging crumbled away from the undersides of the slates, allowing flurries of snow to blow up through the open joints, then down on to our beds.

Father couldn't persuade the estate agents to do anything about the snow leaks so he employed Isaac Hetherington, the joiner, to fit thin-tongued and grooved boarding under the slates, which ended the snow showers in bed then all that Father had to worry about was water running off the board ends and down the inside walls when the snow melted, often on the next baking day.

A blue slate roof had been fitted in the late 1800s, replacing the original thatched roof. Further down the lonnen the other Parker house, as neighbour Hugh called it, had also been thatched. When I first saw it in the early 1930s, all that remained of this older building was the pigsty and a mound of stones; twenty years later I helped to build a small cattle shed and garage on this site, using many of the original wall stones.

I wasn't allowed to see the boarding being fitted under the slates above my bed, but I heard the hammering. I can clearly remember Cecil, Isaac's son, sitting in the living room at a small round table, drinking a cupful of something. His face was black all over because of soot falling from the slates as they nailed the boarding to the spars, but his mouth was clean, the soot likely being washed down by the hot tea. We moved to Haltwhistle in 1938 because the Redpath house was condemned, as was the farmhouse across the road. Almost twenty years after the joiners fitted the roof boards, Hugh Edgar built a hen house with them which, when creosoted, lasted for many years.

I must have crawled and stumbled great distances round the stone-flagged floors, the smooth, ash-covered yard and garden paths, which seemed to go on for ever. Then there was the roadside ditch which ran between the house and the road... That ditch was often blocked, bridged and diverted along its length until Willy Crowe the roadman came along with his shovel and removed all my civil engineering works and put the water course back to normal.

According to Hugh, Willy often asked if that little b... had been on with his water schemes again. He didn't appreciate my efforts, nor did the person who walked over one of my bridges between the road and the byre door. His foot went through the bridge

The site of the Redpath house after demolition, showing garden wall extended to fill the gap, with ditch 'play area' covered over. Old apple trees beyond the wall appear to be all that is left of the once prolific garden. (J Parker, jnr.)

HALTWHISTLE MUSINGS
by Westgate

Mr Edgar took me into the building at the bottom of the bank, tenanted until recent years. Above the door, chisled into the stone is the date 1706, but I have no doubt it was standing long before that. The massive walls, are a yard thick, and the oak beams thick with the dust of centuries are as sound today as they were 200 years ago.

Down below with a flickering candle we explored the dark dungeon-like place into which the cattle used to be rushed at the approach of danger. Mighty boulders formed the foundations, and our feeble light formed strange shadows which danced like dim ghosts upon the rough, damp walls.

On the back wall Mr Edgar showed me an arched opening which long ago had been walled up. A passage driven into the hill side for water, he had been told. Then we went to have a look at what remained of the old farm-house. Only a tumbled gable wall of stupendous strength is left. Gigantic stones bedded together with clay—a monument to time.

Extract from an article in the Haltwhistle Echo January 1950 by kind permission of Hexham Courant. (J Keen)

into the ditch as he carried wood into the byre. I had covered the surface with ashes and soil and he stepped right through it, as a bear through a trap. Cardboard, it seemed, was not the best material for building arches and I knew nothing then of 'Strength of Materials'; design was enough for young Parker then.

Soon I discovered a much better waterway to dig out and alter. This ran through the fir wood and along the bottom of Currys Hill and then tipped through a grating into a large pipe drain under the Wydon Lonnen and Jackson's Well field, then across the big meadow where it emptied into the River Tipalt. Up in the wood, the beck could be blocked up quite easily until a large lake formed between the trees. When the dam started overflowing, the blockage was quickly removed and the race was on to beat the flood to the end of the wood, where the stream dropped about six feet over a rock edge down into the field below. What a grand sight, surely the best waterfall in the world, I thought. It was a great disappointment when I discovered a postcard at home showing Niagara Falls, which seemed much wider than the Redpath one.

Down below the fall was a long stretch of meandering burn alongside the Currys Hill hedge. This hedge overhung the stream like a canopy and provided shelter from heavy rain when I was messing about in the syke. I spent hours straightening this water track to get a good flood going when the blocked water was released, but there were no spectacular rushes of water down to the grating; the fir wood waterfall was the best while it lasted.

As spring moved into summer, the burns dried up and hydraulic engineering was abandoned until the rains returned.

No matter, there were plenty of other jobs to keep me going, such as fetching and carrying at the farm, and when haytime started there was always raking the grass clear for Harry and his two-horse mowing machine.

When this operation was started, the horses were harnessed up with chain tackle for the long-pole mowing machine, instead of the saddle harness as used for carts and bogies. I was not allowed near those bonny Clydesdale horses while they were in the stable being harnessed. Harry promised that after I had started school I could help with 'Betty,' an older, quiet-natured mare; meanwhile, however, I could help with grass-raking.

The horses were positioned one each side of the long draw-pole of the machine. A shorter breast-pole, connected by a centre swivel to the front end of the draw-pole, was strapped to each horse's collar, or breatham, near the ends of the breast-pole. From the hame-stick draw-hooks on each side of the collar, the long draw-chains passed along each side to just behind the horse's rear legs and were hooked to a swingletree: a wood or metal bar almost three feet long with hooks either end for the draw chains and a centre rear link for connecting to the end hook of a larger swingletree, which Mr Dodd of Langley says they called a mastermantree; I cannot remember what this item was called at Redpath. The other horse was yoked in the same way to the other end of the mastermantree, the centre of which was connected to the mower as the main pulling point. After the reins were threaded through from the outside bit rings to the seat position, and the short spacing-rein tied between the inside bit-rings, the outfit was ready for moving to the field, and what a grand procession it was.

Once through the meadow gate and lined up to go round the field edge, the cutter bar was lowered, the many-sectioned knife slipped into the bar and coupled to the connecting rod or pitman. The oiling points were filled, the mechanism was put into gear with the ground drive wheels, the bar fully dropped and we were off.

The angled grass board cleared the cut grass away from the standing crop, leaving a nice nine-inch mown path to walk on, although this was not for my benefit but was a clear way for the next circuit of the mower. When the mower started on its second round, I raked the grass from the first cut in towards the second cut so that it formed a nine inch cleared area. This was required for when the back cut was taken in the reverse direction, which was the last round of mowing, after which a man scythed the grass up to the hedge. It was fascinating to watch the smooth, seemingly effortless sweeps of the curved blade. However, my job was not finished. If, as often happened, the field was 'off the square' the island of grass in the middle assumed a tapering shape, and I had to keep the narrowest end clear of cut grass, to give the mower bar room to finish off without cut grass blocking the knife bar.

When the grass was all mown it had to be raked back over the field to dry. After a day or two the swathes were turned over to dry the crop right through. Usually this was done with a single-horse Lister Blackstone hay-turner, although on steep land such as Wydon Hill, the crop was often turned by hand-rakes because of the danger of the ground-driven machine side-slipping, which also stopped the tines turning the hay. It took two men to hand-turn the hay on this steep part, a long and tiring job

The Redpath water supply of long ago, Jackson's Well (centre). (J Parker, jnr.)

- too heavy for me, so I was forced to watch the great LNER engines steaming past on their way to Carlisle or Newcastle.

This diversion never lasted long; Harry and Hugh were past masters at finding jobs. Harry was the one who, on the days when the haymen were paid, would say to me: "Man, Aa wud've given yi a tip but Aa hev nowt but silver", then walk off, hands in pockets, with never even a suspicion of a grin and jingling his cash as he went. Hugh sometimes got his hand out at the weekend and slid two or three pennies into my pocket - depending on the trade at the mart, I suppose.

I liked making the small 'kyles' of hay, which had to be done quickly if the hay had been horse-raked into sweep rows ready for piking and rain threatened. It was surprising how the hay stayed fairly dry in the kyles but I found them awkward to build with a rake. At my age I was allowed nowhere near a fork in case of injury. Years later I wondered if it was more for their protection than mine; I did poke the others more than once with my rake handle. Harry threatened to fix a bell on the shank end to warn everybody but he never did.

Weather permitting, once the hay was in sweep rows, one man and a horse swept the rows into a long pile up the centre of the section. The hay-sweep was basically a strong wooden plank as a cross-piece, with four or five wooden teeth about three feet long, bolted to the plank at right angles. Also bolted to this main plank were two curved wooden handles. The horse was fitted with chain harness, and with the long draw chains hooked to each end of the plank and the reins from the bridle bit-rings to the handle position, the outfit was ready for work.

In operation, the horse walked alongside the row of hay, dragging the sweep and gathering the hay as it went towards the centre of the section. As one side of the sweep filled up, the horse crossed over to the other side of the sweep row and so filled that side

Hay pikes (right) in the fields north of Haltwhistle. (J Keen)

also. When the load reached the centre of the field, the handles were raised slightly, the teeth dug into the ground and the sweep turned over, depositing the load of hay; the handle ends then dug in and the sweep completed a full somersault, landing with the teeth flat on the ground. From there the horse pulled the empty sweep to the end of the row at the other side of the field and the process was repeated.

The first pike man into this heap of hay roughly forked a channel through the heap to form a first stage of the pike about six feet in diameter, then more hay was added on the top of this base. The next man jumped on to this pile and then started building the pike with the hay forked up to him. When the pike was tapered up to six or seven feet high, a pair of ropes was fitted over the top and the ends wrapped round a 'wusp' of hay, as Harry called it, and stuffed into the pike sides near the bottom, then the builder slid to the ground and went on to the next one.

As the pike was being built, another man pulled the surplus hay out of the bottom edge to enable the hay above to overhang, thus directing the rain on to the ground instead of on to the pike bottom. Pike ropes were often made by twisting hay into a ten-foot length; a wet-day job in the barn and very

13

economical; the cattle usually ate the ropes as well as the hay, if the pikes were not too weathered before they were stored in the barn.

After a rake down all round, it was then pronounced complete and that was when I was allowed to perform. With my rake more or less under control, I cleaned up all the scattered hay between the pikes and carried it forward to the pike builders. This kept me fairly busy and I only managed quick glances at the LNER locos roaring past on the railway.

A very welcome sight in the hayfield was the large basket and tea-can coming towards us on the arms of Mrs Edgar and her helper. The food always tasted so much more wholesome eaten outside but I never tried the tea; I stuck - literally - to the gooseberry-jammed bread and scones; I had another five years or so of water drinking before graduating to tea; the menfolk managed to drink everything quite nicely without my assistance. The sight of a group of hay workers sitting eating and drinking seemed to please the LNER enginemen as they steamed past in their locos; they often tooted the whistle and gave a wave and received the sign of the cup in return. Harry usually put his fist up at them because they frightened his horses with what he described as their daft tooters.

Haytime went on for weeks then, even in a good summer, and no wonder; it was reckoned there were about eighty acres to win at Redpath, Hole House, Hardriggs and part of Wydon Eals Farm which the Edgars took on about the time I started raking the grass for Harry. To me, the Hardriggs and Wydon Eals fields seemed so quiet, there were no long trains to see, only the small Alston train, a long distance away across the valley.

I remember following Harry and his mowing machine up Redpath bank to this Wydon Eals field for the first time. It was always known as the 'black shed field' because of the cattle shed built near the eastern edge of the field. Nowadays there is a tall TV transmitter standing very near to where the shed stood.

This top field was the last to be mown so it tended to be late in the summer before it could be cut. In that first year the raking back was an easy matter. Years of neglect by the previous tenant resulted in there being very little grass so I raced round the back cut in a short time, then I followed the mower to watch the knife flashing back and forth in the cutter bar, which, had there been a fair crop of grass, would not have been visible.

There was a quantity of three-feet-high thistles which dropped like trees when they were chopped through and which were troublesome when the hay was being worked: good for neither man nor beast. It kept me on my toes, dodging them as they fell to the mower, but when I could get hold of them by the prickle-free bottom end, they made great switches for keeping away the flies, cleggs and midges. Unfortunately, clouds of cleggs sucking blood from the horses was not unusual, so whenever the horses stopped and I had time, I flattened as many of these pests as I could - the horses never objected.

Even though the crop was poor, enough hay was gathered to fill two round hay stacks, built in a fenced enclosure next to the cattle shed but after enduring a winter of feeding their cattle from the haystack, the Edgars decided to build a hay barn at this windy location. Hugh reckoned that the wind was so strong that if any of the hay blew off his armfuls as he carried them into the shed, it was whisked away eastwards and fed JP Tweddle's cattle on the adjoining Wydon Fell.

Owing to the demolition of many buildings in Haltwhistle, plenty of suitable beams were available for the barn uprights which were set in concrete and the purlins and the roof principles fitted on top. Harry said that as I liked clarting in water so much I could empty the water out of the foundation holes before they put the uprights in, but as there were ten holes, the water seeped in almost as fast as I emptied them with a calf bucket hanging on a rope; not only that, they wanted the water put into barrels for mixing the concrete.

The site of the 'black shed' and barn to the right of the TV mast at Redpath.

I complained that the barrels were leaking water back into the post holes but Harry said that could easily be cured by stemming clay into the joints of the barrel staves. It was then that I suspected that Harry was a slave driver, like the ones in books. Baling out kept me busy for a day or two and when the concreting of the poles was completed, I escaped from Harry's clarting works.

Willy Crowe, the roadman, came to watch the building operations and said that he had noticed I was in that water again. Then he asked: " Hev yi seen this place where the watter runs uphill frae the Black Burn up ti t'awd quarry crushin plant at Midgeholme?" I told him not to be so daft and he threw his brush after me. It was Willy who told me he had seen the Hanging Gardens of Babylon down at Redpath so anything else he told me I took with a pinch of salt. I remembered, though.

Later on I went into the farmhouse for tea and there they were right enough, darting and swaying over the jam tarts - Willy's Hanging Gardens. The Misses in their elegant outfits had turned up for tea - again. Fascinated by the blooms and foliage stuck into their fancy hats, I watched as they scoffed cakes and knocked back innumerable cups of tea. Mary, the cook, took me aside and told me off for staring but I was only watching and hoping the hat gardens would tip off, then the sisters would go and let me get at the few cakes that were left. Afterwards I asked old Jimmy, another 'card', why they kept their hats on at the teatable. He sniffed and said it was to keep what few brains they had warm enough so they could eat cakes and swig tea all day. Funny, I thought, I had to take my cap off at the table but I could still clear the cake decks. He muttered something about getting their feet under the table so I went and had a look at the fancy shoes these women were wearing. No wonder they wanted them under the table, I thought; their fancy patterned shoes wouldn't be much use in Redpath clarts, but somehow they seemed to match the hats.

Years later, when I acquired a bike, Willy's story about the water going uphill at Midgeholme was investigated - without anyone knowing about it, I hoped, in case they thought I was as daft as he was. And there it was right enough - an optical illusion because the countryside slopes to the north east and the water race alone appears to be going uphill; Willy would have laughed had he known that I had finally fallen for his story.

After the tall upright beams were all concreted in at the site of the new barn, I believe Isaac Hetherington, the joiner, completed the structure using more demolition timber, then covered the roof with corrugated steel sheeting.

Filling the barn with the hay was much easier than building stacks; Hugh boarded-in the west side to keep wind and snow out; unfortunately, that same boarding was one of the main causes of the barn collapsing some twenty years later during a gale-force wind. Hugh and Harry had not noticed that many of the uprights in the western part of the barn had rotted through at ground level, although some were quite sound on the eastern side. The strong wind on the boarded end of the barn caused the building to collapse and the whole of the roof slewed round on the one or two good pillars that were left standing, so that the east end eventually settled on to the cattle shed roof and the west end touched the ground.

By that time I was self-employed and Hugh asked me to lift the whole of the roof down on to the ground without collapsing the cattle shed, so that his man could dismantle it ready for rebuilding; a tall order, I thought: Hugh always said "nowt's impossible" but this was about forty feet long and twenty feet wide and still all fixed together, more or less, in one piece.

Surprisingly, it was much easier to manage than I expected: a long plank set upright in the front bucket of the Whitlock digger lifted the whole roof clear of the cattle shed, then another tractor pulled it over on to the ground with a long steel rope, breaking off the remaining uprights.

After the roof was dismantled and cleared, we fitted telegraph poles into holes dug by Jake's digger and jammed the pole bottoms with large stones, instead of the concrete which had been used in the 1930s and was the main cause of the beams rotting off at ground level. With the roof refitted, the barn was ready for the following haytime.

I forget whether the corn harvest in the 1930s was gathered before this top hayfield was started each year, or if the corn was cut, stooked and left until the hayfield was finished. However it was done, the two jobs usually coincided but they were always completed.

Cutting the corn always seemed a much simpler operation than the hay crop. A two-man-two-horse mowing machine with a swinging gate on the rear of the cutter bar was used in those days, the method being that one man guided the horses as on a normal mowing machine; the other man sat on a separate seat over the right-hand wheel and by pressing a foot pedal he could swing the gate up on the rear of the bar, the gate gathering the stalks of corn as they were being cut. After about ten feet of travel, depending on thickness of crop, the gate was dropped and the heaped-up corn pushed off with an angled rake. Then the gate came up again and another load was gathered, this being a continuous operation without stopping the horses. Other workers gathered the heap up, bound it with a handful of corn straws as a belt, and the sheaf was complete.

The sheaves were stooked upright in batches of eight or ten in a north-to-south direction, so that both sides absorbed some sunshine; these were left to ripen for about ten days before being taken to the stack for storage. In later years I remember corn being stacked in bright moonlight because rain was forecast. Those moonlight stacks at Redpath were, surprisingly to me, as plumb and straight as any of the daylight-built stacks.

I always looked forward to stacking the corn crop; we were allowed to ride on the flat-topped hay bogie from the stack back to the field. The top surfaces of the bogies were well polished by the sliding on and off of hay pikes. In 'hay-pike leading' as this operation was called, the bogie with a horse between wooden shafts was reversed up to the pike, the flat surface tipped so that the tail end fitted under the pike as far as possible. At the front of the surface a hand-hauler arrangement was bolted on. Two long chains were fitted round the pike and hooked together at the back near the bottom, the other ends being fitted to the spindle of the hauler. A small wusp of hay was put between the chain and the furthest side of the pike; this forced the chain to grip the pike and pull it on to the bogie. Then came the hard work, made slightly easier by the horse pulling forward a yard to loosen the pike from the ground. A handle was fitted into the hauler and turned to wrap the chains round the hauler drum, thus pulling the pike up on to the surface, which eventually balanced with the weight of the pike, and returned to the level position. Then it was handle out and off to the barn, but there was no ride for me on this homeward trip. The bogie rides were great, especially if the far away pikes were being moved, such as on Wydon Hill in the thirty-acre meadow. It was a long walk back but it was worth it for the pleasant outward journey.

When the bogies were needed for corn harvest the hauling chains were laid along the surface, one at each side and about six inches in from the edge, over the tail end and under to a hook and then up over the side and along the back about twelve inches in from the end and the end hooks of each chain joined together. When the chains were tightened this made an anchor for the sheaves of corn and kept them in position when they were being loaded and as the bogie moved over uneven ground. We had to beware of jumping on to the empty bogie for a ride and landing on these chains: I had chain-link-shaped bruises on my rear quarters more than once. While the bogie travelled over the fields the ride was smooth but the metal wheels joggling along the stoney Wydon Lonnen really shook me up. I can still feel the chattering of my teeth, totally different from a previous ride on the flat spring cart used by my Uncle Alf.

He carted the contents of his small in-house sweet shop in Wydon Terrace, Haltwhistle, up to Featherstone Show on his flat cart and as Mother had offered to serve on the stall, we also rode on the cart. The stall was set up at the side of a field belonging to Row Foot Farm but for some reason was across a ditch from the main activities; customers blessed having to leap over the water every time, but I didn't. Having had some experience of water works at the Redpath gable end, I wasn't going to miss this opportunity and spent most of the day in that beck. Mother was at hand to keep an eye on me and she probably had given up hope long ago of trying to keep me out of water except on bath nights.

When the show was over the pony and cart appeared, was loaded with Uncle's remaining stock, and we rode on the cart down a hill; I remember seeing people walking up the far side of a valley, then we came down another hill with dark swirling water far below. Twelve years passed before I recognised these places again. One was coming down into Park Burn bottom and the other was on the old route of the Bellister Bank, which went much nearer to the River Tyne before the present road was constructed.

After the corn harvest at Redpath came the potato howking - without the help of a potato digger. The same horse-drawn stitcher or ridger that was used in the spring for planting the potatoes was used to uplift the crop in the Autumn. The stitcher opened out the ridge and exposed most of the crop. The potatoes were then gathered and bagged and the sides of the split ridge kicked back into the bottom, when the rest of the crop came to light. My feet then were too small for this job but my hands must have been capable of picking spuds so I was given a bucket and expected to help.

The turnip crops were partly gathered and the rest left in the ground to be eaten by sheep, in a similar way to strip grazing, that is, moving a fence across the field as the sheep ate the crop off. It saved the bother of pulling and slicing the turnips, then feeding them in troughs to the animals, although some sheep had trouble with their teeth and were unable to gnaw so they were fed with sliced turnip. Some farmers swore by one method and some preferred the other way. I was never personally involved with turnips, I only watched grown-ups 'sneddin the snannies'- chopping off turnip tops with flaysome-looking knives.

With the end of harvesting, I looked forward to getting on with some more ditching along Wydon Lonnen but Father had other ideas. "We will go on a trip to Ullswater" he said. Well, there was plenty of water there - too much for me to dam. During our sail up the lake in the passenger boat I remember water swirling up at the back and found I could look over and partly under the deck overhang. There didn't seem to be anything to stop people sliding over into the lake.

NEAR STYBARROW CRAG

AIRA FORCE.

HEAD OF ULLSWATER

STEAMER ARRIVING AT PATTERDALE
ABRAHAMS' SERIES

ULLSWATER.

KESWICK VIEW FROM PARK BROW

POOLEY BRIDGE

KIRKSTONE PASS.

AT KAIL POT CRAG

I forget what Father bought for my sisters in the Patterdale shop but I came away with a small toy tank loco in LMS red: I could put that to good use at home.

On the return trip we travelled by boat down the lake to Pooley Bridge and then by bus to Penrith, to catch the Carlisle train. Penrith station was interesting in that the tracks were on a curve and were well 'canted' over - and still are. This meant climbing up the slope of the compartment to get out of the train on the southward trip and repeating the process on the northbound train from the west side platform. I wondered that the trains stayed on the line when they were tipped over like that.

To the west was a bay platform for Keswick trains and down there was a nice shiny rail head, just right for a model LMS tank loco. Somehow I got down to the line - there must have been some way round by the original signal box which stood at the platform end in those days. I shunted my loco back and forth on the top of the siding rail until I was discovered and removed from there on to the main platform.

Just then a loud alarm bell started ringing. It seemed an awful row to make just because I had borrowed their rails for my shunter, but evidently the alarm sounded not for small boys but when a through train was imminent, to warn people to keep away from the platform edge. Owing to the curvature of the tracks through the station I heard the whistle before I saw the train. The whistle developed into a roar as loco and trucks came through at what seemed like a tremendous speed. I expected to see the train off the rails and ending up in the town but it disappeared through the bridge at the north end without mishap: it was flaysome.

We caught the Carlisle train, then a Newcastle train carried us to Haltwhistle and from there we had to walk the mile and a half to Redpath. I cannot remember any part of the homeward journey now; I must have switched off at Penrith.

After that trip there was a threshing day at Redpath, which always happened on a Saturday, because my father, and myself of course, were available to help on that day. On the morning of the threshing day, one or two cartloads of corn sheaves were brought from the stack and forked into the long loft and arranged into another stack against the threshing machine.

I had previously explored round behind the loft building and seen this strange pole contraption about twenty feet long and turning on a large central bevel gear in an enclosure behind the building. The long pole was fitted horizontally and about two feet up off the ground, an ideal place to swing on, and it moved round if I pushed hard enough. The large central gear turned a smaller gear on the end of a length of steel shafting. This shaft was fitted through a small tunnel under the horse's walking track, towards the loft building, and I saw that a wheel was fitted to the other end in a boarded-off enclosure in the ground-floor cattle pen, or loose box as Harry called it.

If I was quick enough I could see to the rear of the pen before the beasts came forward to see me, which blocked my view over the half door. I saw what looked like harness leather straps fitted round this wheel, stretching up through a hole in the loft floor; this was a driving belt from the lower wheel up to a pulley on the threshing drum upstairs in the loft.

On Saturday afternoon Harry took two horses round to the swinging pole at the back of the building and yoked them to each end so that they could pull the pole round in a clockwise direction, to drive the gear and pinion. This speeded the threshing drum round and everything then was ready to feed the sheaves of corn through the drum. This is when Father and I climbed up on to the stack of sheaves to start undoing the bands and placing the sheaves on to the thresher feed tray. From there Hugh gradually pushed the loosened sheaves towards the spinning drum which knocked out the grain and fired the empty straws out of the front of the thresher for stacking at the end of the loft. Over the next week the straw was fed to the cattle below through holes in the loft floor above their mangers.

The pile of grain and chaff under the machine was sorted out in a 'deatering' machine where a hand-cranked fan blew the chaff out of the grain as it worked through the shakers to the floor. Should anything go wrong while threshing, the 'power' could be shut off immediately; Hugh only needed to shout "Whoa" out of the loft window and the horses stopped instantly. Harry seemed to be there only for starting the horses and keeping them going; he called the horse circling area a 'gin gang' but unlike many others, it had neither roof nor circular walls: not very pleasant if a snow-storm came on during threshing.

Evidently Hugh had bought all the pieces belonging to the threshing outfit at a sale and fitted them into position himself, so that the Edgars could be independent, save charges and thresh when they wanted. Prior to that time they had to take the corn to the estate thresher at the Spital.

When the 1939 war started and much more grain had to be grown, a threshing machine was hired from Joe Foster at Gilsland as required. The loft-thresher and the horse-pole arrangement were retired but a kerosene engine was fitted in the cattle shed to drive a roller/crusher for grain. This engine could be a beast at times to get started and keep going, many are the times I've seen somebody running from the house to the engine with something being carried in a pair of blacksmith's tongs. Apparently, when the engine wouldn't start, they took the starting plug up to the house and heated it in the kitchen fire, although this rarely helped to start it. Later a mechanic from Longbyre found that owing to a leak, the kerosene was getting into the starting petrol; when this was rectified the engine problems were solved. The Edgars freely admitted that they were not mechanics but give them a horse and they would manage alongside anyone.

In the loft at Redpath there was an interesting model of a hay-pike builder, made by Hugh Edgar, which he had thought would work better than building the pikes by hand. It had a strip of cloth joined in a loop and fitted round cotton reels to represent a hay elevator; this fed into a hinged block of wood hollowed out inside to the shape of a pike. This machine was intended to pick up and feed hay into the pike mould; when filled the whole block swivelled over until the pike was upright, then one hinged half opened out and the pike was left standing on the ground. It worked in model form, but because of lack of financial backing it was jettisoned, then after a few years somebody came to look at it and an engineering firm made some prototypes and tested them on Cumberland farms. They worked, but I believe the man in the pike cage building the pike did some perspiring, because the hay came up too quickly. I noticed one machine standing in the barn for many years at Middle Farm, Brampton but never saw any of them working, and when hay balers became popular the pike-building machines disappeared.

An American visitor watching the pike machine at work was most impressed by the mechanism, although he commented: "I've seen many machines designed to save manpower but this sure is the first one I ever saw for half-killing the operator."

In 1950 Hugh and I made a model of a pike-carrier to be hauled by tractors without hydraulic lifts; this worked in model form but we were 'a bit late in the day' with this invention; nevertheless a Tyneside firm did make some of these lifts, but not for long. Most tractors were fitted with hydraulics by that time and their pike-lifters were much lighter and did not need wheels as did ours. No matter, it was all good experience.

Back at our Redpath house, I found the model tank loco from Patterdale was ideal for making tracks in the hard-packed ashen surface of our backyard. I had no metal rails but on the yard I made a grand display of rail junctions and tracks - all free - by pressing the loco wheels into the yard surface; the 'tanky' pulled and pushed the two trucks I had on many a long shunting operation.

When I tired of shunting I could always look over the wall and watch the LNER engines racing between Newcastle and Carlisle. There was something else though, making a distant 'popping' sound which I thought might be another steam engine. Previously I had seen the pit-heap burning and sometimes steam showing at Plenmeller Colliery, but that was too far away to be heard at Redpath - this sound seemed to come from the Spital Farm area, so I was pleased when one Sunday, Father said we would go for a walk by the Spital and Birchfieldgate, or Bitchelgate as he called it, then round by the College Farm and Smallburn, or 'Smo born', then back home. Now I would see their steam engine - or whatever it was.

Thomas Armstrong with Bonnie & Charlie at Wolf Hills. (C Parker)

Chapter Two

The estate sawmill at Spital Farm with sawbench still fitted. The rear higher part of the building with two skylights housed the large threshing machine driven by oil engine situated in the building on the extreme left. Only the sawbench remains nowadays, powered by electric motor. (D Hunter)

We set off down the Haltwhistle road and crossed over the Tipalt Bridge. That was an interesting place: a gold-coloured river, a road bridge, a railway bridge and a large, half submerged metal pipe in the river bed, passing under both of them. Father told me that the pipe was something to do with the pits but I hadn't seen or heard anything of pits near the Spital... This was stored up in my mind for future investigations. As we walked further on towards the Estate buildings at the Spital Farm, Father reckoned

they had a sawmill and a threshing machine in there driven by a big engine.

Unfortunately, this being a Sunday, everything was closed up, so I had to wait some time to see what was in there. Here must be the thresher that Redpath had to use for their corn before they got their own machine. As we passed through the farmyard Father explained that the main road to Carlisle came past the house at one time; pointing to a stone bridge among the trees, he said that was the way it went. There was no sign of a main road but the mental picture of a stone arched bridge remained in my mind; a bridge to nowhere almost: only a three-sided field with a barn, surrounded by the river on two sides and the railway on the other; a real puzzle to me then.

We walked away northwards from the Spital and through iron gates set in metal park railings. If the gates were banged hard enough, most of the metal fence strips rattled for a good way on each side of the gate... Just as well that Father was rather deaf as a result of World War One or I might have had a 'clipped ear'.

An interesting feature across these fields was a man-made water course - nothing to do with me - directing water from a dam in the Painsdale Burn to the lake, also man-made, in front of Blenkinsopp Hall. This channel was dug mainly alongside the park fencing for about seven hundred yards to the lake. The water was fascinating to me but the ditch was ruined - covered with wire netting nailed to wooden framing over its entire length. Had the estate joiners known that I would eventually find this water? We were wearing Sunday clothes so I could only look at the water and watch the fish struggling along towards the Painsdale Burn.

It seems that the fish in the lake moved up the channel into the burn for the autumn spawning and that must have been the run I had seen under the netting, which was not really to keep me out but to prevent herons - and other poachers - taking the fish as they passed through the shallow channel. The fish would have to take their chances with birds, and men, as they swam up the burn to the Fell End moss. There were some fish under the bridge on the footpath to Birchfieldgate and more further on where the burn passed under the Carvoran road, near Painsdale House.

Our Sunday walk continued up the Back Road from Birchfieldgate as far as the corner of Painsdale Wood,

where we climbed over the wall stile and then by the field path to Wrytree Farm. Before we reached the farm we had to negotiate a hollow near the head of Wrytree Wood and valley, never dreaming that thirty years later the Wrytree coal mine would be put down in this same depression in the field.

At the farm I spotted a type of pony carriage I had never seen before, almost like a very wide poss-tub on wheels with thin, springy, wooden shafts, nothing like the Redpath cart and bogie shafts. This was the kind of pony trap known, I'm told, as a Digby, that many farmers used for travelling to market and wasn't confined to posh people as I had thought. I had a good look at Mr. Brown's pony cart at Wrytree, before we walked on to the College Farm where I noticed the Snowdens also had a similar cart. Redpath lot must be poor, I thought, they haven't a fancy cart like these farmers, but unknown to me, they had one and never used it; it was kept at Hole House, probably to be well away from that inquisitive Redpath lad.

Little time was wasted on the College Farm conveyance because I had noticed the River Tipalt just beyond the farm. We had to walk over the footbridge on our way home and Tipalt was a real river. The narrow bridge spanned the river on the upstream side of the ford in those days before the road bridge was built, and was a good vantage point to look down through the water to the river bed; unfortunately our approach up the path and on to the bridge frightened any big fish well away upstream, so we had to be content to watch, in the shadow of the bridge, pinheads, loachers and minnows but they also moved on after somebody dropped a few small stones into the water from the bridge.

We had to get on to allow other people to cross, so we made for the railway crossing. There was a nice water course at the side of the road up to the railway but not much use for the kind of alterations I liked to perform; it was lined out with flat flagstones over the whole length between the railway and the river.

I had not seen one like this before; I preferred the Redpath kind where I could dig in the mud.

We crossed the railway and turned towards Haltwhistle on the last leg of our walk. Traffic on a Sunday evening in the 1930s was almost non-existent; very few trains or cars passed us. Tar bubbles had disappeared with the cooler weather so we missed the ritual flattening of these bumps on the way down the main road. Two things on that stretch I took notice of: the tall house with large joiner's workshop to match, that Father called 'Smo Born', and the huge oak tree at the bottom of Daleacres Wood that Father had seen struck by lightning as he came home from work one evening.

I don't know how long that walk took; it seemed like ages but was the first one I remember. The miles per hour were greatly reduced on the last half of the trek and I was soon sound asleep under the boarded slates. On other fine weekends we set out on many different routes from Redpath, such as along Wydon Lonnen to Wydon Farm and over the hill to Wydon Eals, on to Featherstone Stone Bridge and up Pinkins Cleugh to the junction with the Redpath road and then back down home.

These long walks created enormous appetites in us youngsters and we made short work of anything available in the pantry. Father tried to slow us down and accused us of eating like 'Hongos', whatever they were.

As we grew older and more ambitious we would go over the Stone Bridge and past the old gatehouse with its gable end stone carved as a rampant lion, now long since demolished. From there to the castle and on along the riverside to Lambley Viaduct, over the footbridge fitted to the viaduct abutments, then up the steps to Lambley pit sidings, over the lines and up to Lambley Chapel. From there we came along the Alston to Brampton road for a short distance, then turned down past Greenriggs to Burnfoot, up Craigs Bank, past Maiden Way farm and into Glencune, across to Pinkins Cleugh and so

to Redpath. That was a marathon walk for my short legs but it must have provided some good training for when I started school, which involved a three-mile round-trip each day, Mondays to Fridays.

I went to Haltwhistle on Saturdays with Mother, who pushed a pram loaded with my two younger sisters, Thelma and Marjorie, while my older sister Anne and I walked alongside. The first Saturday trip I remember with all of us together was in late 1932. The pram was fairly lightly laden on the inward journey but after cramming a week's shopping under and over the two little girls, it must have been at its maximum capacity. After visiting relatives, it was often quite dark before we set off for Redpath.

The gas-lit streets were easily negotiated but when we reached the town cemetery, it was often a case of feeling our way along the further mile of road. The particular pram we had was either a brakeless model or else they didn't work, as we had to hold on to it going down Cross Bank, but after that it was a fairly level run to Redpath road end. I can just recall pushing at the pram at one side and leaning my head against the padded edge at the same time. I must have dozed slightly while walking along, if that is possible, because mother occasionally said "Oi, you're dragging, get pushing". A fair amount of pushing was needed to get the pram up the hill off the main road and on to the last level stretch to the house.

In those days the road was a stone-surfaced track yet to be tarred and have chippings spread over like the main road, so it was rather rough for small-wheeled prams loaded to bursting point. We rarely managed to push a full load up the slope past the gable end of the house, even though Father had put in a proper stoned bridge over the roadside ditch, a big improvement on my cardboard one at the byre door. Usually the shopping was unloaded and carried by hand so that the two young ladyships in the pram could be transported over the yard and into the house while Anne and I carried some of the smaller parcels.

It was amazing that everything stayed on the pram all the way from Haltwhistle - not that we would have noticed anything dropping off in the dark.

It was rare to meet anybody on the road at that time, although I do remember one man called Graham, his wife and two sons walking from Haltwhistle to Greenhead one night. Mother, who when single had cycled round the district collecting grocery orders, thought she might know the house so asked him whereabouts in Greenhead he lived and he replied: "Todholes." Mother laughed and said that wasn't Greenhead, it was halfway to Kellah. It turned out that Todholes was about a mile further up the fell from Greenhead, more than four miles altogether from Haltwhistle.

I was always glad we didn't live in the top house at Redpath when pram-pushing was to be done; we might have had a runaway or failed altogether on the steepest part, which was what happened to some other vehicles one day. Redpath bank proved to be a great place for testing the pulling power, or lack of it, in vehicles.

An early lorry with angled 'Edward R Foden, diesel' nameplate before this was changed to ERF, the type seen by the author on Redpath Bank in the 1930s.

One Sunday, a line of lorries stopped on the Newcastle to Carlisle road then set off in a very low gear before turning up the first short Redpath hill. They were loaded with large semicircular wooden bases, which we heard later were for the floors of bell tents and were destined for an army cavalry camp on Bellister Haughs over the river from

Territorials marching to Bellister Haughs camp down Boat Lane 1911. Railway Terrace in left background, Railway Hotel in centre, Gem Cinema on right. (R Bainbridge)

An earlier camp on Bellister Haughs in 1911. 86 years later a much more substantial bridge was built on the site of this temporary one as part of the Haltwhistle by-pass. (S Blackburn)

Haltwhistle, but owing to weight restrictions on the Tyne bridge, the lorries had been routed up Redpath bank.

At the time I could only think they might be going to that mysterious Kellah City, reputed to have nine roads in and one out, and industries which included cheese quarries and treacle ponds. Hugh had often promised to take me for a ride on the trams at Kellah, but he never had time.

The first lorry looked fairly new with some shiny chrome about it and I believe it had E Foden on the front, so was probably one of the first ERFs. It roared past our house and up the main hill, followed by the other older lorries of various makes and sizes.

Two wagons managed the hill but the third one stopped just beyond Tommy Hall's house and stopped the progress of the rest of the convoy. The following drivers chocked the wheels of their vehicles and went to help with lorry number three. I followed behind but was chased off the road by the drivers, so I climbed into the field and ran to a high vantage point opposite the ailing wagon to watch the performance.

The lorry must have been under-powered for Redpath and I was most interested to see the drivers fitting planks behind the wheels and chocking up the lower end to form a more level surface. Then the driver reversed the lorry slowly back on to the planks.

With engine roaring, the lorry tyres gripped the planks, went slightly forward, then shot all the timber backwards. I was glad to be well out of the way of that rive-up, entertaining though it was.

It was then that they decided to evacuate the Hall family in case the lorry slipped back and crashed into their house. Tommy was not pleased; his Kitchener-style moustache fairly bristled; he was halfway through his Sunday dinner, the highlight of the week.

After many futile attempts to get the wagon forward the first two lorries came back to the top of the hill, having unloaded and returned, no doubt wondering what had happened to the rest of the convoy. They were sent back in reverse to turn near the Paddock Pond beyond the top house and then reversed down to stand in line above the ailing wagon.

Tow ropes were fitted and the fun began again. The wheels on the towing vehicles spun round on the rough stoned surface and dug in. I remember clearly,

watching one man throwing hessian sacks under the wheels, supposedly for grip, but they just flew straight out at the rear.

Finally they unloaded much of the lorry's load and carried it up the hill on to the tow vehicles. Then they made progress up the hill as a roped-together trio, the planks were gathered up and the other lorries roared up after them.

A fuming Tommy got back to his now-cold dinner. My dinner was probably in the farm dog at this late hour but seeing this drama was worth any amount of Yorkshire puddings.

Even at that early age I had travelled on what I thought were gigantic vehicles and anybody else could have done the same by handing over the penny fare to the conductor to ride in style on a United bus for the one and a half miles to Haltwhistle.

My favourite place on the bus was right behind the driver's cab where I could look through the glass

A Haltwhistle group of the 1920s on an outing. The coach 'Lady Belle', run by a local firm, J Mitchinson, had solid tyres, non-electric lamps and the usual opening windscreen used before the days of windscreen wipers. Driver Tommy Railton, to his right George Pepperill. 'Lady Betty' waits behind. (M Henderson)

This group is believed to be Haltwhistle's Vocal Union in 'Lady Betty'. Driver Joe Mitchinson; passengers include Tom Bell, Joseph Hudspith and Ralph Bell. (M Henderson)

division and watch driving operations, a complete mystery then but eventually I worked it out and realised that gear changing was very much slower in those days.

Setting off from Redpath road end in a low gear, the bus gathered speed then the driver pushed a foot pedal down, pulled the gear lever backwards and let the pedal up again. 'Why is he stopping here?' I wondered, but then down went the pedal, the lever was pulled back with a 'clonk' and we surged forward to higher speeds.

After a few more changes and clonks, and if there was nobody at the cricket field stop, the bus, with some vibration and often a 'howling backend', managed a fast run as far as Cross Bank. That was the point where I kept a close watch on the change

down to a lower gear, which was a much quicker change; with a 'rev up' between the gears, the drivers slid the gears in smoothly and with never a scrape, only the odd clonk when changing up - there were no synchro-mesh gears, as far as I know, on heavy vehicles in those days.

They were experts, and no wonder; they would be stopping and starting along the route with hundreds of possible stops on almost 60 miles of hilly road.

Haltwhistle drivers, George Storey, Harry Glenwright, Billy Bushby, Ike Mitchinson (later an inspector for many years) and one whose name I believe was Clark, plus Ike's father, were all part of the team at one time or another.

Always smartly turned out, to us young'uns United drivers were on a par with ships' captains. Although

A United bus like the ones on the Newcastle to Carlisle route in the early 1930s - closely inspected by the author. (E Heslop)

service in each direction with duplicates added when necessary. The Newcastle-bound bus regularly passed the Carlisle bus in the How Burn area, while further west, Upper Denton was the usual passing point, but here the drivers had to keep a sharp look-out for the oncoming bus as the road was so narrow. Nowadays the services are so reduced that there should be few problems.

An early bus operator in Haltwhistle was a Ridley whose garage was on Banks Terrace. This firm definitely had a driver called Clark and they ran a service between Haltwhistle and Hexham. The business was wound up after the garage caught fire and was destroyed in about 1930. The site was later used by Elliotts' for their new bakery.

Further west at Gilsland, Sowerby's ran buses from the 1920s and up to the present day, concentrating on private hire, both locally and abroad. One of their smaller buses, starting from Gilsland, carried miners

not loaded with gold braid, their uniform greatcoats with broad lapels and black leather pieces round the pockets were really outstanding; the shiny-peaked band-master style cap was our heroes' crowning glory.

In the 1930s the United Company used a two-bus garage in Boat Lane, known as Plenmeller Road on some maps, which was situated on part of the railway station house garden and in front of the Gem cinema. This steel-framed garage, on the proposed route and therefore an obstruction to the first Haltwhistle by-pass, was demolished about 1950.

In the heyday of public transport United ran an hourly

Haltwhistle Market Place bus stop. (S Blackburn)

J Mitchinson's garage on Boat Lane east of the Gem Cinema. (M Henderson)

in the 1930s from various places on the way to Acomb pit, near Hexham, the driver also working at the mine.

Robert Elliott of Castle Hill ran a private hire Austin bus powered by a petrol engine, but it was rather slow, and some Haltwhistle wags said that if Robert followed the economic trend of the 1950s by fitting a diesel engine, it would be quicker to walk.

Robert had other ideas and put the bus up for sale at £400 - a very low price. I wondered whether it would be a good buy but its low speed and my lack of garage space changed my mind; it disappeared from the area shortly afterwards.

It seems ages since I first saw the distinctive Red United buses run past Redpath road end.

Lawrence Rushton was a driver on one of the buses but judging by his size when I knew him, he would have trouble climbing into the driving seat. He ran the Gem cinema at one time and after giving up that work he came back out of retirement to drive a Bedford lorry for Robson Brothers during one of their busy spells, and, still being rather rotund, he sometimes had trouble fitting into the driving position and blamed the lorry makers for installing the steering wheel too near to the seat.

At the cinema, Lawrence had the unusual arrangement of a 110 volt generator driven by a gas engine from the town gas supply. Post-war Electricity Board salesmen often boasted to prospective customers that their system was better than gas for all purposes and after all, manufacturers could never make a gas television.

This being Haltwhistle, they should have known better…. Indirectly, Lawrence could have proved them wrong: he managed to run his all-electric cinema from the town gas supply.

Lawrence's bulk came in useful in the cinema for 'packing them in'. The front rows were made up of a series of wooden bench seats or forms, and owing to much use, the seats became highly polished. Before the start of the show, when the forms were pronounced 'full up', Lawrence sat down on one end and gave the row of youngsters a shuffle sideways. The unfortunate at the far end fell off on to the floor but when Lawrence arose, he left room for two so there was some gain; what happened to the far-end boy is not clear.

The few times I can remember sitting on the old seats in the penny end, the sideways shuffle was never tried, for a very good reason. He would have had to shunt Mother as well, who sat with us - with her umbrella.

To return to Redpath bank: the road was resurfaced in about autumn 1932 the holes dug by spinning lorry wheels were filled, then covered with hot tar and whin stone chippings. To flatten this out, a steam roller from Heskett, Cumberland, arrived towing a caravan and water tank. Driver George Rutherford and his wife Hilda set up the caravan on the wide grass verge near the gateway to the Black Wood, just beyond the top house in Redpath, and that was to be their home for many years. George steam-rolled many miles of roads in West Northumberland and travelled between any current road job and his caravan on a motor bike. His first job in the district was Redpath bank and up to the Pinkins Cleugh road. I was lucky enough to have occasional rides in the coal-box of the steam-roller after the steep hill was finished and work progressed on to the more level roads. I was 'learning the ropes' as George rolled tarmac. This was frowned upon by authority but he explained that if he had me in the coal bunker, he knew where the little so and so was.

Unfortunately, coal dust was as black as the melted tar which stuck to everything, including me. Mother despaired of ever removing the tar completely from my clothes and skin but I remember petrol, which

Redpath Bank.

was stored in a small green ribbed bottle, was dabbed on tar marks on clothes and butter was used to remove black patches from my hands and knees, etc. They never told me that petrol was explosive, but luckily none of it splashed on to the old kitchen range, or there might have been more than soot removed from the chimney.

I was regularly warned off the steam roller and mother asked Mrs Hall up the hill to send me back down if she saw me making towards the road operations further up. Mrs. Hall did chase me once, but only once. I only had to walk the other way along Wydon Lonnen, up the small meadow and along the track through the Foxcover wood, across the next meadow and over the top part of Currys Hill and I was at the roadside gate, right opposite George Rutherford's caravan, then out on to the road and the steam-roller - all without troubling Mrs Hall on the way up, but I would likely be spotted going back down.

Eventually the local road tar-spraying was completed and the roller moved to other areas too far away for me to visit. George and Hilda continued to live in their picturesque caravan for many years. George used his motor bike to travel to different road jobs

Willie Milligan (the chemist) and family on Wydon Lane. This Matchless V Twin motorcycle would be one of the first in the area. (M Henderson)

during the week and often he and Hilda went off for a weekend, which was more than any other residents of Redpath could do at that time; nobody else had any mechanical transport other than the buses. I was probably the first resident to have a ride on a motor-bike when, after I had started school at Haltwhistle, George stopped his bike at the bottom of Cross Bank and asked if I wanted a ride home to Redpath. Did I want a ride? I was on the pillion in a flash and off we went. I was surprised how smooth the ride was; I had expected the bike would shake in time with the roars that came out of the smoke pipe. We went up the short hill off the main road much quicker and easier than we did on a Saturday night with the pram. Now, I thought, if we had a length of rope….and if George happened to come up at the same time….but I doubt if Mother would have had anything to do with that.

A length of rope worked for me all right when I could manage to slip it on to the hook at the back of Harry's cart; the horse probably resented pulling me as well as the cart up the bank, and Harry would certainly have made his presence felt if he had caught me but it was great hanging on to the rope, leaning backwards and walking behind out of sight of Harry at the front. Poor horse, I thought...about ten years later.

Poor me, I thought when the time came to start school at Haltwhistle. I could nicely have spent my time at Redpath. It was April 1933 when I first entered the Council, or Board, School, which consisted of two brick buildings, one at each end of the yard; the smaller one housed the infants' classes at the west end. However, the first infants' class was in neither of these buildings; we had to go round

Bike shop at the top of the Castle Hill (F Gents)

into a smaller yard where a wooden classroom was prepared for new starters.

All that I can remember of that class was the huge hot stove behind a metal fence and the nice Miss Cook. What a patient person she must have been, to spend almost a lifetime at the same school easing all those five-year-olds into the discipline of school life. Few if any of us wanted to be there; I certainly did not, but after a week or so we resigned ourselves to the inevitable.

I always looked forward to home time when I could look in the shop windows if my escort could be persuaded to slow down, but it wasn't long before I walked to school and back on my own - it was only a mile and a half, after all. In the mornings I had no time to dally but on the way back, after dodging past the police station at the old town hall, there were two bike shops near Potts' garage which interested me very much, although anything that was not free was usually out of my range.

A few friends had bikes, so I might get one some day, but I doubted if Hugh's two or three pence wages would ever amount to the prices on Mr Forsyth's or Mr Potts' tags. As Harry Edgar said: "Hope's cheap eneugh". Reluctantly, I pulled away from Potts and pressed on homewards, past the smelly window of the Comrades Club; what a whiff always seemed to blow out of their window - from some stuff called beer that you had to be grown-up to drink. I thought at the time that they must have been heroes to stand that if it tasted anything like the smell. Jackson's Well water was clear and cool - it would do for me.

AF Graham's fruit shop, which the author often passed on his way from school - without actually disturbing the potatoes.

Further up was another place with a slight beery smell where the Union Jack often flew above the front door. The next whiffy place up the street had two great round stone pillars and what seemed to be a garden on top in front of the usually closed front door. The smell came from the open windows either side of the door. I could run up to the door pillars, hook my arm out and swing round a few times, then on to the other one and give it the same treatment. I never understood why some brolly-waving old dears objected to my swinging clogs....

Next stop was Arthur Graham's boxes of fruit and vegetables, set out on stands on the pavement. One day there was, on a tray, a pyramid of potatoes which looked like a real work of art. Now if some of those spuds were to roll off, they wouldn't half go down the sloping pavement.... Just then I had the strange feeling that somebody was watching me, and when I looked in the shop window, there was Arthur Graham leaning over the displays of fruit inside the window and stretching his arm with clenched fist, full length and almost touching the glass. I had no doubt what he wanted me to do. His fist waved back and forth, his large thumb pointing westward, and he had a certain look in his eye. Nothing was said so I nonchalantly sauntered along past the stands - westwards....

Arthur's potato pyramids were discontinued in the 1930s when it was discovered that the action of light which turned the spuds green created a poison, so

33

Repairs to cartwheels at the blacksmith's, very wet for the author at one time.

A wintry market place with blacksmith's shop right of centre. Shop and houses left of centre have all been demolished. (J Keen)

they were kept covered to prevent this. Nowadays potatoes are again on open display on illuminated supermarket shelves....

Across the street in the market place, I was sometimes lucky enough see the blacksmith fitting iron hoops on wooden cart wheels - but I kept well clear after the first time. They carried the red hot iron hoop out and dropped it on the wooden wheel; once it was fitted, buckets of water were thrown over the hot iron to cool it as quickly as possible so that it shrank tightly on to the wheel. That was very interesting; a pity all of the water didn't go where it

was intended... I came away with an overflowing clog and sore spots where the hot water from the hoop had splashed. Those smiths certainly enjoyed their work; they kept grinning.

People who recognised me often told me to get away home, it was such and such a time, but one time was as good as another to me and I was going in that direction, perhaps slowly, but going.

Colin Keen shoeing a horse in the blacksmith's shop while Harry Jackson looks on. (C Keen)

The gates played on by the author on his way home. (C Keen)

Old Westgate with horse reversed into original opening of Oliver & Snowdon's warehouse; the other horseman appears to be a continental driver, heading west on the right-hand side of the street.

There was another load of shop windows to see in Westgate plus the Chapel gates; they were great to push back and forth on their rollers. The Mechanics Hall had iron gates but they were forever coming off the runners, they seemed to be poorer quality than the Chapel ones and they eventually fell apart without my help and were removed. On the other side of the street, the Co-op had metal gates that folded to each side but I could never get them to pull out. A tall man, Jack Hall, usually came out and told me to get away home, it was late and to leave the gates alone. Years later it was a different story, when Ted Smith and Jack Hewitson struggled with the gates and asked for help to pull them. I reminded them that I had tried to do that years before and had been chased away - but gave them a hand anyway.

Jack Hall was the man who often asked me to make less noise with my clogs on the wooden shop floor but he never told me how to. I often went into the Co-op when Mother was shopping, to watch the overhead travels of money from counter to cash office. The assistant put the cash in the canister, screwed it on to the carrier and fired it up a wire to the cashier's office by pulling a rope down.

What I and other lads always hoped would happen was that the canister would run out of puff before it reached the office buffers and come whizzing back down again, as happened sometimes. That was usually the time when we jumped up and down with excitement and annoyed Jack Hall, among others, with our clog dance. The force which fired the canister along the wire could be adjusted and I'm

Carnival float passing the Fair Hill mart. Passengers include Ethel Thompson, Norman Banks, Rossi Fleming, Anne Noble, Pam Stevenson, Margaret Telford, Derek Armstrong, Gerald Armstrong and Eric Smith. (G Armstrong)

sure one of the older assistants altered the settings when we went into the shop, to get us going and possibly to annoy Jack.

As I came round Ernie Carrick's sticky-out fruit shop on one occasion, I was amazed to see that the right-hand window of Joe Brown's watch and clock shop was smashed and jagged pieces of plate glass were scattered about. A break-in, I thought - this needed looking into - but the strange thing was that nobody was clearing up or in the shop. Had Joe been kidnapped? As I went nearer there was a sudden shout from behind the window backing, "Keep out o' there, it's not safe." I jumped back and stepped in some vital evidence lying on the pavement. This would have been at home in the middle of Hugh Edgar's field but gave a clue to what had happened.

Less destructive animals being herded along Westgate to the mart. (S Blackburn)

It was mart day along at Fair Hill and as usual cattle were herded down the street to the railway siding for dispatching, when apparently one beast saw its own reflection in Joe's window, didn't like what it saw and charged through the glass and in among the barometers. The 'crack' was that the beast only wanted to see what the weather was going to be like, but it had made a right mess, in more ways than one.

There was a curved window, which was broken more than once, on the corner of Willie Milligan's chemist's shop at the junction of Aesica Road and Westgate, where cattle were often squashed into the narrow lane-opening. Willie tired of these disruptions among his medicine bottles and had the lower half

Old Westgate showing the curved corner of Milligan's shop which often had the window broken by cattle coming and going to the Fair Hill mart. (C Keen)

of the curved corner window built up. He blamed the out-of-work miners sitting on Liddell's wall for frightening the beasts into his window but some of the miners whispered - loudly - that Willie's face would do that. That happened before my time so I never saw Willie's damaged window - or medicines.

After quick glances into the unbroken shop windows up to the station corner, there were shunting engines to watch in the station yard, although it was better if I went as far as the Metal bridge and climbed on to the wall top just over the bridge; it was much higher and provided a better view and was well out of the way of station porters. After struggling to get up the rather smooth stone wall, often somebody would come along and chase me off there and as usual, tell me to go home. There would be other times and I could always watch the trains steaming alongside the road to Redpath. Once when I managed to clamber up I was lucky enough to see an engine off the rails, but not far off. This engine, a J39 I thought, had been coming from the Alston side of the platform in reverse towards the turntable, but the points were open for the main line; the loco came on and into the trap points when the tender wheels became derailed and dropped on to the ballast. Reluctantly, because of heavy rain, I left the driver and fireman jacking up the wheels and headed for home, before somebody blamed me for the derailment.

Splashing along the West End and coming down Cross Bank, I remembered about the beck under the road, having noticed it on our shopping trips to Haltwhistle; a stream my earlier escort seemed to think was out of bounds, whatever that meant - now was my chance to see it. A jump over the roadside wall and I was down to the beck side, from where I could see right through the square-shaped tunnel to the other end. It only needed two or three flat stones thrown into the pool at the lower end and I was across into the tunnel and by bending down I could walk through and out into the wood at the other side, then up on to the roadside wall and back on to the

Haltwhistle Station from Metal Bridge with turntable in foreground; Alston Arches can be seen in background. (M Henderson)

road. I would remember that this place made a good shelter from the rain providing the beck didn't flood and wash me out.

Next stop was the stream near the cricket field where the Painsdale Burn came under the railway and the road, in one very long and curved tunnel, so consequently I couldn't see through to the other side. I remember eventually paddling through this conduit and out into the Spital Lodge wood, when the water was only an inch or two deep along its length. About the halfway point I could just see light from either end and, strangely, some water dripping out of a hole in the roof.

This was a very well built tunnel, just like the ones on the main lines, but scaled down in height to about three feet, so I had to keep my head down. The floor was stone-paved like our living room above the byre, but some of the stones must have corroded or washed out as there were deeper pools in places which filled my clogs. Some time later I realised that the water dripping from the arched roof was from a drainpipe under the railwayman's house up above, and as they had an iron hand pump on the gable end next to a rain barrel, both would overflow into the gully and thence down below. I often wondered where the pump drew the water from and whether it was just a case of recycling some of the Painsdale Burn water from round the tunnel.

The house was built tight alongside the railway tracks and it could be very entertaining when a visit to Kit Carrick, the occupier, coincided with the running of express trains, especially at 7:40pm when two expresses often passed the house. All the ornaments on the sideboard rattled about as the whole house shook with the combined weight of two heavy engines and their trains at speed. Although

38

it meant a return walk from Redpath at that time of the evening, I always tried to be there at the right time for the shake-up, which neither Kit nor his wife seemed to notice, and I once heard Kit ask his wife if the express had run yet, just after a rattle-up fit to bring the house down - and Annie wasn't sure. This was most likely a show put on to amuse young Parker. I wondered if the house shook as much when the all-black train, known as the oiler, came past Kit's; with not much smoke and no steam, it seemed to be a loco and two or three large van-like vehicles and made little more noise than a bus. Father reckoned it would be an oil-engined set on trial out of Armstrong's works at Newcastle but he could not say where the 'bus-train', as we called it, came from. This was a single carriage with what sounded like a petrol engine; the driver sat in the centre at one end and moved to the other end when they reversed.

Another unusual sight was of an 0-6-0 loco, perhaps a J27, pulling three low-loading trucks, each with a shiny black steam loco on top and with a guard's van on the rear. These apparently new locos seemed to be of a different gauge and slightly lower in height than LNER locos; a load came from Newcastle on their way to Carlisle, each Friday afternoon, for many months in about 1936. They often stopped at Haltwhistle platform-end signal and I tried to beat them to the cricket field by running through the West End and down Cross Bank, but the train usually disappeared past Redpath road end before I got anywhere near the 'cut end' at Kit Carrick's. These locos could have been from Hawthorn Leslie's works in Newcastle and were being taken to the docks for shipment to India.

These diversions on the way home from school took such a long time that they had to be spread over several days and were the reason for some very late tea-times for me; my sisters often had been home for ages when I strolled up. Time meant nothing to me; but it seemed to bother other people. The walk to Haltwhistle in the mornings was often under way by eight o'clock but I had a reason for getting a move

on at that time. If I could get to Kit's ten minutes before the Carlisle train passed I was in time to watch the guard standing in his open doorway to fire the rolled-up daily newspaper over the fence and into the house doorway, while the train went past at full speed. He rarely missed the house doorway and never missed the yard.

If we had slept in and were late setting off we missed the newspaper flight but we did recognise the different drivers and waved to them nearer the Redpath road end. Their engines were usually painted green, with LNER stuck on the sides and were always clean-looking, almost polished, and if we passed them near the Tipalt bridge where the tracks were higher up, we could see right under them and through part of the ash box if the damper was open. I thought the drivers must be the lucky ones, all they had to do was sit and ride all the way to Carlisle and wave at the odd schoolboy trudging along to another day of discipline. I vowed I would be an engine-driver some day.

Some days as we walked along a car would stop and give us a lift; we called the driver 'Mr. Brown from Brampton', because he had a brown car. The back seats were always full of new clothes, dresses, suits and other pieces. As I recall the shape of the car, I would say it was most likely an Austin 10 or 12 of about 1932; the leather seats had a lovely smell and squeaked as we sat in them. That ride saved us a long walk but got us to school far too early, so I often spent the time looking at Potts' bikes and came on to school when the other lads appeared.

Like all the long-distance walkers, I always carried sandwiches with me in a satchel; town boys went home at bait time but we ate ours in one of the school rooms. Mr Liddell, the caretaker, had a big black cast-iron kettle for making tea but I took Jackson's well water with me. I rarely ate all the bread in the bag but a friend from Town Foot always cleaned up any surplus; he was a big lad and he never had any trouble devouring the spare sandwich. He went home for bait but he always seemed to come back

An early view of Pott's Garage (left), Central Place. (C Keen)

hungry. More than 50 years after our schooldays, John remembered the sandwiches but had forgotten the time when, as an eight-year-old, he accidentally swallowed a pin. Somebody was sent out of the school to Brian Bowerbank's house on the Fair Hill for two slices of dry bread and John was told to eat them. He grinned and scarcely believed that this extra grub was for him but he wasn't long in shifting Mrs Bowerbank's home made-bread. As far as I can remember, we never heard about the pin again but teacher warned John not to make a habit of swallowing haberdashery. I had never heard this haberdaber word before so it was explained and we learned something extra that day - as well as not to swallow pins.

Miss Cook's class was pretty informal, but in higher classes, when that whistle blew in the playground, we had to stop where we were and on the second whistle we lined up in orderly rows near the classroom doors, then we marched into our class in readiness for lessons.

The second infants' class was run by Miss Johnson, another nice person who tried to teach us letters of

Haltwhistle Silver Band in the Church School yard: l-r from the back row: Tommy Jarvie, John Forrester, Norman Smith, Howard Smith, Percy Tyers, Victor Little, Wilf Robbie, A Wanless, B Milburn, C Hall, Joe Robson, Billy Naisby/Pears, Harry Adamson, Dennis Noble, G Rutherford, Sidney Fletcher, R Wright, ?, A Wilson, Jim Robson, L Banks, B Bell, J Mitchell, Albert Teasdale, Herbie Hunter, J Bell, A Burns. (E Coates)

the alphabet and sums and even some croaky singing. We can't all have been croaky though, or Haltwhistle's famous St Cecilia's Choir wouldn't have had any members. Dr Hutchinson, the well-known musician and conductor, was involved with the choir, and Kathleen Ferrier joined them at a concert early in her tragically short career. I well remember a member of Hylton Seymour's Record Club telling me that she still treasured a hair comb which Miss Ferrier had borrowed on that visit. The choir, like the equally famous Singing Waiters, is heard no more, and Haltwhistle Silver Band disbanded a few years ago, but there is still music in the Churches.

More sums and spelling followed in the next class under Miss Fleming, or perhaps she was Mrs Birkett by that time, but the thing that stands out in my mind in this final class of infants was when I was hauled in front of Miss Fleming because I had socked another boy from the next class up and he scraped some skin off when he caught the wall.

Miss Fleming said she thought it was terrible to go round fighting and it would not be allowed in her school. I explained that he had pinched my bag of marbles and when I tapped him he let go of the marbles and they scattered all over the yard and the others pinched the lot, so I bumped him and he shouldn't have been in our yard anyway. None of this seemed to impress Miss Fleming; I was wrong for hitting him and would have to be punished - but I don't know what that punishment was.

I doubt if it would be the strap or stick, she wasn't that kind of teacher, but there was plenty of that to come in the big school across the yard. I always thought Miss Fleming was all right but she couldn't remember this incident and asked if I was 'pulling her leg' when I asked her....about 55 years later.

When I moved to Standard Two in the main school, the strap and stick were brought to the fore and often left their mark. For some reason, I missed Standard One with Miss Mansfield, later to be Mrs Teasdale, and went to Miss Ridley, who let me know what she thought was right and wrong, and none of us lads got away with much in her class. She wore spectacles and we always thought her eyes appeared to act independent of one another, we would think she was looking away from us but she always seemed to know instantly what we were up to and consequently, I often felt the strap in her class.

My younger sister started school when I moved into Miss Fleming's class and I walked to school with her and managed to get home again at a reasonable hour, for a time at least. I had investigated most of the burns and ditches between Haltwhistle and Redpath over the previous two years, as well as the alternative routes, public rights of way or otherwise, so I didn't mind giving them a miss, there were always the becks along Wydon Lonnen and up in the wood for after tea.

I had walked to school with my older sister on occasion but she lived with other relatives for a time and she was confined for a long time in an isolation hospital at Longtown suffering from scarlet fever, so I usually felt like a lone ranger stepping out, and more or less pleased myself which route I took; only hunger urged me homewards. I always enjoyed the walks there and back, except in deep snow. Clogs were the usual footwear in those days; they had a disadvantage in that snow packed into the 'cokers'- the metal strips nailed to the wooden soles of the clogs - and built up, sometimes as thick as four inches. Just as you'd got used to this, one snow clod would fall off and until the clod came off the second clog, walking was a "dot and carry one " affair. With both clods though, it was just like walking on stilts, and I could see over higher walls and look into windows in the railway houses at West End.

My clogs were fitted with double coker irons at one time, one set inside the other; these lasted much longer between removal and refitting of the irons by Joe Hudspith at Station Corner. The double irons did have a drawback. I accidentally walked along a cement footpath in Wright's glasshouse at West End; the path had only recently been renewed and was still fairly soft, so good impressions of the double cokers were left for grown-ups to identify the culprit.

Our ankles must have been very flexible and surprisingly never broke while cavorting about in the snow. If I had stuck to normal walking and not raced about so much, I could have avoided some of the knocks I suffered.

One day after I had eaten part of my bait at school, I thought I might run down to Auntie Connie's house near the gasworks; I might get a close-up view of the quarry loco and trucks which passed near the house. I thought I could be back in time for lessons, so with a clatter of clog irons, I raced along the High Row towards Town Foot. Near the Primitive Chapel my clogs slipped on the curbs and I partly sailed through the air and struck my head on something sharp and suddenly blood seemed to be everywhere.

Somehow I struggled to the gas works house and Uncle Joe then took me to the hospital, where a nurse put stitches in and wrapped a turban bandage round my head like the one Syi, the Indian, wore when he came round selling stuff from his suitcase. I was off school that day but went with Uncle to watch the

Olympic Hall being built beside the paint and varnish works down the Haughs.

Another calamity for us was when Mother had to go into hospital and was away for over four years, then shortly afterwards my younger sister suffered a broken leg. Everything seemed to be going wrong and more was to come.

Helping on the farm still went on at weekends and some evenings, when I could spare time from my beck and burn digging.

During haytime one year, we were up at the Hardriggs Farm putting the hay in the barn. Hay bogies were not used there because the field almost adjoined the barn and the system was to put a long chain round the pike, and the horse merely dragged the pike along the ground to the barn, so the team forking hay into the barn had to move quickly.

I was at the back of the building stamping the hay down, or 'possing the mow'. Mr Lattimer, or Jim as Hugh called him, forked the hay to me after taking it from another forker at the front. How it happened I'm not certain, but a heap of hay built up between me and Jim's position so I leaned down to grab the heap. At the same time Jim turned round and, not seeing me behind the hay, gave the heap a good push with his fork. Neither of us realised that it was only a very loose and thin mound of hay and consequently his fork came right through the heap at speed. I would have to be there when that happened - but it could have been worse. His fork could have hit me anywhere on my head but I was lucky - if there is a lucky way to be hit with the points of a hay fork. One tine of his fork hit me between the eyes and slightly to one side of my nose. Of course, blood was spilt and somebody said that people a mile away in Haltwhistle heard my howling. After bathing the wound in cold water and wrapping it up, I was off to hospital once again with Mrs Edgar. Everybody we passed on the way down

Elliot's West End Garage. (A Burns)

Comb Hill and along Banks Terrace asked what had happened.

At the hospital a dressing was applied by the nurse who I am sure was the one who once gave me a piece of gingerbread, then we walked home to Redpath. Apparently Jim could not do any more at Hardriggs that day and had to go home, he was so upset. He couldn't sleep that night and the next morning, as I was bringing a bucket of water from Jackson's Well, I saw Jim coming across the fields, having walked from Haltwhistle, carrying a large paper bag full of apples and oranges, "to help you to get better," he said. He was very upset and went off, shaking his head. I was upset that he was upset and I felt sorry for him, not for myself. I never saw him again and I have always hoped that he got over it.

1935 was the year of the jubilee of King George and Queen Mary and I remember bringing home a jubilee mug and a sixpence which, some suggested, brought us a lot of bad luck. So many things seemed to go wrong for us in 1935: Mother and Anne in hospital; Thelma with a broken leg, also in hospital; myself at seven years old almost a regular outpatient at hospital. Luckily my youngest sister Marjorie, a three-year-old then, avoided accidents at that time.

My accidents didn't keep me from school, unfortunately. I carried on walking alone to school, often seeing nobody on the road until I reached the outskirts of the town, apart from the LNER enginemen and Mr Elliott at the garage when I called to give him another starting handle which I had found on the road. I wonder how many handles and other parts I handed in during the years I walked that road. If there had been rewards in those days I might have been 'in the money'.

I often took the long way home in summer, coming out of school and down the Croft path, over the Haltwhistle Burn by the footbridge and up to the quarry line, hoping to see the small engine and trucks. I had seen the trains from the school yard and at Aunt Connie's during the day but rarely saw them after school time; the Toon Futters reckoned

the line was going to close, anyway. After walking up the line, I had a good look round the old South Tyne Colliery buildings if there was nobody to chase me off, then I walked over the pit bridge near Rudstone Cottages and back up Willia Road to the Fair Hill. From there up Woodhead Lonnen to the farm, along the footpath to Birchfieldgate, over the Back Road and down through the woods to Spital Farm and on to the main Carlisle road and so to Redpath.

I doubted if my young sister could have managed daily treks like that, so I came home by the direct route, for a time. Unfortunately, she only walked for about six months before she broke her leg, went to hospital, and when she recovered, went to stay with Aunt Connie for about four years. My youngest sister started school in 1937 so she was to walk to school for over a year until November 1938, when we moved to Haltwhistle.

Fair Hill looking west: Haltwhistle workhouse on left in middle distance and Woodhead Lonnen in centre at the end of Fair Hill houses. (J Keen)

Chapter Three

NER delivery van. Driver: Mr Graham.

It came as a blow to Father when he learned that we had to move out. Our extensive garden, almost a field, was everything to him. He asked the landlords if he could buy the house but they said that authority had ruled that it could not be used as a dwelling and it was really only a one up and one down house, not suitable for a family. Father pointed out that he had bought a large steam-roller-type caravan and this was set up in the corner of the yard for extra living accommodation; he had to use it for himself when a

live-in housekeeper was employed to look after us while Mother was in hospital.

Many years afterwards I learned from the Edgars why Father didn't want to leave Redpath; evidently Parkers had lived there for centuries as yeoman farmers and are mentioned in local history books, as lookouts at river fords where marauding Scots - and English - were likely to cross, so it seems possible that the Land Enclosures changed the

Parker status. Redpath hamlet merits a book of its own, there is so much ancient and often violent history attached to it.

Hugh reckoned that our pewter plates and their number had some significance but he never learned what it was, and I have failed to find anything in history books about them, but they made a rare clatter when they came down. If the number of them was important Father must not have been bothered because I can remember looking over the top of the staircase door at Redpath when I was supposed to be in bed and seeing this man from London with his wife, again, pleading to buy just one of these pewter plates.

I had seen him a few times before and I discovered his wife was the daughter of a man that often chased us off his fields, old Joe Hetherington of River House at the West End. Eventually Father gave in and sold him an odd-sized plate that didn't match the others. Because Father was rather deaf I heard the stranger bellowing at him - and when I heard five pounds mentioned I thought he must have bought the lot but no, he went off with one plate only, wrapped up in brown paper. The couple would have to walk back to River House in the darkness that night and then carry the plate all the way to London. I thought they must be daft, five pounds sounded like a fortune to me and probably would to most people in the 1930s. Father would expect the rest of the plates would always be there at Redpath, but we had to move.

I would miss the becks along the lonnen and in the woods and the caravan had such a grand play area underneath. Our caravan had four wheels and was made for hauling by a horse; wooden shafts were folded up the end and partly hidden by the van when it was pushed into the corner. The wheels were properly wooden-spoked and iron-hooped, almost a half-sized farm cart wheel and fitted to iron axles with the luxury of leaf springs. Space under the van was ideal for my excavations, etc. and for storing my shunter and trucks (as well as odd, unwanted breadcrusts) on the cross timbers; there would be

nothing like this at a council house. The living part of the caravan was almost identical to George Rutherford's steam-roller van but ours had more windows, and rambler roses grew out of the garden at one side, up and over the roof and down the other side.

What a miss that would be - then there was the byre under the house, often used by all of us for playing in, although Father objected to my finding his aunt's wooden leg in one of the boxes and bending it back and forth, pretending it was walking. I don't know why he made such a fuss about a wooden leg; his aunt had been dead a long time and it was full of woodworm. Hugh told me many years later that aunt Jane had never used the leg anyway; she put her shortened leg on a wooden chair and hitched herself round the place on that and was able to work in the beehives, lifting out frames full of bees to inspect them; she had to look after everything herself while Father was in the army. One of the curios of Redpath at that time was Aunt Jane's chair, she had trailed it about for so long in the garden, on the road and over the stone-flagged floor, that the rear legs had worn away with the result that it was useless for sitting on.

I never found the chair in the byre but there was a pair of her old crutches. I often wondered what other treasures were hidden away in there which we could not manage to penetrate. There was a large bike hanging upside-down from the beams which I was warned not to touch. I believe Father bought this bike from Doctor Williams at Haltwhistle but found he couldn't ride it and stored it away in the byre. Eventually, somebody from the West End took it away, about the same time as George Hepple, also from West End, took all the bee-keeping appliances away. Father had not kept any bees since he had lost all his stocks in the 1920s owing to Isle of Wight disease. I remember George, who was lame, had to make quite a few trips on foot carrying the stuff along Wydon Lonnen, like Father Christmas, with a great sack on his back which rocked violently from side to side as he limped along.

On flittin' day we stayed off school to 'help'. Father had some shares in the railways and always bought our household coal from the railway station, thinking it would help his dividends, so when he needed a carrier for furniture, he hired a LNER lorry with Mr Gibson as driver. With the help of the two Edgars and one or two others, the heavy furniture was loaded.

Heavy was the word for the big oak sideboard, which was over six feet long and like a solid block. Four men tried to lift it, but they had to have others to help them and it only just scraped through the narrow Redpath doorway. Over the years, its weight had caused the whole of the sideboard to sag in the middle because the legs were fitted at each end, consequently, the two-inch gap, through which our marbles disappeared, was much reduced in the centre of the six-feet span. Hugh thought it would never fit into the council house and Harry said that if it did, it would likely go down through the modern wood floor.

As it happened, the sideboard was up-ended at Haltwhistle and dragged along by strong ropes on some thick cardboard; happily the wood floor survived and stood the weight for many years. The old plate rack was found to be unsafe to fit on the sideboard, so it went for firewood, and only one row of pewter plates stood at the back of the sideboard. Because the top was smooth and slippery, we often had clatters of pewter plates after we found the floor also bounced like the Redpath one if we happened to jump about. Unfortunately, at Haltwhistle the plates seemed to make a clean sweep of all the other things set out on top of the sideboard; one of the large round pewter mugs assumed an oval shape after one of the crashes.

I had planned to nail a strip of wood moulding near the back as a support for these plates but the oak was so solid and hard that the rail was never fitted. The grandfather clocks stood in opposite corners of the living room but sadly the wooden cases were not in the best of health and in fact, one of these towering clocks fell over, missing sister Thelma by a hair's breadth. Marjorie had been reaching behind to rescue a marble when over it went. After that near scrape, Father moved the clocks into the yard; the wood was used for kindling and I played with the works for many years. I have one of the bells and some of the gears somewhere. My sister was lucky but could have been killed if that great heavy clock had hit her; had our luck changed for the better? My jubilee mug was flattened out before the flitting; coronation mugs were issued in 1937 and these also disappeared; perhaps somebody thought that they brought bad luck and got the hammer out to change it. I am sure Aunt Connie, who was superstitious, had something to do with it.

In the evening of the flitting day, the men sat in the living room having a drink, some on chairs, some on stools. Meanwhile, we bairns ran upstairs and down, switching this newfangled electric light on and off. I was stationed at the bottom stair light switch and if somebody at the top switched the light on, I immediately switched it off and tried to anticipate when they would try again and moved my switch. This was great fun and we had some near misses. Suddenly, there was no light whatsoever; all was in darkness. What had we done now? Harry said later that there was dead silence; everyone stopped racing about and Hugh said into the firelight, "That's stopped the little beggars." It turned out that it was a penny-in-the-slot meter, so when the coin was inserted, on came the lights. To us, this was magic.

Laughter from the living room increased as the liquid in the bottles reduced; I happened to go in just as Harry threw his head back and gave a great laugh. Suddenly, there was a crash. The stool he was sitting on gave way and flattened out from twelve inches high down to about two inches. Father reckoned we needed more firewood anyway and carried on with the bottles; very heroic of them, I thought, to drink that stuff.

We were glad to go to our beds that night after all the excitement. I slept in a little back bedroom; my sisters and housekeeper sorted themselves out into the larger main bedroom and Father occupied the small front bedroom. This front bedroom was to become a special place to me and my wife, 27 years later when our daughter was born there (ushered in, coincidentally, by one of 'my' midwives Nurse Riddle) , our son having been born the previous year in Haltwhistle Maternity Hospital.

It was a bit strange using a flush toilet inside the house before we went off to bed; at Redpath we felt our way along the garden path in the dark to the wooden 'netty' but we did have 'modern' chamber pots for emergencies during the night; here at Haltwhistle we had no need of the pots or the wooden hut, everything just flushed down the hole to - somewhere. Another improvement was the hot-and-cold water taps; no need to fill the setpot at the side of the fire range; no more carrying buckets of water from Jackson's well, everything was indoors - even the coal - but what a daft place for a coal-house: under the stairs in the middle of the house. There was already some coal in there when we moved in but I was looking forward to seeing the coalman getting the stuff into that low and awkward coal-house.

Aunt Connie had organised everything before we got there: coal delivered, the new house cleaned out, some extra bedding and blankets, etc. We only had to bring the Redpath stuff down and we were established. Aunt Connie directed some of the items into the back yard; she wasn't having anything in the house that would get in the way of cleaning - or perhaps bring bad luck. Each house was supplied with a smart kitchen cabinet which I believe was assembled on the job by the joiners working on the building. It was a nuisance to us as we had trouble getting our furniture set out owing to the extra windows, compared with the Redpath house. These cabinets were very useful for people who had very little furniture when they moved into the new houses and are known nowadays as 'collectable'.

Greta & Connie Hunter, the author's mother and aunt.

I remember one family who had nothing at all, their house had burnt down and, as was often the case in those days, was not insured, so they had been allocated a house immediately. Neighbours gave them some blankets to make beds on the floor, some coal to heat the water, and somebody supplied them with a heap of small envelopes on which they wrote what had happened to them and asked if anybody could spare a coin to help them to buy some furniture, etc. They put the envelopes through as many letter boxes as possible in the town and they got their furniture: a very grateful family; very generous neighbours.

Each house was also provided with a large Burco electric clothes boiler, to make up for the lack of wash-house and setpot boiler. When washing was in progress in the kitchen and water spilled on the cement floor, I was always intrigued by the blue flashes reflected under the boiler when the switches were turned off. I found out years later that these were the old AC/DC type that made minor crashes when they were being switched off and on - but they carried on flashing satisfactorily for many years and of course the boilers cost less to run if filled from the hot tap.

We didn't have a wash-house at Redpath so the washing was thumped about with a poss-stick in a barrel filled with soapy water - in the open air. The bump, bump, bump could be heard on Monday mornings and after a while all the washed clothes were fished out and put through the large iron mangle, its great wooden rollers squashing out the soapy water which ran back into the poss-tub for re-cycling. The clothes were rinsed and mangled and put out to dry. Some people carried on with poss-tubs when they moved into council houses but the tubs had to be kept in the yards because of lack of space; the mangles were out there anyway. As newer and smaller washers such as the 'Jiffy' became more popular the posser was used less and less, and poss barrels were often used on their sides for storing firewood until they fell apart.

The fixed bath was a big improvement and much more private than the old tin bath we used on the flagged floor at Redpath. We couldn't tip the council bath, unlike the Redpath one which I tipped a few times but as the mats were cleared from the bathing area beforehand, any floodwater quickly disappeared down through the cracks between the stone flags, into the byre below; we speculated on what the cows would have thought of it.

We quickly got used to the new house and it was much closer to school. I will always remember Standard Two teacher, Miss Ridley, as Miss Strap, because she always seemed to have it handy when I was near her and she knew how to use it - on me at least. I always wondered why, others probably didn't need to wonder. This proved to be an incentive in the learning process because I jumped a class and moved up to Standard Four. I had not been looking forward to Miss Watson's Class Three, but I never found out how good or bad she was and I passed on to Harry Graham's in Four.

He was the first master I had encountered since starting school and I was a bit wary of him. He seemed a giant of a man and likely would stand no nonsense. In that classroom stood a science cabinet full of interesting items which, I was told, he knew how to use, and he had a good knowledge of mechanics, so I decided to put up with him. When science lessons were held, the girls in our class joined the girls in Standard Five for a sewing lesson with Miss Keenlyside, and the Standard Five boys joined us in Four with Harry Graham.

In one of these lessons we made a crude form of fire extinguisher with glass outlet tubes, heated and bent to shape, threaded through a tight-fitting cork in the top of the container. The extinguisher pressurised all right, it blew the glass tubes out of the top with some force up to the ceiling and we never found all of the pieces; the caretaker, my uncle Joe, probably wondered what we had been trying to blow up and swept the pieces up after we went home.

Somebody brought in a live steam model of the Rocket and we fired that up and got it going along the floor; what could I not have shunted with that machine on the ash surfaced yard at Redpath. It used methylated spirit but I supposed I could have used small 'duff' out of the adjacent coal shed... These lessons were very interesting to me, and during a subsequent lesson, Harry decided that we should learn about petrol engines; he asked if anybody could make a drawing on the blackboard of a car or lorry engine. Somebody suggested that John Bowerbank from Standard Five could do it but John said he couldn't, so I said I thought I could do it.

Harry gave me the chalk and told me to get on with it, then went to the rear of the class. I started off drawing the outline of the engine and adding fan, pulleys, flywheel, clutch, carburettor, inlet and exhaust manifolds and finally I stuck the oil filler on the top. I drew this from what I remembered of Robsons' Bedford lorry engines, and after I had drawn in these items, I hesitated, looking at the board and wondering if that was the lot. Teacher asked from the back of the class: "Have you been taking somebody's engine to pieces?" This raised a titter from the rest of the class.

When I said I thought it was all there now, he came forward and said it was very good and asked the rest of the class if they could tell him what I had missed out. Missed out? I was sure it was all there. Nobody said anything, whereupon Harry said: "He's forgotten the sparking plugs," and drew some in with the chalk. "But sir," I said, "I think because of the hot exhaust they're fitted on the other side of the engine." Harry looked up at the ceiling and just said "Thank you, now would you just go and sit down." I always remembered that: me beating - or cappling - Harry, in front of two classes - or at least, I thought I had. That was a great lesson, perhaps for both of us.

Harry would certainly have taken a dim view if he had caught any of us climbing over the school roof, although he was probably more aware of what went on than we thought. This exploit required us to change our clogs for sand-shoes, as used in PT lessons; we could then grip the down pipes and walls to gain access to the long flat roof between Standards Two and Seven. At the far end of this roof, after dodging under the hall windows, it was an easy matter to run up one lead valley gutter over on to the north side, down to the large vent pipe from the teachers' toilets, swing over on to the pipe and reverse down to the playground. Sometimes we ascended on to the flat roof officially, to recover footballs, when Harry brought out a cissy ladder for us to climb.

One boy, making his way over the roof top and down the vent pipe almost to yard level, was very surprised to feel six of the best from the cane belonging to headmaster Johnny Smailes. Unknown to the boy, JS must have spotted him through the high hall windows, grabbed his cane, gone through the boys' cloak room into the yard and waited round the corner for our intrepid roof walker to appear. We came to the conclusion that the teachers must have known all about these adventures beforehand; Johnny knew exactly where the boy would be descending into the yard.

Some time later we thought that some of the boys had gone too far when a large roof ventilator was discovered lying in a crumpled state in the girls' yard; climbing over the roof seemed harmless enough to us but wrecking the school roof was going to cause us some trouble until they found out who was responsible. Oddly, there was no investigation by the teachers; the police were seen at the school so we thought they must be really 'going to town' about this damage. Later we found out that a wartime barrage balloon had broken away in Scotland and headed down to England, trailing its mooring cable over the Roman Wall, across Lees Hall Farm and the Burn then over the school roof, removing the ventilator in the process. I believe it went over Plenmeller Fell and reached County Durham. Apparently the police had been checking for damage caused by the cable; some of us wondered if they would pin the blame on us, but Clydeside was out of our range.

Soon after the blackboard drawing, I was disappointed to hear that Harry was leaving Standard Four, but pleased when I heard he was staying at the school to take over Standard Seven because Mr Peggs was moving to Hexham. This meant a new teacher for Standard Four; a younger man arrived, who seemed to be lacking something, so the pupils more or less took over. He tried for about six weeks and finally gave it up as a bad job; he must have had his eyes opened while he was at Haltwhistle.

Harry Graham and 'the gang': Summer Camp at North Seaton Hall, Newbiggin, July 1939: l-r: back row: Albert Weir, Tom Shield, Billy Wallace, Dennis Dent, Dennis Simpson, Teddy Butler, Sid Wanless, George Smith; second row: Lawrence Elliot, Jim Robey, Derrick Reed, Victor Little, Edmond Phillipson; third row: Ronnie Henderson, Arnold Hepple, Raymond Nixon, Harry Graham, Bobby Hunter, Derek Pape, Roly Pape; front row: Kenneth Gill, Pearson Bell, Ronnie Laidlow, Jonty Carruthers, Norman Moss, Tom Maughan, Tom Tweddle, Joe Penrose, Bob Dixon. (M Hunter)

Boys and some girls were quick to take advantage if they thought they could get away with anything. One of the Toonfutter girls refused to come out to the front when ordered to by the new teacher, and when he made to haul her out, Frances climbed over the desk into the next row; when teacher made for that row, she merely stepped back over into the other row. He gave up and just shouted "Sit down then!", and she did, waiting another chance to get the better of him. He used the strap often enough but most boys put their hands out for the strap and when he swiped it down towards the outstretched hand, they clicked it down to their side; consequently it was not unknown for the teacher to lose his balance. He started aiming nearer the boys' shoulders so that he could still hit their hands when clicked back down to their sides.

A counter-offensive was mounted by wrapping papers round the arm muscles and then putting on our jackets. When the strap was seen to be aimed towards the shoulders, boys would hold their arms out as usual and keep them in that position. He could belt away all day at the papers for all we cared but he was getting near the end of his six-weeks visit by that time and the strapping slackened off. We had gone far enough; we had some fun at his expense.

Learning had almost come to a standstill but the next teacher changed all that. She was a Miss Somebody, whose name I can't remember, but as she was a no-nonsense person, we had to get on with some work, although science and mechanics were not taught in Standard Four after Harry Graham moved on.

It was about that time that we moved from Redpath, and after the main flitting day, a Friday I believe, we still had some things to bring, most of which were carried on Harry Edgar's cart; bushes and garden plants were trailed behind us as we walked down the road. The long rambler roses had to be dragged; Father and I took one each as we walked down the main road, then by the shortcut over Cross Bank allotments and on to the Back, or Park Road near the football field, now covered by Westlands houses.

It was dark by the time we reached the football field gate but I recognised some of the voices of a group of cheeky lads. Father didn't seem to hear anything, but I did, so I gave them as much as they sent. Just then the lads started jumping on the long rambler that I was dragging along the road. Father was in front and his roses were out of their reach so he just walked on unaware of the carry-on I was having. I managed to pull one or two gowks off their feet and got the roses up into the air and swung them round and into these West Enders. Their ouches and arghs were music to my ears as they retreated while I hurried on to catch up with Father who was still walking on as if nothing had happened. I suspect that he would notice what was happening in the dim street lamp light and likely thought I was managing all right.

There were some scratched faces in class the next week but no comments were made about rambler roses. Their wounds have probably healed by now.

One of the last items to come from Redpath was the big caravan; unfortunately I missed that drama. Father had sold it to Mr Liddell, the former caretaker at our school, for use as a store shed in his Flowers Close garden; the removal was kept dark at the time so I missed it. Apparently, David Railton, driving a Robson Bros. Bedford lorry, managed to pull the van out in reverse, on to the lonnen at Redpath, and then coupled the horse shaft-ends to the back of the wagon for towing to Haltwhistle. Slow progress was made down the main road - and somewhere near the town one of the wheels became defective; having stood for years some of the wooden spokes had rotted, the iron hoop came loose and fell off and the rest of the wheel crumbled into a sorry heap next to the rim. The top part of the van was shuffled on to another lorry and delivered into the gardens almost opposite Robson's Comb Hill garage. The remaining undercarriage probably ended its days in Joe Lee's scrapyard. Our old van stood in the gardens for many years and always reminded us of happy times at Redpath.

By moving to Haltwhistle I had more time after school and at weekends to explore the district's industrial sites; people always seemed willing to explain what had happened at the old collieries in 'their days' when a great number of folk were employed. Walled-up shafts still showed at South Tyne, Plenmeller, Fell End, Blackett at Melkridge and other sites; a bike, I thought, would be an asset in the investigation of all these places. I hadn't long to wait.

One day I walked down the street and there it was: a bike rear wheel and mudguard sticking out of a full load of ashes on Kennedy's cart on the way to the tip. It looked very interesting and I was sure the front part of the bike was buried in the rest of the ashes. I followed the cart to the tip and asked the horseman if I could have the bike. He laughed and said it was all but rusted away and was only good for scrap. I said I could repair it so he pulled the bike out before he tipped the cart, stood it upright, stepped on the seized-up pedal and promptly shattered the rusty chain. Again I said I could repair it, hoping to get it away before he did any more damage, so he said I had better take it away then. This, I thought, was my lucky day.

The front wheel turned but the rear one was jammed, so I wheeled it home, carrying the rear wheel up off the ground. A cousin had plenty of spanners so we dismantled the bike, cleaned, oiled and re-assembled it in our back yard, and checked the tubes and tyres, which, amazingly, held the pressure. I had found a puncture in one tube and repaired it with the sticky tape off a Bournvita tin. Old Ned Windsor, who was breaking-in our garden, just shook his head and thought I would have to get a proper rubber patch and throw the sticky tape in the ash pit. Ned happened to have a patch in his bike tool bag so he showed me how to do the job properly and the bike was soon ready for a first run out.

I had learned to ride on a lady's cycle some time before, so the crossbar on this gent's bike caused a few problems, but these were overcome and the bike worked all right, although owing to rusty wheel rims, I used quite a lot of home-made rubber brake blocks; they were sometimes worn out in a few days but this improved as the rims became polished. These rubber blocks were cut from old lorry tyres and it was thought by some that proper blocks would last longer, but this wasn't the case; our own manufacture lasted much longer but they were fiddly to shape and cut; nevertheless, the bike was rideable so now I could begin exploring. The bridge to nowhere at the Spital had puzzled me for years so I went and had another look at it and was promptly chased away by the estate workers, although one kindly man, who must have been about retiring age, told me that Father was right about the Carlisle road passing through the farmyard. Seemingly the raised wooden

The 1816/18 bridge at Spital which carried the main road for about 20 years. (J Parker, jnr)

crossings put up over the old river fords were gradually replaced by stone bridges. These permanent structures enabled much heavier loads to be carted on the highways, although not all changes went according to plan.

This good strong stone bridge was built about 1816/18 at Spital Farm, which is on the modern Grid ref.687638, on the then main Newcastle to Carlisle highway; it had a life of about 20 years as a main road bridge. A date can be seen on the parapet and although slightly weathered, the lettering seems to read : 'Built by the Commissioners. 1818 (or 1816)'. This bridge has been used merely for access to the west field at Spital Farm since the arrival of the railway.

Previously, the highway ran north-west from Cross Bank west of Haltwhistle, towards what is now Blenkinsopp East Lodge, crossing over the present position of the railway and bearing slightly left, passed over the site of the modern farm buildings and sawmill, then crossed the River Tipalt in the vicinity of the 1818 bridge and continued alongside the river towards Greenhead.

53

When the railway was constructed, a new road was formed on the south side of the line to Greenhead with a new bridge over the Tipalt alongside the railway bridge (G 687637).

Like so many smaller bridges built by the railway company, the deckings and spans were made of timber, although the stone abutments were built at the time, ready for the later addition of stone arches in the case of the railway, and the cast iron spans in some of the road bridges.

The railways developed civil engineering using mainly manpower, with some help from the horse and cart and windlasses for lifting heavy stones used in bridge building. Fuller mechanisation came later with contractors' locomotives and eventually trains on the line.

Iron foundries did well out of railways. Railway engineers had no choice other than to use cast iron for many of their road bridges where height was restricted.

I remembered noticing the railway bridge at the west end of the town, the aptly named Metal Bridge, with cast iron spans and railings, which carried the main road over the railway. Using cast iron girders here, much less bulky than a stone-built archway, helped to keep the top finished surface down to the line of the road on either side, avoiding the need for a humped-back bridge. The original open type of cast-iron railings had boarding added, presumably to prevent smoke and steam blasting on to pedestrians as they crossed the bridge, although this didn't stop me from jumping up and peering over the top on one particular occasion, but I had a shock when I realised I was looking straight down the chimney and blast pipe of a stationary loco, so I dropped down pretty smartly in case the driver opened the throttle and showered me with oily steam.

All the structures that the old man at the Spital told me about were there and, I thought, just needed looking into more closely.

Haltwhistle Tyne Bridge; a bridge of all sorts. showing brick pillars, steel structure and service pipes sometimes used by boys to cross the river, hand over hand, to the far side. This was classed as a 'capple' or an 'I'm better than you'. (D Hunter)

When much later a road bridge was required over the Tyne, to line up with the station railway bridge in the 1870s, this consisted of stone abutments, circular brick piers, steel girders and lattice spandrels, cast iron railings, oak timber decking and tarred road surface: a bridge of all sorts. The bridge also carries the main water supply pipe to Haltwhistle from Coanwood together with a gas

Remains of south side stone abutment of the old wooden span bridge opposite Kilfrost Ltd., Albion Works. (D Hunter)

pipe, both of which are bracketed from the framework under the decking. Certain schoolboys who felt the need of a challenge sometimes crossed over on these pipes, hanging by their hands, which I believe was quite exciting if there happened to be a high flood at the time. I preferred to edge over on the outside of the girders and never came across on the pipes; neither did 'Chippy' Slater... Haughan's lad came across fairly quickly but Chippy got tired on the final pipe span and dropped into the fast-flowing Tyne. With arms flailing, he grabbed the willow bushes and was out on the banking within a very short distance, but he was rather wet. Boys were often wet in those days.

This river bridge replaced the old timber crossing situated further downstream, near the present Kilfrost factory. The south-side stone buttress for this older bridge stood until the 1970s, when it was partly removed to provide an access road to riverside gravel workings. Many of the large buttress stones from the north side were built into the river banking to prevent erosion near Kilfrost's works.

Temporary timber bridges built for the opening of the line were gradually replaced by the Railway Company with mainly stone arches, except where low headroom existed. These were replaced with steel girders as at Lanty's Lonnen and near the station, where the old road to Whitfield and Alston passes under the railway and over the Tyne road bridge.

This station bridge was double track for many years but an extra steel girder bridge with a third track, bridge number 1 of the Alston branch line, was added alongside in about 1900 to enable Alston trains to proceed from the station to Alston without having to go out on to the main Newcastle-to-Carlisle 'down' line. Another section was added to this railway

Looking towards the railway from Boat Lane, station bridge on left. (M Henderson)

The Railway Station bridge, with four steel girders furthest from the camera supporting the double main line tracks; the two foremost girders added for the Alston branch about 1900. (D Hunter)

bridge on the north side to extend the Newcastle platform.

The cast iron girders of the Tipalt road bridge carried all the east-west traffic until the 1940s, when a heavy electrical transformer, on an equally heavy transporter, broke some of the girders in passing, leaving a rather depressed-looking road surface. Owing to hot weather at the time, the loaded trailer left deep wheel marks in the tarmacadam road surface for many miles. The broken cast iron girders were timbered up with props of about 12" diameter, and these carried the traffic until the early 1950s, when the whole of the bridge and abutments were renewed.

Many a time, when the water was low, I walked along the big metal pipe that was laid under the two Tipalt bridges but luckily I was elsewhere when that load came over. Surprisingly, the same load that broke the Tipalt bridge passed over the Metal Bridge at Haltwhistle's West End without incident. This bridge had the same cast iron girders and the span may have been about the same but was at an angle to the railway.

Subsequently, alterations were made to the Metal Bridge to improve the flow of traffic, the original width being almost doubled. All of the cast iron was removed years ago and now it has steel reinforcement buried in the concrete decking.

An older chap who liked a good crack was employed in the railway telegraph department for many years and he explained that railway building involved a lot of engineering, and as the system developed, railway companies were the first organisations in country areas to use electricity on any large scale for their electric telegraph and signalling. He thought railway companies intended to run a nationwide telephone service in those pioneering days, although they are only now, in the 1980s and 90s, providing communication facilities through their cables for some of the private telephone companies. There were no telephones in the early days as we know

The Metal Bridge at the west end of the station. First formed with timber and then cast iron girders, the abutments have been lengthened over the years. The blackened stonework shows the original width of the roadway. The newer building work was added in 1973 to take concrete beams. Consequently, the distance between parapets is almost twice that of the original bridge. (D Hunter)

them now, but some properties were later connected to the railway telegraph; some of these connections still existed locally in the 1950s.

Electrification progressed in cities and industrial areas in the late 1800s but this area saw very little change until mining expanded and electricity generation was then used extensively. This was very different from the railway telegraph, but one ex-colliery electrician reckoned that one of the earliest users of electricity in the area was the South Tyne Colliery (G.707646), which generated its own power from steam, produced by coal-fired Lancashire boilers. Four of these boilers were each thirty feet long, one of them fitted with a superheater. A fifth boiler was much shorter at 16 feet, but with 80 smoke tubes fitted was probably more efficient than were the longer tubeless models.

A small upright boiler was set up to work the winding drums for sinking the shaft, in about 1905. As the mine expanded and generators were installed, steam was required in increasing volume, hence the five boilers. This overloaded the chimney stack to such an extent that a forty-two-inch-diameter, induced-draught fan had to be installed in the smoke ducting to the chimney, to boost the furnaces. I can remember the hole in the side of the chimney where this fan ducting was fitted. The boilers were tested in rotation; one boiler at a time was descaled and inspected while the others carried on providing the steam.

By the 1920s the power house had three 550 volt generating sets installed: a 300 horsepower, two-crank, compound steam engine driving a 265 amp, 3-phase alternator: a 400hp steam engine driving a 370 amp alternator and a 400hp engine driving a 300kw alternator. This led to the need for a large steam-raising plant with eight and ten-inch-diameter steam feed pipes. Foundations and signs of this machinery were still visible at the pit site when we investigated during school holidays although, unfortunately, most of the plant was gone before our time. This installation, Haltwhistle's first

South Tyne Colliery looking north.

big Power Station, together with another of similar capacity at Plenmeller Colliery (G.705628), which we also investigated, provided the initial impetus for Haltwhistle's expansion into industry.

Much of South Tyne Colliery machinery was made to be compressed-air-driven but electricity was exploited fully both on the surface and underground, wherever possible, except for the winding gear which remained steam-driven. This was mining on a large scale for the Haltwhistle area.

Officials during the 1926 strike; output would be minimal at this time. (M Henderson)

At the closing-down sale in 1931 almost 40 electric motors were itemised, some 100hp up to 340hp. Many of these motors must have been kept in reserve, as the generating capacity was not high enough to run all of them simultaneously; why they kept a 340hp motor is a matter for conjecture. The shaft winders were steam-driven and there would be no other work requiring that amount of power.

Possibly this motor was acquired for the future conversion of the cage winders to electricity if the steam engine broke down, although converting a steam winder was not just a matter of fitting an electric motor alongside the drums; steam cylinders and rope drums were usually all built as a unit and took time to alter, so if the change-over could be avoided, so much the better.

At the sale, the 340hp motor made £20, a bargain for somebody. Daily output of coal from South Tyne pit reached 600 tons at one time but this figure may not have included boiler fuel for the generators. Assuming that this was shaft output and according to our calculations, the cages would make 300 trips, possibly more if each load was less than 2 tons, so it seems that the cages often travelled over 28 miles at maximum daily output. If 600 tons was the amount of coal sold, then the cages would have had to run even more trips to raise additional coal for the steam boilers.

It was a similar situation at Plenmeller which had a high-capacity power-station, but they also had an unconventional winding system capable of raising a much higher output than South Tyne, even though the Plenmeller shafts were about 50 per cent deeper. This colliery was the first pit in the country to have the 'Koepe' balanced type of shaft winder, a type of pithead gear that I had not given much thought to for some years until I happened to meet Mr Teasdale, a former winding-engine man at the pit.

Steam for the Plenmeller generators came from three Lancashire boilers, about thirty feet long, without smoke tubes, but with super heaters in the brick-built combustion chambers between each boiler and the adjacent chimney-stack. Boiler fuel was stored in stone and brick-built bunkers at the firebox end of the boilers, with rail connections via the shaft top gantries or the yard network to the loading hoppers. South Tyne boiler fuel went to the boilers direct from the shaft 'as raised' without screening.

Plenmeller shaft-sinking started about 1909 on the site of a borehole sunk in the mid-1800s to a seam of coal, 27 inches thick at a depth of 775 feet. This seems to be a long way down to sink two shafts for such a thin band of coal, although nowadays we tend to think too much in terms of modern mining methods and forget that labour was relatively cheap in those days,so that prospectors thought it worthwhile to go for thin coal seams.

Plenmeller Colliery. Steam boilers on settings, chimney stack completed, super heaters partly completed at rear of boilers, steam pipes to power house and boiler water feed pipes not yet connected. Brick and stone-built fuel bunkers in progress at right side of photo. Separate building in background appears to be an explosives store, rather close to the boiler house, which probably explains why another store was built on the far side of Gowk Hill. (R Bainbridge)

To visualise shaft depths I always compare them with something local like the 110 feet of Lambley Viaduct or the 300 feet of the modern Hopealone TV mast. Plenmeller shafts are about the same as seven Lambley viaducts, one on top of the other, or two-and-a-half TV masts. Comparing heights with objects further afield, South Tyne shaft is about as deep as Blackpool Tower is high.

Two shafts were required at Plenmeller; one for coal winding and the other to provide an alternative way out and for air circulation, unlike South Tyne where the older drift mine workings connect with the new shaft bottom.

The Plenmeller Company should have known what to expect in seam thickness, as the drilling of another borehole, about one-and-a-half mile to the east, past Unthank Hall gardens, (G.733633), discovered a

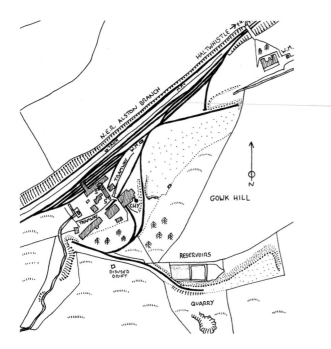

Plan of Plenmeller Colliery yard 1925. (R Hunter)

invaluable vignettes to a wider audience. South Tyne generators also supplied power via a line of large poles alongside the coal tub tramway to screens at Town Foot railway sidings, (G.714642), a distance of about half a mile.

Another row of poles with 3-phase supply cables stretched alongside the burn upstream, to power the ventilation fan in the older drift.

Had the colliery companies been more adventurous, increased their generating capacity and extended the poles and cables into the town, supplying electricity should have proved profitable, which might have been an incentive to exploit the lower seams which were said to exist, although none of the borehole plans that I have seen show any lower seams hereabouts, and of course many drilling details were never published. These, understandably, were often kept secret by the company which paid for the expense of the borings.

coal seam of 30 inch thickness much nearer the surface at 130 feet, which they calculated to be the Plenmeller seam. This last borehole is in such a position that it might possibly be against the east-west whin dyke of about 20 yards thickness which separates the Plenmeller mine from the South Tyne workings.

With all this activity, Haltwhistle forged ahead into the industrious 1900s. Haltwhistle folk being what they are, I picked up all sorts of information from ex-miners and other interesting people - memories of their early days at work and at home - and enjoyed many a good crack. Most of my informants are now long gone and their accumulated knowledge with them, so I am pleased that I kept a record of our conversations on times past, and grateful to have the chance to pass on these irreplaceable and

Early days at Plenmeller. Railway siding with trap points, laid into the site from the Alston branch line near the 'one mile' post. Some internal track fitted but no building work appears to have been started. (R Bainbridge)

Plenmeller shaft sumps were said to be so constructed that further sinking could be carried out at the same time as the existing coal-winding, so perhaps they had intended to go lower down. It would have been most interesting to know how they proposed carrying out this further sinking below a working Koepe winding installation, although it would have been possible to sink the south, upcast, shaft further without complicating the coal-winding in the north shaft. The drum winder was retained over the upcast shaft after the sinking and kept in good order for emergencies and could have been used for further sinking operations.

Evidently there was a company which thought it would be profitable to supply electricity, and so, after being almost surrounded by our own local power stations for about 20 years, the national supply came from Tyneside to the town in late 1920s and early 1930s and was extended to Greenhead Walltown quarry shortly afterwards.

One of the main reasons put forward for the closure of Plenmeller was the cost of transporting coal on the railway, a distance of one mile only, to Haltwhistle. South Tyne Colliery was not burdened with this extra charge. If some of the coal had been converted into electricity at Plenmeller and cabled over to Haltwhistle, maintenance costs on the supply lines would have been minimal compared to rail charges. South Tyne electricity poles were already into the Town Foot and could have been extended from there.

Further east at Mickley, the Coal Company generated electricity for some years before the Haltwhistle mines and supplied the village with metered electricity, and that system worked profitably. Perhaps these ideas were somewhat ahead of their time but apparently Dunston Power Station did not think so, and its managers were anxious to bring their supply 36 miles to Haltwhistle, even to the extent of providing free house-wiring installations, to secure the business. Three lighting points and a socket were offered with free fitting.

Almost 800 feet still to go. The start of shaft sinking at Plenmeller about 1910. The 27-inch coal seam was at a depth of 775 feet. (R Bainbridge)

I believe that any large mine with a foreseeable future should have a small power-station adjacent, to save transport costs and to be sure of a market for their coal. When seams at these pits become exhausted, coal could be brought from elsewhere to the generators, as happens nationally.

It seems curious that nowadays coal is mined, transported to the power station, converted to electricity which is then conducted back to the mining machinery to extract more coal and so on.

There must be an advantage somewhere, but then, the coal transport industry would be much reduced if all electricity was generated at the mine.

Plenmeller generators were different from those at South Tyne; the power output voltage was higher at 600v and most of the equipment was more modern, although some of the 3-phase switch gear recovered from Plenmeller and reused, would certainly be condemned nowadays and would never pass modern regulations.

Because of essential renewals in the late 1920s, South Tyne Colliery ended up with some generators more modern than Plenmeller's, when both pits closed down in about 1931.

Another example of a self-contained unit started working in the 1930s at Ventners Hall Colliery, (G.724707). This venture, always known as 'Wardle's Pit', was started by GR Wardle and partners, a few miles north of Haltwhistle, in the outcrop of a coal seam which dipped back towards the Roman Wall and the whin stone

area. The drift mouth was at a high elevation of about 900 feet above sea level. More important to me was the fact that it happened in 'my days'.

Mrs. Wardle told me that the first time she saw Ventners Hall area in the 1920s, many years before the mine was started, she thought it looked like the end of the world, it seemed such a desolate place. Mr Wardle, whose family had run the Gilsland Bakery business, followed by some lorry haulage for many

A view of South Tyne Colliery from what is now the old school playing field. (F Gents)

Plan of South Tyne pit yard. (R Hunter)

Bob Sample & George Carr - South Tyne Colliery workers. (M Henderson)

years, and Miss Robson, as she was then, rode out on a motorbike over some very rough tracks to see these old mine holes they had heard about in the outcrop on the north side of the hill facing Hopealone. Mrs Wardle said she always thought Hopealone to be well named. However, from those early explorations, a mine was developed in the late 1930s, which provided much employment for the area when times were particularly hard.

Mrs Wardle's brothers, as well as Mr Wardle, were in the haulage business, so after some road repairs, they managed to transport some machinery to the pit and to lead coal from it. Could the lady see the area in the 1990s, she would probably say, as before, that it rather looks like the end of the world. All traces of the mine other than the gateway are gone and the site is grown over. Looking to the north now, there are miles of fir trees stretching into Kielder Forest and many of the former farmsteadings are redundant; a slightly different landscape but equally as desolate as the one Mrs Wardle saw so long ago, but at least there is now a good hard road.

After a year or two of preparation, the mine first produced coal in quantity in about 1938. An upright boiler supplied steam to drive a twin-cylinder steam hauler for pulling coal tubs out of the mine on to the screening plant; there was also a steam-powered generator for supplying power to the underground and surface machinery.

Ventners' own generators kept going until the late 1940s when mains electricity was extended from the Haltwhistle area. In the late 1940s, after nationalisation, the screens were rebuilt further north from the drift and a new hauler house was built over the drift mouth with the direction of pull facing away from the mine. This necessitated fitting a return wheel behind the new screens, to enable the rope to haul tubs up the drift.

In the early 1940s Cecil Crowe was one of the stokers of the steam boiler in the north-side building;

Matt Maughan performed with the saw bench in the adjacent joiners' shop. Geordie Hepple was the blacksmith who made all the iron fittings for the new wooden tubs produced by Matt. Tub irons were only a small part of Geordie's work, which, as usual at pits in those days, required many skills. Geordie seemed to be well endowed with talents and after work these stretched into the musical field. He was a very accomplished Northumbrian Piper - his son also was keen and shared his father's remarkable ability on the small pipes.

There was, if I remember rightly, a Mr Armstrong, or Robson, living near the pit, who looked after the pony and horse-power. One of his jobs was to feed the animals over the weekend, so it seems that he was like the pumpmen: a seven-days-a-week man.

I don't know the name of the haulerman whose head appeared above the clouds of steam escaping from the cylinder-packing glands, when hauling was in progress. On one occasion I saw Bob Lattimer, Isaac Brown and Ernie Hunter in the picking belt department, which had a cast iron stove that vibrated so much when the coal-screening jigger was running that it wore a deep recess in a two-inch-thick concrete paving slab; it was said that the stove never needed poking...

Mention of concrete reminds me of the time during the pit holidays, when the ponies were out to grass and Matt Maughan had just completed a new cement floor in the pit stables, another of his many skills. During school holidays young Alan, George Wardle's son, often spent time at the pit with his father, and what better place for a young lad?

Matt was just admiring his smooth cement floor when Alan raced in past Matt and straight into the still-wet concrete. Alan got a shock and Matt seemed to swell out to an enormous size and bellowed: "What the blooming heck's going on?" Alan shouted: "You're sacked, you're sacked!" Matt suddenly spun round and stamped out and away up the yard.

Alan scraped concrete off his shoes, inspected the great howks out of the floor, then he was summoned to the office where a stern-faced father sat behind the desk and a very forlorn-looking Matt stood with his bait bag, ready for home. "Now lad,what's been going on?" demanded father. "Matt says you've sacked him - so who's to make the tubs if he goes? The sooner you get him set on again, the better, before he gets away and we lose him, right?". Puzzled, young Alan mumbled :"Yes" and wondered why they were making such a fuss about a sack. He departed to the sound of the two men laughing.

I was always glad to get away from school if there was a chance of visiting the pits or quarries; after moving to Haltwhistle participation in farming had to take a back seat in favour of 'new industries'. School work deteriorated because, owing to the war, we were left with women teachers who knew little or nothing about science or mechanics; we quickly got through the arithmetic and the composition was not so hard, but one thing I objected to was so many words in the dictionary meaning the same thing: why learn up to half-a-dozen words when one would do? It was a plot laid by teachers to try and catch us out.

I was not really interested in whether he was William the Conqueror or Bill the Loser at that time, then I read that Henry Ford had said that history was bunk; I wished that he could have come to our school and tell them that, but gradually my attitude towards history changed as I realised that it wasn't only about old battles - otherwise I might not have written these notes.

Miss Keenlyside in Standard Five must have noticed my great interest in industry because one day she took a book from a cupboard, handed it to me and said:"Read that!" 'History', I thought. My heart sank. Then I saw the title 'Coal and the Miner' and suddenly she was the best teacher in the school. At home-time, I was only part-way through, but Miss Keenlyside told me: " You'd better take it home to read - it's a wet night anyway, so you won't be playing out tonight. Remember to bring the book back though." It was a great book and I read it a few times, then it was mislaid, but turned up many years later and I still enjoy a glimpse through it now, more than fifty years after I first read it. Miss Keenlyside didn't pester me to return the book - presumably she was encouraging my thirst for knowledge; she is long gone, and houses have replaced the school on Fair Hill.

In the next class, Standard Six teacher, Miss Mary Milburn had a strap and a stick which I occasionally encountered, and someone commented that had I passed the exam for secondary school, I would have avoided Mary's belts, etc. I never sat the exam, having stayed away in case I passed and would have to go to Hexham school and end up in an office job, when there were all these other outside jobs. No - I would put up with Mary's strap, which seldom appeared later on, perhaps because she was a good geography teacher and I liked those lessons. Given the chance, I would have taken the exam later on, instead of which I enjoyed a few years studying a wide variety of courses at home, after work - and sitting exams.

We had geography in Standard Two, mainly about Northumberland, and in Standard Four it was about the British Isles and some of Europe. As we reached Standard Six Miss Milburn dealt with the rest of the world. She made the whole class repeat names up to four times, which usually made us remember them; the unfortunate pupils in the front row got an inadvertent shower from Mary when she repeated such names as Athabasca, Athabasca, Athabasca. There were other lakes, the names of which escape me now, surprisingly, but which were almost guaranteed to produce a shower or two from Mary. Bella Watson in Three was also said to produce a few sprays when agitated but I missed her class so this is hearsay.

By the time I reached Standard Seven Harry Graham had left to join the RAF and I was looking forward to Miss Hall, who was said to be a good teacher; also - like the other lads, I had a bit of a 'crush' on her, but she left, I believe to become head teacher at Langley School. About 20 years later when I was working in the Catton area we enjoyed a chat; it was nice to see that she hadn't changed a bit, apart from the wisps of grey hair not uncommon in school-teachers. Miss Hall was replaced by Mrs Walker, who managed to teach us some things - but Harry Graham's absence was a great disappointment. I had been expecting more science and 'mechanicing' in the top class. A Mr White came to teach us for a time and he seemed to be a decent teacher; certainly a no-nonsense man, but I forget whether he was in Standard Four or Seven; perhaps he moved from one class to the other and he didn't teach any science or mechanics but was good with arithmetic, which I rather liked.

As it happened, much of my spare time was spent at Robson's garage, at the soap works, and doing more cycle-repairing for other people as well as myself. Some of the quarrymen who cycled to work brought their bikes for repairs after they had finished work, three-speed adjustments being a regular fault easily rectified, and collected them either later at night or early morning. I never charged them for the work but they usually gave me more than I would have had the cheek to charge them in any case, so it was a nice little business while it lasted. This was all mechanical experience even though not very scientific.

During a school holiday I remember one particular day spent at Ventner's pit with one of Robson Bros.' drivers with his two-ton, 1939, ML model Bedford lorry, on what they called 'time work'. The small Ford yard lorry at the pit had disgraced itself, split the engine block, in fact, so a Robsons' Bedford had been hired to help out. There was not a lot of work involved in this yard job, mainly moving the stone picked off the belt, out of the hopper and over the tip. As a 12-year-old, I liked this work because it gave me a chance to drive the lorry.

The expression on Ford driver Alan Johnson's face was worth seeing, when driver Harry Roberts handed me the keys for his Bedford and told me 'to look sharp' and bring the lorry, so that we could empty the stone hopper. I shot off across to the dump, jumped into the wagon and brought it down into the yard, swept round in a half circle and reversed under the hopper without any damage to the lorry or the screen supports, but with just a little bit of showing off, knowing that a concerned-looking Alan and a grinning Harry were watching me.

It was then that I realised that other people also were watching this performance; the miners had come out of the drift while I was shunting the lorry, but as I hadn't made any blunders, I felt like 'Mr Big' that day.

This mine, under the NCB, was closed in 1959, which meant that more than 160 men were made redundant; however, some were transferred to other NCB pits and the proposed Spadeadam Rocket Establishment was expected to absorb much of the local labour force.

About the time that the NCB took over Ventners Hall pit, George Wardle changed to fluorspar mining, and together with George Ridley, won this ore from a number of old lead mines in the Allendale, Nenthead, Garrigill areas, and they formed a company by the name of Allendale Metalliferous Mining Company. George Wardle and John Liddell also restarted Langley Barony Fireclay Works, (G.828611), in the 1950s, to manufacture bricks for the house-building industry, but they gave up making the white earthenware sanitary fittings, for which the Barony Co. was renowned in the past. The works closed after a few years; the kilns were dismantled and the old bricks used on some Haltwhistle buildings.

In about December 1958, GR Wardle & Co., who were by that time running a coal mine at Tarset employing 22 men, applied to open a mine at Bank Foot (G.663644) in the Blenkinsopp seam. This was welcome news for the many miners still unemployed after the closure of Lambley and Ventners.

Bedford lorry similar to the model the author learned to drive.

Unbelievably, this proposal was objected to by four local councillors; I know not what reasons, if any, they gave for opposing this venture.

The same Council advertised industrial sites alongside the railway line, presumably to create employment, yet here we had four councillors causing a delay in the starting up of this mine, which would have provided many jobs, almost overnight. Later the NCB refused the application, perhaps swayed by the objections from our local councillors; then suddenly they changed their minds and allowed the development on condition that the Tarset mine was closed. Somebody must have persuaded the objecting councillors to change their minds also; the Council later approved the opening.

Back on the north side in the 1970s E Dodd and Co. opened out the old fan drift, (G.729708), and mined coal east of Ventners Hall workings for a few years before poor roof and working conditions forced its closure.

An earlier mine had worked the coal from the outcrop at Wallshields pit, (G.714702), in the same seam as Ventners Hall, with a steam boiler supplying power for haulage in the drift. There is a fault or 'hitch' in the strata between these two mines; George Wardle always said that there was a big difference in the quality of coal between the two pits.

This older pit did not generate electricity on the same scale as the later Ventners Hall mine. Wallshields closed in the late 1930s and the only man I knew who worked at this mine was Jackie Atkinson, blacksmith with other talents. In later life he worked as assistant to his brother-in-law, electrical contractor Albert Philips at Haltwhistle.

Wallshields Mine was reopened in the 1950s by Jimmy Bell from Haltwhistle and a partner (who also prospected for coal on Rockhouse prior to NCB open casting) but after a short time they gave it up; the small amount of poor machinery they had seemed to be continually breaking down and they got off on the wrong foot by trying to sell poor quality shale, discarded by previous miners, instead of extracting the existing good quality coal.

About twenty years later Treloar Bros. reopened the mine and installed diesel generators and compressors to work a coal cutter, hauler and picks. The drift was arch girdered and tubs were used for carrying coal to the surface, but after a relatively short time, the mine was closed because of disputes with the landowners, but I believe Treloars eventually came away smiling.

Later the outcrop coal between Wallshields and Ventners Hall was mined by opencasting in the late 70s and early 80s.

All of the output from these north side mines had to go by road, which caused some trouble in the 1930s on the poor track beyond Caw Burn in the case of Ventners Hall Mine, but this was the age of the motor lorry: the road was rebuilt to take the heavier traffic.

A Nuffield grant was made for this roadwork, which involved diverting the route between Edges Green (G.723688) and the Dipper (G.729698) on to a

The road to Ventners Hall near Edges Green; the road straight ahead is the 1930s road; the narrower one to the right is the track via Wealside. (D Hunter)

shorter and higher route instead of the older track via Wealside. The road to Wallshields was made up from the gate at Benkshill (G.710691) to the pit and finished off with two wide concrete strips over the worst parts, spaced to suit lorry wheels. This concrete was laid by the previous colliery company at Wallshields, but the opencast operators laid much more stone over the original road and were obliged to add lay-bys on the road between Benkshill and Cawfields.

In the 1920s and 30s, haulage firms sprang up all over the district to transport coal from these small mines and road stone from local quarries. The firm with the largest fleet of wagons in the early days was Robson Brothers at Station Garage.

I remember Bert and Stan, brothers of Mrs Wardle, saying that the work that really started them off in haulage was the rebuilding of the road from Greenhead via the Temon to Low Row and then the upgrading of the Military Road eastwards from Glenwhelt top (G.668655) before the start of Ventners Hall pit. There was also more work for lorries when some of the main telephone cables were put underground on these roads.

Mr Robson senior, who was a winding-engineman at Roachburn colliery until the disaster in January 1908, later moved from Shanters to Haltwhistle, where he started selling bikes, then motor bikes and cars. A taxi and funeral car hire business was set up with some great cars complete with running boards, just like the ones that the American gangsters raced about in, on the local cinema screens. One early black hire car had a most powerful engine with eight cylinders and I often thought the engine was more suited to a lorry; with only light loads to pull, two cylinders would have been adequate; the hearse that I remember was a much lighter Austin.

When the Station Garage was first built, using a redundant military building from Gretna, an underground tank was installed and a hand-pump set in position on the road side. Apparently, they overstepped the mark with this pump and it had to be moved back to make room for a pavement, whereas at J. Potts' garage the pump was clear of the pavement, but after road-widening, the pavement was put round behind one pump so that it was isolated on the roadside kerb, just as Robsons' had been in the first place.

The lorry haulage business was in operation at the same time as the taxis and in about 1940 I noticed 'No.27' on the front mudguard of the 1939 Bedford ML, mentioned previously at Ventners Hall pit and driven by Harry Roberts. Some of the earlier lorries had been sold on or scrapped, so they would not be running 27 trucks at that time, possibly 15, which was a good-sized fleet in those days. Robson Brothers carried some of Ventners Hall Colliery coal in the early years, then moved mainly on to quarry stone, especially in the early 1940s, when wartime aerodromes and munitions depots were being built.

For this work, existing wooden wagon bodies were replaced with steel backs and hydraulic tippers. These were fitted at Edbro's works in Lancashire, which involved the driver delivering the chassis and

The original petrol pump at Robson's Station Garage, shown on the right of the photo and on the edge of the future pavement. (C Keen)

cab, minus the body, to the works, staying there until the job was done and then driving back to Haltwhistle with the refurbished lorry.

Some of the lorries had to have underfloor hydraulic tippers fitted to the original wooden bodies because of steel shortages, although the metal bodies were fitted later as they became available. I remember the ram of one of these tippers pushing its way up through the floor and cargo of the overloaded wooden body, instead of raising the load; as driver Norman Hogg said: " Aa thowt it wis tekin a gey lang time ti tip".

Steel bodies were a great improvement; they could be well overloaded without mishap but they had underfloor rams, which we thought inferior to the front upright rams. Although the latter type used more oil, the pipes lasted much longer, because of lower working pressure.

About that time industrious Robbie Pape, an apprentice mechanic in the garage, built up an extra lorry out of all the parts lying about in the stores and the garage yard in his spare time: this wagon was then added to the quarry-stone fleet. Robson Bros. also started a coal mine at Morwood

A fine gathering of Commers from Robson Bros. The photo was taken at Featherstone Castle, possibly to underline the permanence of both the castle and the firm. Unfortunately, the firm of Robson Bros. no longer exists at Haltwhistle, although the castle appears to be as stable as ever it was. (R Bainbridge)

(G.796673) in the 1940s using some of the output to burn lime at Crindledykes quarry (G.781672), which they reopened.

After the 1939-45 war, road repairing programmes kept Robsons' lorries busy until government subsidies opened up another useful industry: spreading lime on the land. Robsons carried lime in the much larger Commer 2-stroke-engined lorries to much of Scotland when lime spreading was at its peak; round trips of 350 miles were not unknown. From Haltwhistle to farms on the shores of Loch Fyne in Argyll was one of the long runs I recall in the 1950s and 60s. This business carried on until Robsons went into partnership with Harrison's Shap

Lime works, after which the Haltwhistle activity ceased when the lorries were transferred to Cumberland.

Two earlier lorry operators were Bob and Tom Kennedy who took over from Lees' and parked their solid-tyred wagons at the wooden garage next to the town cemetery, on the site now used by West End Garage.

Parts of this older wooden garage, although modified, were still in use 60 years after I first saw it through clouds of smoke from Kennedy's wagons, which may have been Sentinels. Photographs of 1914-18 and even Boer War army vehicles are reminiscent of the Kennedy wagons; they could well have been ex-army and carried anything that would fit on the lorries - and much that should not have done.

Many years later Tom said that if the wheels still went round after loading, that was all they bothered about. He also said that they couldn't make much sense of official papers - log sheets or whatever they used then - so they just ignored them. I understand that it was Bob and Tom who ventured as far as Liverpool to collect cattle food for Oliver and Snowdon Ltd. of Westgate, Haltwhistle. This was a very long distance trip in those days and they were often away for many days, depending on the number of breakdowns; at least they were not troubled with punctures on the solid tyres.

Eventually they gave up that work, which was taken over in the early 1930s by T.H. Sharp from Coanwood, whose sons, Teddy and Howard, each had a more up-to-date WL Bedford lorry with pneumatic tyres and petrol engines which could race along at over 50 mph, greatly reducing the time taken on the Liverpool journey. It was hinted that they didn't bother with log sheets and such trivia either; they just went down, loaded, and came back home as fast as they could. As Teddy said, they had lights on their wagons, what more could anybody want? The green-painted corrugated-steel garage they used at Watchtrees, Coanwood, lasted for 50 years, but this has now been replaced by a modern farm building.

Yet another transport firm, Laidlow Bros. progressed from horses and carts. One of the brothers, Wallace, kept on with horses until he retired in the 1950s. Brother Arthur, also a horseman in the early days, changed to lorries; his sons later following on with Bedford-2-ton hand-tippers plus a Commer fixed-bodied wagon with Sammy Mitchell as driver.

Once I thumbed a lift in one of Laidlow's Bedfords with Willie Wilkie as driver, via Greenhead Walltown quarry (G.668660) to Brampton. The lorry reversed under the hopper, the body was filled, then

Arthur and Wallace Laidlow with early lorries. (E Laidlow)

it groaned up to the office to be weighed and to collect the ticket, then we were off. "What weight you got on there Willie?" "Plenty." End of conversation. The lorry shuddered from the quarry to Glenwhelt Bank top where the gears were changed down into first and we set off down the hill.

The most alarming thing to me was that the footbrake went right down to the boards and the

Billy Laidlow with pre-war Bedford outside Smith & Walton's works. (E Laidlow)

Arthur Laidlow next to Mill Lane. (M Henderson)

Glenwelt Bank. (M Henderson)

level), and up the other side towards Naworth railway bridge. A fairly fast run followed through Naworth woods with another coast down past New Mills and back into gear again to get over the severe hump (now level) next to the reservoir west of Red Gables, then a coast right down to the Sands at Brampton and into gear through the town.

I stepped out in Brampton after Willie managed to stop, well past where I wanted to be off, but very glad to escape unscathed and with Willie's words ringing in my ears: "Normal, just normal."

Those Bedford engines, and indeed the entire vehicles, must have been built like tanks to stand that punishment day after day. I noticed a '6' in the tons column on the quarry ticket, although those wagons were said to be two-ton-capacity models. The braking systems appeared to be poor performers but often they must have been trying to hold back three times the weight for which they were designed. That was likely 'Normal, just normal.'

engine almost screamed its head off trying to hold the lorry back. I slackened my door handle ready to abandon ship if that gear lever jumped out of mesh but 'Wendle' just sat there grinning and saying: "Normal, just normal."

We screeched down to Glenwhelt Bridge, where he changed straight through from first to top gear, shot through Greenhead like a rocket and up the other side but was back down into first gear just past Gilsland road end. I thought we would never get up this hill and slackened the door handle again but with more screaming from the engine we reached the top and struggled up to Gap Shields and past Reaygarth, when out went the 'stick' into neutral, and we coasted almost to Temon Lodge.

Into gear again and we struggled over the top past Closegill, then out with the stick, hoping to coast over the next bump at Cleughhead road ends, but needing another boost in gear. A longer coast now into Low Row bottom and a climb up to the top of Scarrow Hill, then a mad race into the bottom, (now filled up almost

Greenhead Bank. (I Hunter)

Willie joined the police force a year or two later and could be imagined in traffic police, knowing exactly what faults to look for in two ton Bedfords, etc. Even though the Bedfords appeared to be built like tanks, we never imagined that in addition to the 250,000 military vehicles they turned out during the 1939-45 war, Bedford would construct over 5,000 Churchill tanks with 12-cylinder, horizontally-opposed, 350hp engines.

Bedford WTL model. (E Heslop)

Chapter Four

Gordon Burns with twins Billy and Helen Wilkinson on his wagon, 1942. (E Burns)

When the Churchills were on training missions in the Haltwhistle area, they occasionally tipped upside-down on the fells but they never seemed to be much trouble, apart from the time it took to start the engines; the soldiers blamed poor quality petrol for this.

The first tank to arrive at Haltwhistle set out from the depot in Flowers Close, near the present Police Station, and turned up Comb Hill on very icy roads, with the engine spluttering and banging and almost stalling. I happened to be on my way to the hospital, again, to have some dressings changed, and was allowed out of school, so I was in a good position for surveillance. I heard and saw the tank before it trundled out of sight round the corner and by the time I ran along Fair Hill the noise had changed and then stopped.

It seemed that the tank had slipped off the road into the deep roadside ditch above the old Lady Capell School room - later used as the bandroom - on the

A Churchill tank.

right-hand side of the road and was stuck fast, one track down in a deep gully and the other not able to grip on the icy tarmac; in fact as far as I could see, it had 'bottomed' on the roadside verge.

Looking at this predicament, I didn't think much of their chances on the battlefields but in retrospect realise that the young driver was probably a learner and had pulled the wrong lever.

The hospital visit looked as if it would have to be delayed; much more important matters had arisen for this schoolboy.

Closer inspection showed the tank at such an angle that I could walk right on to it from the bankside in front of Hawthorn Villas. A hatch above the driver's position was open and I remember noticing that the steering levers appeared to be fitted downwards, unlike the D8 Caterpillar working on the new road at Town Foot; this had levers fitted to the floor. Before I fell into the tank, a soldier suddenly looked over the rear end and shouted: "Hoy! Out of there - the sergeant's coming and you'll get me shot".

Ah well, it seems that I was the first Haltwhistle schoolboy on a Churchill tank - and nearly in it.

My schoolmates couldn't believe me when I retailed my adventures. The teacher put my late return down to the hospital being very busy, although he didn't ask and I didn't enlighten him. Harry Graham often had that look in his eye which clearly said: "What has he been up to this time?"

Will and Dick Sloan, trading as Sloan Brothers, garaged their lorries at Rose Villa and like Laidlows worked mainly with tippers to and from the quarries, their flat wagons being used to carry a variety of loads.

James Potts & Son, motor engineers, of Central Garage, had a haulage depot, in addition to their motor-repairing business. They ran a 1930s Dodge lorry, with what we thought was an unusually luxurious cab, the rear panel being covered with chamfer-edged, tongue and grooved boarding, so of course we called it the mobile hen hut. Driver Geordie Hepple (from Plenmeller, not blacksmith Geordie) blamed Jimmy Potts for it.

Potts also had a WL Bedford driven by Percy Noble, plus two short-wheel-base Bedfords, driven by Jack Potts and Frank Henderson, which were requisitioned for the army in the 1940s, because of wartime shortages of vehicles. The short-wheel-base Bedfords, Internationals and the Reo at Robson Brothers also went to the army, never to return to their Haltwhistle depots. About 25 years earlier, the army took horses and hay etc. from farms for the war effort but as far as I know they didn't take fuel for lorries in the last war. They did use spare underground tanks in the Haltwhistle district, although later on much of the fuel came in very thin sealed containers which could be opened with a knife and easily burst if they were dropped. 'Jerry cans' were much safer and usually leak-proof.

It is possible that some of the short-wheel-base lorries were returned after the war to local sites such as Walltown Quarry. They used some very rough and ready lorries in the quarries for internal haulage; these were often described by drivers as 'well and truly shot' in more ways than one.

John Weir Elliott revived the lorry business alongside his motor engineering activities from West End Garage. He bought two big WTL Bedford semi-forward-control wagons with flat bodies from Nixons of Kellah, who were giving up lorry haulage, to concentrate on farming in the Roadhead district.

These lorries were classed as three-tonners but in reality they carried what could be loaded on to them.

Both of these wagons were used to carry coal from local pits to Carlisle Power Station and one of the drivers, Tim Venables, was often unlucky enough to have to load six or seven tons with a hand shovel at Ramshawfield and then unload at Carlisle, again with a hand shovel. The other driver, Jimmy Carruthers, usually had a second man, either Bobby Butler or John Pattinson, which speeded up any hand-shovelling, but both of them later went to work in the mines. I could never understand why they went so often to pits with lorry-loading hoppers where they only had to pull a lever and watch the coal drop into the lorry, while Tim, working on his own, had to hand-fill his wagon.

Overloaded wagons were normal then and often coal lorries travelled to Carlisle without the driver being aware of the weight he was carrying, simply because few pits had a weighbridge capable of weighing heavy loads. It was only when they reached the power station that they found out how overloaded their wagons had been - they said.

Double capacity seemed to be in order but treble was stretching it too far. When coal was destined for places such as Carrs Biscuit Works which had no heavy weighing machine, the lorries often used the public weighbridge on the city side of Eden Bridge, Carlisle.

Tim Venables and his brother John, who later drove a Bedford for Sloan Bros., had their own lorry in the early 1930s and delivered household coal in the district. I am not certain whether this was a Bedford or a Morris Commercial but it had a spiral tipper: a long threaded shaft in a large nut up the front of the body and worked by crank handles. They seemed to keep on turning forever to tip the coal from the body when they came to our house at Redpath, instead of the usual LNER man, but it must have been better than unloading with a shovel; the railway lorry had no tipper.

Most spiral tippers were replaced by rack and pinion gear which was easier to use but still hard work compared to today's hydraulic systems. The racks were much quicker on the downward movement: lift off the ratchet pawl and keep well away from the spinning handle for a steady drop - or pull the handle off and the body came down much quicker. I didn't see any lorries in the early 1930s with hydraulic tippers, I noticed only the hand-wound sort, known locally as 'Armstrong' models and further afield described as 'sweating handles'.

Irvings had a small lorry and carried coal etc., much as the Venables did but I don't know the make of the lorry. Both firms were 'Toonfutters' and they must have cursed Castle Hill as did most drivers, who knew it as 'half-shaft hill' because in trying to climb it, they broke so many drive shafts, which was a calamity in those days; hand brakes were not always effective and the gears couldn't hold an overloaded lorry with a broken shaft. If they ran backwards, most lorries ended up leaning against the stone walls on Castle Hill; it was often the only way of stopping them. In the event of the near-side shaft breaking, the lorry had to be unloaded then pulled away from the wall to allow access to remove the broken shaft from the hub. They were often considerate enough to break down after school so that we could watch proceedings.

John Kennedy, who had a small coal mine at Coanwood, used an old Bedford for delivering coal in the Haltwhistle area. He was known as 'baldy tyre' to us young'uns; on wet days the almost white canvas, showing in the centre of the tyres where the tread used to be, made such a nice contrast with the black rubber on the rest of the tyre. How he evaded the law for so long and avoided having endless punctures, is a mystery; he often had canvas showing on all six tyres. He must have beaten us to the tip to retrieve the tyres before we did.

John Weir Elliott also had two smaller WL Bedford tippers driven by Watty Fairbairn and Jack Dodd, neither of whom had been in a lorry prior to JWE asking them to try the job. They both refused but JWE said: "It's easy enough and you'll learn as you go along." Evidently they did and drove for many years but they were not fussy as to how they got their lorries through narrow openings or under awkward quarry hoppers. Watty had been known to get out of his lorry and kick any obstructions his wagon came against. What Jack did is not recorded.

Watty was a master at rolling a lighted cigarette from one side of his mouth to the other without touching it by hand; if he lost his temper it almost broke the speed limit.

Jack smoked a massive pipe which seemed to produce more smoke than the lorry ever did and perhaps was just as deadly.

These two drivers often disagreed and ignored each other for long periods, usually because of quite trivial things, but one incident they regarded as very serious indeed, almost sacrilege.

One of the lorries, which had a posh chrome radiator shell, broke down and the other driver, who had driven past ignoring the broken-down wagon, was told to go back and tow the lorry to West End for repair. The tow rope was fixed and the rescuer then raced off recklessly. The vacuum-assisted Clayton brakes on the Bedfords were sometimes inadequate even with the engine running, but without the engine, they were fairly useless, so when the towing lorry

A Bedford lorry bent into a similar state as John Weir Elliott's. (R Bainbridge)

stopped suddenly, the tow-ee kept going and the coveted chrome radiator grill, attached to a broken-down engine, was altered beyond all redemption. This was another blow to JWE's finances and led to yet more shaking of heads back at the garage from mechanics Bobby Hunter and Brian Bowerbank.

Not long after this incident, one of the drivers needed water for his lorry but in the hard frosty weather the tap against the large wooden garage had frozen during the night. A blow lamp was brought out but the driver had not realised that the petrol pump was so close behind. Part of the pump caught fire and the handiest item to smother the flames was JWE's heavy top coat. The coat was thrown aside and the smouldering cloth stamped out. Whoever did the stamping out evidently had a light touch; when they remembered the coat some time later, just before JWE appeared, all that was found were buttons and a spanner or two among a blackened mess against the cemetery wall. It seemed an appropriate place for it to end up but I wonder how long JWE looked for that coat; nobody seemed to know anything about it.

In later years JWE took an interest in the Croglin Lime Quarry; he used a short-wheel-base, OST model Bedford in the quarry. This vehicle returned to Haltwhistle when the quarry closed but was not used on contract work. Brian Bowerbank, demobbed from national service and following a spell jointing electricity cables under London streets, returned to Haltwhistle and used the Bedford occasionally during the construction of Elliotts' new garage at Edens Lawn.

The last JWE Bedford, an M model, was used on quarry work and driven by Jack Askew, presumably until both man and machine retired.

John Weir built up a garage business from the 1930s in the wooden garage of the Lees/Kennedy era. He always seemed interested in lorries and started running his own as soon as he was able to buy them. He should have had plenty of spare starting handles in the collection young Parkers rescued from the road and handed over on the way to school.

The first transport JWE was involved with was the narrow-gauge steam locomotives and trucks on Cawfields Quarry railway line soon after he left school. If the engines broke down anywhere on the two-mile run, the drivers set to and repaired them and quickly picked up mechanical skills.

When a larger garage was needed at West End in the 1950s, a trip to a redundant aerodrome produced a hangar, which was erected on the site and the front and back walls built up to form the present-day facade. I believe Mrs Elliott was the main designer involved in this new garage and showroom and she certainly showed a talent for utilising the materials available, in a time of building supplies shortages.

Naturally, jokers asked JWE how he was going to get his aeroplane inside. That was when the hangar was visible, before the facade was added.

After I found out about JWE's early work on steam locos, we often chatted about his experiences, between operations at the petrol pumps on his evening shift. One thing we could never agree on

Rear of West End Garage showing the hangar to the left and part of the old pitched roof garage to the right. (D Hunter)

was how to bank up the fire in his ex-Featherstone Prison Camp central heating boiler. He insisted on having a fairly thin fire, about six inches deep, over the grate area, which would have been perfect for a free-steaming Kerr Stuart loco clattering up the Cawfields line, but was not ideal for keeping the garage warm throughout the night. I said: "Fill her up - the thermostat will keep it right during the night," but he wasn't convinced. JWE's brother Robert also went into the haulage business with a garage on the Castle Hill and used Bedford tippers, mainly on quarry work.

One of Robert's drivers, George Rutherford, previously in the caravan at Redpath but later living in a house in Haltwhistle, had driven a steam-roller all his working life and the only driving he had done on rubber tyres had been on his motor-bike. He had never driven a lorry but probably 'learned as he went along' like Watty and Jack. He was very precise with his driving and never had a bump that I know of. Perhaps a steam-roller - or motor-bike - were good machines on which to learn the finer points of driving.

Tom Elliott, a cousin of JWE, started with a small lorry in the coal retailing business, working from the old South Tyne Colliery buildings and moving later to a yard on the Aesica Road site of the old Working Men's Club, which had burnt down in the 1930s. Tom later built a new timber garage and workshop up Willia Road but it also burnt down in the 1980s.

Tom and Fred Storey of Comb Hill were two of the first Haltwhistle hauliers to carry cattle and sheep on their lorries and in addition both ran small coal merchants' businesses. Tom had a very early Bedford WLG model of about 1933 vintage. Fred's first lorry was a Ford which was almost identical to Tom's Bedford; the radiator grills and wheel centres were the only noticeable differences. Both models, although made in Britain, showed their American origins in their styling.

Fred said he 'got lived' all right with only one lorry but Tom expanded his fleet to carry coal from the pits to Carlisle, as well as moving household coal, furniture, cattle and sheep. Fred had a cattle container which was damaged at one time so he took it to John Liddell & Son's joiner for repairs; the story goes that when Fred got what he thought was an over-priced bill for the work he was very upset and complained at the office. He was told it was quite in order and that, after all, the job had been 'Liddellised'. That stopped Fred for about two seconds, then: "I don't know about Liddellised, but I'm b... paralysed," and stalked off. Tom Elliott did the repairs for Fred after that.

For much heavier haulage, Kitchener Burns ran two big American International trucks with very long bodies, unusual for those days, which he parked at Scotsfield Terrace. It was said at the time that these two lorries were the first of the type imported from USA in the early 1930s. No doubt they were the first in the Haltwhistle area until Thubron Son & Kirkup of Sedgefield commenced carrying loads of trees through Haltwhistle, from the west to the east

Gordon Burns' Thubron Son & Kirkup Ltd. truck, June 15th 1940. (E Burns)

of the country in the late 1930s; they used two International long-pole timber lorries.

Kitchener's brother Gordon was one of the Thubron drivers and if I remember rightly, Norman Pigg was the other. One of Kitchener's lorries caught fire on Shap Fell but was repaired and used again. The Internationals were fitted with prop-shaft hand-brakes and these, or the oily parts near them, were prone to catch fire if the brake band or shoe caught the drum on the propshaft when the vehicle was moving. Fortunately, when this happened, the

The Wilkinson twins with Gordon Burns' wagon at the end of Scotsfield Terrace; the wagon was part of the American 'lease and lend' scheme for the war effort: note the blackout covers on the lights. (E Burns)

smoke from the brake usually came up the rear of the cab and was noticed through the rear view window before flames appeared. Kitchener must have missed that one on Shap.

These lorries were sold when he was called up for service during the war - he would be, with his name - but he started again a few years later with an OW model Bedford lorry to which he fitted a turntable and a pole with third axle for hauling large trees to the east coast mills.

Robson Brothers used another unusual lorry in the late 1930s: a Reo Speed Wagon. I never heard how it compared with other lorries and thought it was the only one of that make in the district until I discovered that Frank Bryde of Bardon Mill also used a Reo. When Alf Surtees started driving for him Frank bought another, so he must have found them satisfactory.

Later Frank and Alf formed a partnership and when Frank moved away from the district, Alf took over the business and expanded his lorry fleet to carry stone from quarries, coal to the power stations and to develop a household coal business. For many years now he has been a dedicated Bedford man with TKs etc. and was still using them in 1996.

Robson's first diesel lorry was a rather worn Thorneycroft or Atkinson, with a flat body and without electric starting; a dreaded starting handle was provided. The performance of starting the engine from cold was not to be missed on our way to school.

Being a forward-control type, the engine cover was removed inside the cab: pieces of cloth, well soaked in diesel fuel, were placed in a gallery along the side of the engine and under the air intake; they were then set alight and with the valves lifted by the decompression lever, the engine was turned over with the starting handle, to draw the smoke and flames into the cylinders. After a while, with the handleman cranking the engine fast, somebody knocked the decompression lever down and it started up - sometimes. The sudden release of 'drag' on the starting handle when the engine started often sent the handleman sprawling across the yard.

If they were lucky enough to start the engine, exhaust smoke then poured out of the pipe, to add to the other clouds coming out of the cab from the burning rags. The exhaust cleared somewhat as it warmed up but it would never have passed today's emission tests.

Tommy Trotter was the driver, and being rather short in build but fairly wide, he sometimes had trouble clambering up the side of the tall cab to reach the driver's seat and then had more trouble getting out of it. He often carried small coal to Carlisle, hand-shoveling it off at the far end. Pointing to the smoky exhaust, drivers of petrol-engined lorries often asked Tommy if he filled up with fuel at the tar works.

In the 1970s or 80s, Treloar Bros. (nephews of Robson Bros.) used two large American Mack lorries

Drivers Kenny Dent and Geoff Turnbull with a GR Wardle Bedford lorry at Crossfield Garage in the 1940s. (R Bainbridge)

but unlike Kitchener's or Tommy's flat wagons, the Macks had very high-sided bodies more suited for carrying bulk coal and coke; I believe they were thirsty machines, like the Internationals before them.

GR Wardle ran lorries from a garage near Crossfield in the 1930s and 40s, which were used mainly for coal carrying from Ventners Hall pit and for general haulage. George Warwick used a GRW lorry to take miners from Haltwhistle and district to the pit, carried coal during the day, then brought the men back to the town afterwards. A Bedford WTL was also used by drivers Kenny Dent and Geoff Turnbull for GR Wardle.

Geoff Turnbull later went into the lime-carrying business and I always thought that indirectly, he caused me to lose what I regarded as a record in that I learned to drive a van as an eleven-year-old.

This loss came about because of Geoff's custom of calling at his home in Central Drive, Haltwhistle for tea before going further on to load up at ICI, Prudhoe, for the next day.

Whenever he arrived at the house, his young sons had to have a sit in Dad's wagon so he usually braked it, left it in gear and removed the key for safety. Presumably the lorry had been converted to diesel from petrol at some time and possibly could be started without the key. However, on this occasion it started up in gear with the boys in the cab and slowly went across the street with the engine 'ticking over', mounted the pavement, pushed over a garden fence and stalled climbing the slope of Matty Hetherington's rose garden.

Geoff, having a meal in the kitchen at the rear of the house, didn't see this so he got a shock when he saw where his lorry had ended up. He reversed the wagon out on to the road and the young apprentice drivers were sent indoors in disgrace. Matty said later that he wondered if he was at the right house when he came home from work and saw a flattened fence, the bent roses and wheel marks in the garden - until Mrs Turnbull explained.

'Peace' and 'Mrs Miniver' were spared to bloom again but my record was dashed - here were Geoff's sons driving, if inadvertently, a great lorry before they started school.

Wilf Teasdale often had some fun delivering coals to remote farms north of Ventners Hall pit over almost non-existent roads. He always took his bait in case of mishaps. It is ironic that when most of the farms have gone, good hard roads exist throughout the forest area. Wilf would have been pleased.

Ike Bell was 'blessed' with a very high-geared Leyland lorry which caused some trouble when negotiating the steep hill out of the Ventners pit yard - usually in the over-loaded state. One way of solving this problem was to have Ike race along the level yard with the loaded wagon, charge up the hill and at the point where the engine started labouring, eight or ten men pushed the lorry up the last section. Once over the steep part, Ike managed the other hills on the way to Carlisle. I never saw this operation but I have been assured that it happened. Another of the GRW wagons was a steamer, which seemed very sensible, as George was involved in coal mining at the time. To get this machine into the garage at

Crossfield, part of the door frame head had to be cut away to clear the high exhaust pipe. I remember Fred Lamb as one of the drivers but I am not sure of the name of the fireman, possibly a Mr Dodd.

Parking the steamer inside during frosty weather was a very effective way of heating any garage, but more important, prevented freezing of the many water and steam pipes on the lorry.

The next owners, Smith and Walton Ltd, Hadrian Works, found this out to their cost when they parked the steamer overnight in the open when they first bought it. A severe frost damaged the pipes and it took a few days for a plumber, not a mechanic, to repair the vehicle. Smith and Walton Ltd. used the steam wagon during the 1940s war years, to deliver their paint and varnishes over a wide area, and it was not unknown for machine and crew to go 'missing in England'.

On one occasion, fireman Stan Hankin, with I think Fred Lamb driving, returned to Haltwhistle after a

Steam lorry similar to the GR Wardle/Smith & Walton wagon. Jameson's new lorry in the photo has solid tyres and a short wheelbase compared to Wardle's steamer, which has pneumatic tyres and was longer overall. (R Bainbridge)

The Smith & Walton's model - a six-wheel Sentinel. (A Burns)

few days in the 'wilderness' of Lancashire with tales of woe. Most things that could go wrong, did, but they thought the hardest day was when they had to barrow their cargo a considerable distance because the customer wouldn't let them near his premises in case they set fire to them with 'that flaming chimney'. They were refused accommodation more than once because of their filthy state, which was mainly caused by the coaldust stirred up while firing the lorry's steam boiler.

Smith and Walton later retired the steamer and Jakey Strong carried on deliveries with the Leyland: it was much less bother.

The Cement Marketing Co. had some fairly modern steamers which they still used in the 1940s. These steam lorries were kept in good mechanical order and carried massive loads of cement between Tyneside and the West.

The last time I saw a CMC steamer was on the Castle Hill. I was walking up Mill Lane towards Castle Hill when the lorry, loaded with a fair mountain of cement, went up the hill, past Joe Henderson's shop, as easily as most lorries travelled on the level. The airspace above the wagon was blackened with the large amount of 'clag' being lifted up in the exhaust pipe from the firebox; what a powerful sight that was. The law would have had something to say about the black smoke - if the culprits had been caught, but steam-lorry firemen knew where they could get away with a bit of hard firing; Haltwhistle was one of the places and Greenhead bank was another.

Haltwhistle's Castle Hill was a great testing place for all types of transport since horse and cart days when a second 'chain' horse was often required in front to get loads up the hill.

Later steam and petrol-driven vehicles brought their own particular problems such as broken drive shafts etc., and mishaps such as the steam-roller which ran back and tipped into a garden near the Town Foot Bridge and the large military gun which broke loose,

The crashed steam-roller next to the Town Foot Bridge. (E Coates)

rammed the front of one house and removed part of the gable end.

Motor bikes in pioneering days were frequent victims of Castle Hill - most of them were belt-driven and geared far too high; few of these machines managed the steep rough stretch up to the 'Spotted Cow' entrance. Drivers often had to turn back down and ride over the bridge, up the short hill into Weir's old slaughterhouse yard for a short downhill start.

If this failed, the 'Toonfutter' lads had a nice little business going helping bikes up Castle Hill. No 'Upbyers' were allowed near when there were tips to be earned.

One local character, who had a sidecar of sorts fitted to his motor bike - usually with a fair load of furry carcasses on board - very rarely had trouble negotiating Castle Bank, especially when the police were after him. Johnny's bike probably had a more powerful engine or lower gears, more suited to local roads.

Many are the tales of how Johnny avoided the police, such as the time when he drove towards the waiting PCs shouting "Fire! Fire! - find fireman Joe Bowes - emergency! Look out!" and raced on up the bank. If he had gone to the doctor's every time he yelled "Doctor! Emergency!" it would have cost him a packet in those days, but apparently it cleared a way through for him. Sadly, both Johnny and bike are

George Denwood, behind Shepherd Terrace, with a Brough Superior motorcycle rather like the well-known model of Johnny's day, but without the 'box' sidecar. (R Hunter)

long gone and modern bikes hardly notice the hills. Sidecars full of 'furry carcasses' belong to the past - few people eat wild rabbit meat now. Johnny would have been devastated.

P. W. Sharp, coal agents, built up a fleet of lorries, mostly carrying coal from local mines to Carlisle Power Station. The drivers were some of the first to be on bonus payments and more loads meant more pay, so on the roads it was best to keep clear of PWS wagons. Most of them were 'flyers'. Generally, these drivers were quite capable of keeping their lorries on the road at high speeds and some put up incredible records of loads to Carlisle in a day. The name 'Toola' or 'Tulla' springs to mind in connection with these speed merchants but all the PWS drivers seemed to be infected with the racing bug.

Apparently some drivers had been 'burning the road up' many years before the P. W. Sharp era. I heard of two lorry drivers who were always trying to beat each other on the runs between Ventners Hall Colliery and Carlisle Power Station. One of them was Norman Hogg but I cannot recall the other so he will have to be driver B.

After much rivalry over a considerable period, driver B thought of a cunning plan to beat Norman; he would go to Ventners and load up during the early hours and go straight on to the power station; this worked well and he was parked against the locked gates at Carlisle when he spotted Norman coming up behind him with his lorry load; 'Aha - he must have loaded up last night,' he thought. Still, he was sure he had beaten 'Hoggy' this time.

Eventually the weighing machine attendant appeared and unlocked the gates. Unknown to driver B was the fact that the far side gate had to be opened first, whereupon Norman reversed slightly and then drove through the open gate on to the weighing machine. Driver B was stuck behind the closed gate and was hopping mad and vowed to get even with him during the day.

Norman unloaded and raced back to the pit pursued by B; when they reached the Military Road beyond Greenhead, B passed Norman, then they continued to overtake each other alternately until they went neck-and-neck over the hill between Glendale and Four Laws, keeping up the race, side by side towards the bridge over the Haltwhistle Burn. One of them gave way on this single-carriageway bridge but

P. W. Sharp coal wagon. (A Burns)

Billy Banks' P. W. Sharp lorry on Shepherd Terrace, with John Murray's 'pop wagon' in the background. The girl is Shirley Calderwood, from Scotswood, visiting the place she was evacuated to when five years old. (A Burns)

Norman gained the lead and kept it along the narrow road to Ventners Hall, B closing right up behind him, ready to dash past given the chance. After Edges Green and on the hill near the Dipper, B saw what he thought was a golden opportunity to beat Norman; he steered his lorry on to the grass to cut the corner while Norman continued to drive round the long curve. A grinning B sensed victory and raced even faster, but failed to notice one or two hefty rocks concealed in the grass. The lorry lurched and stalled just short of the tarmac.

A now jubilant Norman raced past, tooting his horn and roared over the hill to the pit. Hopping mad, once again, B threw the bonnet up to find out why the engine had stopped. After a while he noticed a battery lying in the grass: his own, which had bounced out of the carrier when the lorry hit the stones, broke away from the cables and stopped the engine. This incident didn't stop the rivalry or the speeding. The fastest ride I ever experienced in the two-ton Bedfords was in No. 27 owned by Robson Bros., the same lorry I sometimes shunted about Ventners Hall pit yard. Schooldays were put up with

from Monday to Friday; Saturdays were reserved for lorry trips and on this particular day, the loads were of whinstone penning from Walltown Quarry for constructing the runways at Crosby Aerodrome, now Carlisle Airport.

I made a key to fit the door and the ignition on No. 27 so that whoever arrived first at the Comb Hill lorry garage on the Pinfold, (now covered by Woodhead Lane housing), could prepare and start the lorry engine...with the starting handle. The six volt batteries fitted to lorries in the early 1940s, even when they were new, were not powerful enough for starting engines from cold in frosty weather so the handle had to be used.

Cranking the engine required all the schoolboy strength I could muster, so this encouraged me to find any easy way of doing this. Fortunately, four half turns on full choke with the ignition off, then switch on and a single sharp click-up almost always started the engine. There was no antifreeze available in those days so engines had to be drained in frosty weather and refilled each morning. If the tap was frozen, water for the radiator came from the Woodhead beck which flowed past the garage and under Joe Lee's garden and scrap yard, (now partly covered by housing).

By the time I had driven the wagon out of the garage, official driver Harry Roberts usually turned up and on this particular morning appeared to have had a very rough Friday night 'on the pop'. He grunted "Water? Oil?" and I replied "Yep!" and off we went to the quarry.

Later when Harry was driving the loaded lorry across the penned area of the main runway at Crosby, the rear wheel sank into a gap in the penning which had been mistakenly filled with ash, and progress came to a halt some distance from the tipping point. This did not improve Harry's head, especially when a passing labourer suggested that an adjacent steam-roller would likely pull the wagon out. The roller was coupled on and then with much revving from the lorry and clouds of smoke and steam belching from the roller, the lorry remained where it was, stuck fast. Stone chippings were thrown under the slipping rollers but these were merely ground down to dust. After some bumping and shunting, Harry raised his hand and then walked to the tailboard and opened it. Then up went the tipper and the stones cascaded on to the ground, enabling the steamer to move the now lighter lorry out of the hole; Harry unhitched and waved the roller back to his runway job; jumped into his lorry and drove off, shouting from his cab: "Now you've got plenty of stone to fill that gap".

This brightened him up and he managed a grin when he noticed that the Ruleholme car park was overflowing with Robsons' lorries - on Saturday mornings the drivers often called here after their last trip of the week. Harry parked and hurried into the pub. Ennis Little had travelled as passenger in one of the other lorries and he came across to have an inspection of 'my' newer No. 27. We were sitting quietly in the passenger seat when suddenly the pub door burst open and all the drivers came running to their lorries.

Battle of Britain pilots scrambling to their Spitfires would have recognised and heartily approved of that exodus at Ruleholme. Harry raced over shouting: "Get the engine started!" That was easy; I reached over, turned the key and pulled the starter. Harry leapt in and we were off; the race was on. Ennis stayed with us; he would never have caught his driver. As we raced over the Irthing bridge, Harry noticed how many wagons were in front and demanded to know how that lot had got so far ahead?

Ennis mumbled :" Thy wagon's too slow man!" That stirred Harry up; he crouched over the steering wheel, foot down... Mile after mile the lorries overtook and were overtaken. This was the first time I had seen the speedometer pointer near the bottom of the right-hand side of the dial; the pointer jumped

about so much that it was impossible to judge our speed. As we came through the cutting at Gap Shields and along the downward slope to Greenhead top, the pointer was hitting the stops. This we thought was 'flat out' and then amazingly Willie (Timmer) Rushton gradually overtook our lorry with his older 1937 Bedford WL. We guessed that it had higher ratio gears or bigger wheels.

Willie's higher speed surprised us because a week or so previously he had been driving fairly fast in a convoy of wagons over the same road when suddenly a wheel shot past him, fortunately missing the sparse oncoming traffic and ending up in the far side wall. Willie laughed and thought: 'Some poor beggar's lost his wheel', then realised it was one of his own double rear wheels, so he had to drop anchor before he lost the other one. Apparently this previous mishap did not deter him in the least from joining in the present race. We all hoped that he had checked his wheel nuts this time…. There were no winners: the race was the thing; all heady stuff for a young lad. Bedfords were well trimmed in the mid-1930s to get the tare weight below two-and-a-half tons so that they could speed along at 30mph instead of the regulation 20mph for lorries over this weight.

Willie Timmer and Co. evidently knew not of this regulation; 60 and 70mph was more to their liking. The speeds they would have managed with modern lorries can only be imagined.

In the 1950s and 60s Nicholas Elliott used the Crossfield garage for his lorries, which worked mainly on lime spreading but also on other long, distance deliveries, including most of the plastic bottles produced at Cascelloid's Plenmeller factory in the early days.

A transport firm was started by Dennis Crawford and Frank Henderson, at one time a driver for Jimmy Potts and then mechanic for John Weir Elliott. Dennis did the driving and Frank retained his job in the Cascelloid works but later the partnership was dissolved. Since then, Dennis has expanded his

Crawfords Transport business at Plenmeller yard, together with storage depots.

A similar type of business has been built up by Martin Oliver at Melkridge with his lorries travelling to most parts of this country and Europe.

Many transport enterprises were built up from small beginnings; one was started by farmer John (Jack) Foster of New Hall, Gilsland.

Up to the 1920s, if a farmer wanted to expand his milk sales, he could take his milk cans to the nearest railway station and send them to Newcastle by train. This was acceptable if the farm was near the station. Jack thought New Hall could not be described as near so he arranged to transport his surplus milk, together with some from neighbouring farms, to the Tyneside dairies. This was the start of milk-can collecting in the Gilsland district. For some reason, officialdom described the milk cans as churns and printed this on the labels, confusing country folk who knew full well that a churn was for the manufacture of butter. One of Jack's lorries was a forward-control Commer with what was very

Border Rambler collecting the milk. Driver: Ernie Bainbridge. (R Bainbridge)

unusual for the 1930s: a Perkins diesel engine, which must have been one of the earliest Perkins engines made. The lorry was an early thirties model and it was 1930 before the Perkins factory started producing engines. Jack also had a cattle container to fit this wagon for moving other farmers' stock as well as his own.

Ike Bell, driver of the high-geared Leyland at Ventners Hall Colliery, did some driving for Jack Foster in the early days and they eventually became brothers-in-law.

Jack expanded milk collection over a wide area and after a few years he sold the business and lorries to Fred Laidlow of Gilsland, brother of Arthur. When Fred retired from milk collecting he sold out to Robson's Border Hauliers at Carlisle. This firm opened the Mill Bridge Service Station at Haltwhistle together with a lorry repair depot and parking area on what had been the old South Tyne Colliery railway sidings and the blast furnace field.

GR Wardle and Son, who had built up a large fleet of lorries since the 1930s, established a garage and

John (Jack) Foster's 1934 Dennis wagon. (P Howe)

repair depot for their lorries nearer to the Castle Hill on the site of the South Tyne Colliery screens which had been demolished in about 1932. In later years GR Wardle took over all of this area and lorry park.

Some of the bodies fitted to Volvo lorries today are massive compared to those of fifty years ago, and looking now into the long bodies of the coal wagons, many of 60 cubic yards capacity, I wonder what Tim Venables would have thought if faced with hand-filling twenty tons of coal duff.

There are still many one-man, one-lorry firms in the area, all presumably making a living out of the work available.

In all this transport activity since the 1930s there was one period when everything seemed to be 'out of gear' for a while, and that was when road transport was nationalised. BRS did not respond quickly enough to requirements, which resulted in many manufacturers buying their own lorries so as to have control over transporting their materials.

Modern monsters. Tailboards are now almost equal in width and height and the bodies hold about 60 cubic yards - approximately tenfold in capacity and weight-carrying - a long way from the two-ton Bedfords. (D Hunter)

This made it much more difficult for haulage firms to regain business after the nationalised period, although increased demand for manufactured goods created a need for more transport, and local firms soon picked up from there.

Most of the purely haulage firms were nationalised but such as coal merchants, livestock movers and manufacturers with their own vehicles carried on as before. Some haulage firms were started up during the nationalised period and expanded into very big operations.

One man in particular, demobbed from the RAF, used his gratuity money to buy one lorry and soon built up a fleet of lorries which was never nationalised. I remember each lorry had the firm's name on the chassis in very small lettering, but on the cab top was a roller type indicator board bearing the names of all the firms they had contracts with; the driver merely moved the roll to the name required for any particular job. This would enable the firm to stay private.

I often wondered where that firm found its drivers. They appeared at Greystonedale works behind the wheels of old ERF, Foden or Leyland tractor units and trailers to load up sacks of hydrate of alumina, usually to be delivered to Barking in Essex; for many of them it was their first experience of driving an articulated lorry.

They could not have been sent to a worse place; the road down the yard to one of the loading areas was a 'dog-leg' and the vehicles had to be reversed. Many were the 'knot-ups' created by these tractor units and trailers and their inexperienced drivers.

To save time and trouble for the drivers and to avoid damage to their lorries and vulnerable parts of the factory, I offered to position the wagons at the loading area. There seemed little difference between manoeuvring these artics and the long-pole timber lorries I had driven, and so it proved. Before long most drivers gave up trying to reverse; they just left

Not all transporting went according to plan. Here a Scammel tractor unit and trailer loaded with a heavy metal casting seems to have missed a gear on the short but very steep Cross Bank, west of Haltwhistle. A crowd of 'Westenders' gathers to watch as Dick Kennedy cycles through, quite unconcerned. PC Sandy 'Fists' Forsyth takes particulars. Another of Currie's Scammels has arrived to assist and can just be seen behind the delinquent tractor unit marked 'Road Engines'. (R Bainbridge)

their lorries at the top end in charge of the 'resident shunter', which suited me; I got the chance to handle all kinds of weird and wonderful vehicles. I never asked them what they did at the delivery address.

When the Greystonedale firm gave me the grand title of millwright, there was no mention of shunting.

I could fully understand how these 'non-artic' drivers felt when they saw the twisty road to the loading area, having been in a similar situation myself, on changing from mechanicing to driving a timber-carrying lorry between Northampton and Willesden, London, of all places. Until then I had never seen London traffic, and I quickly concluded that it was driven by suicidal lunatics. Perhaps they thought the same about me but I never expected to see a little

MG driving partly under my twenty ton load of oak tree trunks, and in the fairly long gap between the tractor unit driving wheels and the rear trailing wheels. This particular hero apparently wanted to dodge through past somebody while we were all moving along at about 10mph. He was lucky and did a marvellous manoeuvre but if he had stopped his MG would have been telescoped. 20-ton loads took some stopping in those days.

This was on Edgeware Road, which was then partly dual carriageway with a central metal barrier and two lanes each way, and the only safe way I could think of to turn right at Cricklewood, if there were no police about, was to edge over and drive astride the two lanes well beforehand and just ignore the orchestra of car horns behind. My left-hand drive lorry with no indicators apart from a railway-signal type of arm pulled by a cord across the back of the cab made right-hand turns a bit of a lottery anyway.

At the crossroads I steered the lorry almost into the oncoming traffic in the northbound lane; the sight of a huge aggresive-looking 'Studebaker' grill and wheels with a towering load of oak logs approaching, always seemed to have a great calming effect on the traffic and most vehicles stopped quickly, except for those London buses; they just ignored everything.

By driving the lorry up the centre of two lanes, I must have saved a lot of road signs from being mown down by the overhanging tail swing of the load of long trees when turning across the road. The police would pounce on people trying that sort of manoeuvre nowadays - then, it was just another of many challenges.

On the return journey there was often more fun getting back out with the empty pole-wagon on to the northbound lanes of Edgware Road. Even with the rearward axle pushed in to make the outfit more compact, it was surprising how many car drivers seemed to forget about this rear axle when the vehicle was emerging from a side road; there were some near misses.

Unlike the visiting drivers at Greystonedale, I left the timber caper after ten days, before I became a nervous wreck. I should have stuck to mechanicing instead of taking that job but it paid a much higher wage. Traffic was not as heavy in the late 1940s but it was increasing. I wonder how timber-lorry drivers cope with present-day conditions; it would make more sense to take the sawmill to the trees.

One good thing about the petrol Studebaker was its speed. The return journey north was covered at up to 60mph, in the absence of police; the back trailing wheels sometimes following, more or less in a straight line. Later on, after my few days driving, Perkins diesel engines were fitted to these machines and I believe the maximum speed then became 40mph, but fuel costs were halved; however, the size of the loads had to be reduced.

Some time after the artics first appeared, a driver arrived with a four-wheeled lorry for a change; from the cab he asked if I would reverse the wagon down the yard as he couldn't twist round to see where he was going.

Before I got the chance to ask him what was wrong with his looking glasses, as mirrors are known in our family, he started to struggle out of the cab. I could hardly believe what I saw. He had a leg in plaster and had driven the lorry from Newcastle to Haltwhistle. This firm seemed to have a hotch-potch of drivers but that capped everything.

After works staff had loaded the hydrate, somebody tied the load on for him and managed to shove him back into the cab. He drove the lorry out of the yard but I noticed that when he stopped at the road end, no stoplights showed, so presumably he used the hand brake to stop the wagon, instead of risking his broken leg on the foot brake. He drove all the way to Barking like that.

The drivers soon learned to reverse their vehicles and consequently, I lost my little excursions down the yard. After a year that haulage firm was displaced by local firms, privatised once more.

Haltwhistle appears to have been one of the lorry capitals of the country - and still is. There must have been more wagons to the acre in this district than in most other areas and the trend now seems to be towards much longer distance haulage; many local firms cover much of Europe, a far cry from the old two-ton Bedford days.

I heard of one transporting job, carried out by three of GR Wardle's lorries, which involved driving through six countries. The lorries got to Seville in Southern Spain where the drivers were put up for the night, with instructions to be ready for a 5am

Another crash, this time at Cates Garage, Low Row. Stan Waugh (left - driver of the Bedford) gives details to the AA patrolman, while Alan Coulson 'lights up'. The other driver (Billy Banks) is missing from the photo. (A Burns)

start. At dawn the lorries arrived at, not an orange orchard, but the potato fields, to find a multitude of workers waiting with baskets, ready to load the wagons.

The drivers imagined being there for days while their great lorries were hand-filled with tons of potatoes but apparently the locals worked like Trojans, picking spuds into baskets and tipping them into a hydraulic loader bucket which was kept going continuously, lifting potatoes into lorries. By 11am the workers had loaded 75 tons into the three lorries in six hours. The land was so dry that the lorries could be driven over the fields without any fear of being bogged down.

From Seville the Haltwhistle men travelled across Spain, France and Belgium into Holland, where the potatoes were supposed to be unloaded - but the customer rejected them and the potatoes were eventually delivered to a German town where the buyers were not quite so fussy.

Although transport played a great part in my young life, I still had much investigating to do round industrial sites - both local and further afield if I could find the time. Mysteries from my Redpath days were still there to be poked into - such as the thump of machinery at the Spital Farm. I was now sure it would be impossible to hear shunters from Plenmeller pit even though I had seen steam showing over the hill. This steam, I discovered later, was from the Alston train on the run up to Featherstone.

I had heard about an alleged gas engine at Blenkinsopp Hall but there were no gas works there. I had seen the one at Town Foot, Haltwhistle, near Auntie Connie's house, which seemed miles away, but investigations proved that in about 1900, the estate owners had gas pipes laid from the Park Road via North lodge to the Hall and also had electric lighting fitted. I am not sure whether the generator was town gas or oil-engined originally, but an oil engine was used just prior to the mains being installed in the 1950s. By that time the gas was disconnected, although the underground pipe from North Lodge was re-used for another purpose. Two new Estate houses were built behind the Spital Farm and it was decided that the new water supply could be brought from the water mains on the Back Road, through the old gas pipe to the houses. This did not work.

When the water was coupled up and turned on, all the residue and settlement from the previous gas flow in the pipe had turned the water an odd colour, almost white, which refused to clear even after some days running. Finally, a farm labourer said: "Why not shove a plastic tube doon inside the pipe?" and they did, saving much digging and ensuring a clean water supply to the houses.

The puzzling regular thumps I had heard came from the oil engine used to drive the sawmill at Spital Farm; this engine was also used to drive the large built-in threshing machine - when they could get it started. In winter weather up to four men, pulling on ropes wrapped round the flywheel, were sometimes needed to turn this powerful engine.

Blowlamps were used at the cylinder-head end of the engine during frosty weather but I was never allowed near enough to see exactly what they were heating. Some old engines had a metal rod that unscrewed from the cylinder head, was heated until glowing red, then screwed back in again. Sometimes this helped to start stubborn oil engines and was the forerunner of the hollow-ended rod with ignition paper which glowed after lighting, then was screwed in for handle-starting the much later, single-cylinder diesel engines fitted to the Field Marshall tractors. In fact without the ignition paper the engine was liable to start up in the reverse direction and although it would run, if anybody tried to drive the tractor,

they found that they had only one forward gear and three reverse speeds.

To remedy this, the throttle was pushed into the stop position then opened full out just before the engine stopped turning; this caused the engine to bump back and forth a time or two and it generally started up in the right direction; if it still went the wrong way, the process was repeated.

Sometimes the starting handle would stick in the flywheel when the engine started; the safest way to remedy this was for the driver to run clear, by a circuitous route, away from the spinning starting handle and knock the throttle off with the longest pole available. A successful driver had to have his wits about him.

No doubt, the easy way of starting the Marshall was with the 12-bore cartridge made specially for the job. The cartridge was fitted in the chamber, locked, then the striking pin hit with a hammer and away it went.

Marshall tractors could be fun or frustrating but I think the one that capped the lot must have been Jake Johnson's bulldozer.

I had used this machine and was amazed how these powerful, single-cylinder engines managed to push all the weight of the tractor, tracks, blade and whatever was being bulldozed. However one day, instead of the engine firing and pushing the piston down in the cylinder to turn the crankshaft, the piston stayed put and the force burst the crankcase and pushed the front part of the tractor off by the crankshaft. That stopped it - permanently.

The new joiner's shop at The Spital, with machinery driven by line-shafting, powered by a new single-cylinder horizontal oil engine was put into commission as late as the 1950s. What a picture to see those belts running from the drive shafting to all the wood-working machines.

A factory inspector wouldn't have approved, but then, I saw it before most of the guards were fitted and it would have to be inspected later. The layout was unusual in that the line-shafting was fitted on pedestals about two feet high, against the rear wall of the workshop, and the driving belts were almost horizontal between the shafting and the machines.

This arrangement was necessary because of fairly light construction in the walls and roof of the building, rendering it unsuitable for carrying line-shafting. Mains electricity came a few years afterwards and a large motor was installed for the sawmill. By the 1990s, the shafting, belts and the oil engine in the joiner's shop were replaced by a small unit electric planer and saw bench. At the sawmill, the big oil engine and shafting were long gone; only a built-in plummer block, once used for the line-shafting, remains in the wall of the building. The circular saw is still used occasionally for estate work.

What seemed to be a curious feature of the old wiring in Blenkinsopp Hall was that much of it was single-core, lead-covered cable, the centre wire acting as the 'live' and the 'neutral' merely clamped on to the outside of the cable. This must have been normal wiring practice for low voltage supply at one

Unthank Hall. (M Henderson)

time; it was the only place I know of which had this system. This old lead cable was removed many years ago.

Unthank Hall also had a gas supply pipe laid via How Burn and under the railway and River Tyne but I have no details of a generator being installed.

Unthank estate sawmill (G.725626) up the Lynn Burn valley had a horizontal-cylinder oil engine when I first saw it and was originally built in that position for a waterwheel driven by the burn water.

There were no signs of a dam near the sawmill but about half a mile further up the Linn Burn, a man-made lake exists in a wood called Milldam Plantation. Working the mill would have involved a man walking up the burnside path, opening the dam sluice gate to increase the flow in the burn, which would then act as a very economical mill-race. At the small waterfall nearer the mill, the water was diverted via a wooden-troughed leat from the burn on to the waterwheel.

This system saved the expense of constructing a long mill-race and worked well enough; the only drawback was the long walk to open and close the sluice gate, but in stormy weather the flow in the burn from the fells was adequate without relying on extra water from the dam.

Blenkinsopp Hall. (M Henderson)

Estate owners also used the lake for private boating and fishing, whereas I often 'kittled' trout from the burn below the lake without rods or lines, but they were only - literally - small fry.

The only local waterwheel I saw working was at Featherstone estate sawmill situated near Park Burnfoot (G.684621). The dam was still across the burn in the 1990s and the race can be traced under the road bridge but beyond that, all the sawmill building, saw benches and waterwheel were cleared away some years ago.

I first saw this wheel working in the 1940s and as it was one of only two turning in the north, I watched it for a while before going into the mill to see the cutting operation.

On the next visit to Burnfoot Sawmill I found that one of the waterwheel gear sections had broken; the wheel was probably scrapped later because of the cost of replacing this big iron casting. To dismantle the mill seemed like vandalism when a farm tractor could have driven the saw from its belt pulley. Nowadays the casting could have been welded quite easily, probably free of charge if it resulted in the mill remaining in working order.

Further afield a waterwheel drove a water pump in a valley to the north of Teppermoor Farm. A dam across the Crook Burn (G.856722) supplied water via a very long race to the wheel of about six feet diameter, which pumped spring water to a number of farms in the area. I discovered this wheel while at a nearby camp for the Army Cadet Force during the 1940s. The pump also supplied water to the camp and when the supply went off one day it was found the wheel had stopped turning because no driving water was reaching it from the dam. Further investigation revealed that the sluice gate at the dam was closed, and the pin for holding it open was missing.

The Cadets immediately thought: 'Saboteurs!' but presently someone found the pin some distance away with a piece missing; we decided that an enemy force would have made certain we couldn't find it. Our explanation was that because the steel plate targets for the 900-yard rifle range were just above the dam near the sluice, a bullet from the previous evening's practice had rebounded off the plate, knocking the pin out, dropping the sluice and stopping the water, which eventually was restored.

Teppermoor seemed to be one of those places where unusual things happened. Those same target plates caused a ricochet bullet to spin up a long valley at right angles to the line of fire and strike one man on his tin hat. The bullet made a groove in the steel which the wearer was very pleased about: "Better the hat as my head", he reckoned. I remember hearing a section of a hand grenade strike another man's steel helmet, a 'sticky' bomb being thrown and breaking in two instead of exploding, and the same thing happening to a much larger missile which I believe was called a Blacker Bomb. A Mills Bomb was detonated one night as we took cover in the adjoining wood and it showered us with leaves and small branches, scythed off by the shrapnel. A grenade that failed to explode when fired over the fields went off as another exploded near it. A 'molotov cocktail' missed its target and failed to burst into flames but was safely disposed of by Major Douglas Smith with his second bullet from a 303 rifle over a long distance. I saw my first 'Mustang' fighter plane skimming the wall tops across these fells and to cap it all we had some of the best meals ever, prepared by a great cook, Mr West from Banks Terrace in Haltwhistle.

Returning to waterwheels, Jake Johnson installed one of four or five feet diameter, many years ago in the burn behind Wolf Hills (G.728589) to generate power for the farm. It had been damaged by floods when I saw it, and as mains electricity had arrived, the wheel wasn't repaired, so I missed that one working.

These waterwheels were all smaller than most of the wheels on the Haltwhistle Burn, although the ruined Wall Mill (G.707663) north of Markham Cottage on one of the tributaries cannot have had a very big mechanism and may have had an overshot wheel. There is not much to be seen now at this site, which is reputed to be of the Roman era. The long water channel, with stone-built sides carrying water from a mossy lake near Peat Steel crags, appears to be too low to work a wheel on the ruined mill. This channel is now for drainage only; what could have been a mill-race shows as a long depression on higher ground to the north of the present channel. Perhaps this was high enough to work an overshot waterwheel. The present stone-built channel could well have been used to drive an undershot wheel.

One mill was situated near Cawfields and another near the Military Road bridge, both worked by the burn water. The next known site downstream is the High Mill (G.706650) a woollen mill at one time, near Broomshaw Hill with a catchment up near Herding Hill crags. Part of the line of the race is visible; unfortunately, the buildings were demolished in the late 1930s when there was a mania for knocking down historic structures instead of repairing them.

Lower down near the bottom of the Cat Stairs, the Low Woollen Mill and a group of houses stood; the race for this almost certainly used the water from the High Mill tail race, in addition to the burn water. The buildings were classed as unsafe and removed about the same time as the High Mill.

Remains of the next dam downstream could be seen for many years in the river bank a short distance up from the footbridge on the Fair Hill/Pike Dyke Neuk footpath (G.709645). The dam was built of stone in the form of a semicircular topped wall about eight feet thick at the base and about six feet high, which must be the strongest of structures for holding water. Unfortunately the small remaining part of the built dam has now been removed, presumably by floods. Constructing this would be an interesting job, like building up the space inside a tunnel but with no

Part of the waterways at the Wall Mill, now almost completely demolished. (D Hunter)

form work needed. Even though it was of such a very strong section, it has gone now. It is doubtful whether even the highest flood was responsible for ruining such an extremely sturdy dam; only a few squared stones remain in the river bed.

The race from this dam was formed on the south side of the burn and tunnelled under the Pike Dyke Neuk footpath near the footbridge, then along between the gas-works site and Crofthead field before passing under Mill Lane, from where it ran straight on towards Shepherd Terrace and into the Burn. When power was required for milling, water was diverted to the left on to the Manor Mill wheel (G.712643) which was on the gable end of the building, the marks on the wall suggesting that it was about twelve feet diameter. The tail race also ran back into the burn towards Shepherd Terrace. Both of these races were stone-built and covered over with large stone slabs to enable the 'battery' embankment to be formed for the coal tubs from South Tyne Colliery.

The Manor Mill was later used as a farm building but has gone the same way as the others and it is now difficult to find where it was situated.

Above: High Mill and house.
Left: Route of the water race to High Mill. The mill position was behind the camera; the race veered round to the right and to a catchment under Herding Hill crags. (D Hunter)

The Low Mill and three houses, Haltwhistle Burn. The bridge, which was wide enough for horse and cart, partly collapsed at a later date, the wooden beam nearest the camera breaking near the centre. People still walked across on the far side until it was replaced by a footbridge. Straight ahead and over the burn, both clay and coal drifts were worked at one time.

Manor Mill dam with race in the foreground. The buildings, chimney and pithead gear of South Tyne Colliery are in the background. The 'rolleyway' to Town Foot is on the right of the photo. (S Blackburn)

Manor Mill dam position today; most of the dressed dam stones have gone. (D Hunter)

Another weir, almost opposite the Manor Mill race outfalls, directed water from the burn into a covered race behind Shepherd Terrace. This last culvert carried water under the back lane of Shepherd Terrace, over the main road and to the cloth mill (G.713641) at Town Foot.

I have no evidence of the size of the waterwheels, except for what I saw at Manor Mill, but they wouldn't be small judging by the nature of the work they had to do and the buildings to which they were attached.

It is doubtful if many of them were much larger than the disused waterwheel at the old Bardon Mill woollen mill (G.779647) which, according to Mr Reay, is about 18 feet diameter and also appears to be wider and deeper troughed than most.

The mill, which was used by the family who also ran the Otterburn Mill, was, according to reports, 'maliciously burnt down in the 1870s by a disgruntled person' and owing to the financial situation at the time was not reinstated.

William Reay, then employed at the fireclay works (G.713640) at Haltwhistle Town Foot, walked down

to Bardon Mill and looked over the burned mill remains. Clay was available nearby so he and Robert Errington decided to start their own works.

That happened in 1878 and the buildings have been used ever since by Errington Reay for their fireclay works and pottery. Subsequently, other Haltwhistle fireclay workers followed to work for the new firm.

Many employees spent much of their working lives in the fireclay industries and some at Bardon Mill knew no other place of employment.

In the 1950s, on South View, Haltwhistle, a retired Mr Hudspith came out to show me this marvellous pocket watch. "Whaat's ti think of that, then?" It had been presented to him for very long service and part of the inscription read: 'From Errington Reay'. He certainly was proud of that watch - I wonder where it is now.

View from the original position of Manor Mill waterwheel. The fairly level path at the left was the route of the mill-race which flowed behind the right-hand houses and in front of the centre house. Grassland in the foreground was the site of the mill and farm buildings which stretched up to the houses on the right of the picture. (D Hunter)

There must have been many Reays who have worked all their lives at Bardon Mill, one of whom, I suspect, did not think much of some new factory regulations that had to be complied with.

One new ruling was that a separate 'bait cabin' had to be provided; nobody was permitted to consume food at their workplace.

The boss thought nowt to that. However, the cabin was arranged, and while the men were having their first meal in it, Mr Reay came through the door and enquired whether the place was comfortable, and to their satisfaction. They all agreed that it was a grand place. "Warm enough?" "Aye - grand." "There's bound to be something..." Mr Reay glanced at the puzzled workforce. "A bit o' music mebbe - aye - that's what's missin!" and picking up an imaginary fiddle he played an imaginary tune, bowed, and departed.

Errington Reay's products can be seen throughout the district - and indeed the country; from large water troughs to the still unsurpassed Bardon Mill patent chimney pots for curing down-draught.

Socketed glazed wall cappings were first developed and made here and many old gardens have glazed ornaments and path edges that are still as good as new. The major production of later years cannot be seen: miles of underground drainage pipes. Plastics seem to have taken over this market but perhaps clay pipes will make a comeback. Some councils would like to see the more durable, glazed earthenware pipes used again but at present the cost of fitting them is higher than the cost of laying long plastic ones.

The old 18-foot waterwheel is enclosed in a building and is not easy to see, but must have carried a great weight of water in the wide wheel troughs when running and would be capable of developing a very high power output. There was another wheel of about 12 feet diameter in the mill at one time.

The main-axle bearing and centre of Bardon Mill water wheel. (D Hunter)

Unfortunately the mill water race, from a sluice gate up the burn (G.777650) to the mill, has long since gone back to nature and is partly covered by a road by-passing Bardon Mill village.

There was also a corn mill, on the low side of the road (G.778645) nearer the railway station, with an unusual feature for this part of the country: a mill pond. Regrettably this mill was dismantled and the parts seem to have been dispersed throughout the

Preparing clay products ready for firing. (D Hunter)

country and the building is now a private house. The village by-pass was planned to go over this mill site at one time and the mill would have had to be removed, but the road route was changed.

The tail race from the woollen mill kept the pond topped up through a culvert under the main road. It would have been interesting to see these wheels turning, using some of the potential power of the burn.

Clay for the later fireclay works came from a hillside (G.777651) up the burn near the present Westwood; it was carried by tubs on a narrow-gauge tramway laid near the race from the mine to the mill.

The chimney, round kiln with mechanical stoker and some of the finished products. The original cloth mill building, adapted and used as a fireclay works since 1878, is on the left of the photo. (D Hunter)

Chapter Five

Walltown Quarry workers, l-r: Donald Nicholson (plant operator/fitter), John Broadbent (joiner/ blacksmith), Allan Hodgson (fitter), Fred Hall (driver), Les Howe (head fitter), George Nixon (plant operator). (R Bainbridge)

Another narrow gauge tramway was used to carry limestone to the kilns (G.780647) on the east side of the burn across from the fireclay works.

This line, about two miles long, carried stone from quarries (G.776672) near Bradley Hall; it crossed the Stanegate Roman Road and the newer access road to Chesterholme and continued along the east side of the burn gorge towards Westwood. The track crossed the road (G. 774651) near Chineley Ford and along the north side of the valley to the kilns.

Some of the burnt limestone from these kilns was carted over the main road then loaded on to railway trucks at Bardon Mill station.

From Bradley Burn Quarry down to the kilns, the line was on an average falling gradient of one in 35, which was managed by the horses; any stone moved between Crindledykes and Bradley was worked by a hauler or self-acting incline. The higher quarry is less than a half mile from Bradley but rises over 200 feet in that short distance.

The older lime kiln at Crindledykes, now preserved. (D Hunter)

Crindledykes had a large old-type kiln near the quarry, although in the 1940s and 50s, Robson Bros. built a more modern kiln.

An earlier Birkshaw Colliery (G.772658), situated about halfway along the lime tramway, might have supplied the coal for the Bardon Mill kilns via the tramway, although the fuel was more likely to have come out of the lower seam, later to be mined from Bardon Mill drift. There were at least five known drifts and shafts into this coal, up the burn from the kilns, in addition to the clay drifts.

The lower quarry at Crindledykes, now closed, looking west from the kiln towards Haltwhistle. (D Hunter)

In the early 1900s, an aerial flight conveyor system from Birkshaw carried coal in skips, hanging from a continuously moving endless rope, running over pulleys up on pylons, down to the railway sidings (G.773646) between Redburn and Bardon Mill. The redundant lower terminal of the flight and the coal screening area was utilised by the Henshaw Drift Co. for their Bardon Mill mine, opened in 1940.

A water wheel situated at Chineleyford (G.773651) was supplied from a weir further up the burn; nothing much remains here.

Small rivers were made to work to their utmost over short distances in this district in the 1800s and earlier. Bardon Mill and Haltwhistle Burns were two excellent examples of this, and I spent many weeks 'ratching' about these burns and their industrial remains.

While visiting my aunt at Town Foot, one interesting place I had to visit was the Haltwhistle Gas Works (G.711644) of the mid-1800s, which didn't need water from the burn for power, although it was used for coke cooling until piped water was installed. These works were built down Mill Lane between the Manor Mill race and the Burn. This area was first widened out by diverting the Burn on to a fairly straight course on the north side of the valley.

The coal-gas-production process at Haltwhistle was the standard system. Coal from local drift mines came via a tub tramway, crossing the Burn alongside the ford for horses and carts, and into the retort house. Later on, coal came by motor lorry from small mines in the Coanwood area.

Each retort was fired with an unusual hand-shovel, which instead of having the blade cranked forward from the shank, had the blade in line or cranked slightly backwards. This shape was necessary when firing the high retorts: a normal cranked shovel would hinder the coal leaving the blade when thrown upwards. Firing was carried out by casting about three cwt of coal through the 24 inch wide

The gas pumping house shown here and the former manager's house are the only buildings remaining of the gas works established in the 1800s. The road in the foreground continued straight on through the wooden fence down to the burnside and the original works was situated to the left of that road; the footpath was much further to the left and the Manor Mill race flowed along next to the hillside on the extreme left. Trees now showing over the pump house are growing on the position of an earlier gasholder. (D Hunter)

opening. The coal had to be spread evenly along the 10-feet length of the retort, which was quite a feat, especially in those with higher openings. The sectional shape of the retort was almost circular with a flat base and was of very thick gauge metal and fitted between the front and back walls of a large heating chamber.

A few of us lads tried firing but much of our coal landed on the floor; however, we did get some coal into the lower openings; it was far more exciting though, to watch a professional stoker send the first shovelful right to the far end of the red-hot retort and see the resultant smoke and flames belch back out into the firing area with a great 'whoosh'.

I always associated this activity as something to do with the Devil - but fear didn't stop us from getting in the way of the stokers, who retaliated by squirting water and brandishing shovels at us - for our own good, they said. In the 1940s two semicircular troughs, fitted at one end to a framework running on overhead girders, made stoking easier. The troughs, looking very like a giant double-barrelled

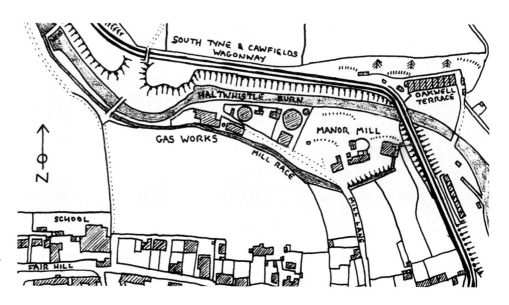

Plan of Gas Works and Manor Mill. (R Hunter)

Grassland in the foreground is the site of the later retort house of about 1900; the small trees behind are on the position of the large gasholder erected about the same time; the tar tank was beyond the gasholder, near the burn side; manager's house on extreme left. Large trees on left background across the burn are growing on embankment formed for colliery and quarry lines. (D Hunter)

a charging hole at floor level, to keep the retorts heated.

A by-product was black tar, which ran through a metal pipe from the building to a tank; it was drawn out of this tank into barrels which were sent to roadwork sites for tar spraying and chipping coatings. In winter weather, this pipeline, heated by constantly running tar and sheltered by the gas holder, made a nice warm seat for local youngsters.

Coke was crushed to size and sold for heating purposes. This was lightweight and required two sacks to hold a hundredweight, however, it burned away very quickly so it was not a great deal cheaper to use than hard coke.

The gas-holder, a large open-bottomed cylinder, free to rise and fall in a close-fitting and sealed outer tank, rose up as the gas was pumped in and fell as

gun with the barrel tops sliced off along the 10-feet length, could be lowered almost to ground level, filled with coal from the stockpile then raised, turned and pushed into the open retort to the far end, where the troughs were revolved. This emptied out the coal evenly over the length of the retort, causing much more spectacular displays of smoke and flames than did hand-firing.

The retort was then sealed up for some hours; the resulting gas from the heated coal was pumped through various washing and refining processes and into the big metal gas-holder. When the retort was unsealed, hot coke was drawn out into wide metal barrows, pushed outside, then drenched with water. This produced clouds of steam and, if they got too near, showered onlookers with hot water; this amused the staff. The empty retort was quickly refilled and sealed again.

At other times the yellow-hot coke was emptied into a funnel-shaped guide, directed down and through

Bridge abutment at Castle Hill. Stone-built part on right was used by the South Tyne Colliery tramroads which terminated at the screens, behind the camera position. Later brick-built wall on the left supported the bridge carrying the Cawfields Quarry line which terminated at a main-line loading dock beyond the colliery screens. Small boys, reaching from the embankment, occasionally blocked the house chimney on the right; evidently they welcomed a chase by the householder. (D Hunter)

106

demand increased. The inlet from the works and outlet pipe to the town supply network were fitted under and up into this gas holder; the weight of this metal 'cap' maintained the pressure in the pipelines throughout the town and into surrounding areas.

The smaller gas-holder, used occasionally when repairs were needed on the main holder, was positioned in a large circular pit about ten feet deep which was partly filled with water to form a seal. It also was free to rise and fall and was adequate for the amount of gas used in the 1800s. Originally, the gas-holder was further west, near the first small retort house.

With increased demand for gas a much larger holder had to be installed at the site and this was used until the works changed to the Butane gas system, later to be changed again to North Sea gas. Nowadays pressurised supply pipelines from the coast and throughout the country act as reservoirs and are kept at a constant pressure.

By the 1900s, the Burn Gorge was to have another role for which water was not required as power. With the upgrading of more roads, demand increased for hard whinstone surfacing, in preference to the softer limestone. Stone was plentiful at Cawfields Quarry (G.712666) on the whinstone dyke; transporting it over any great distance was the problem.

With the Newcastle and Carlisle railway in the Tyne Valley some two miles to the south, the quarry company wisely decided that the best way to transport stone was to construct their own branch line up the Burn Gorge from Haltwhistle.

At Town Foot, some narrow-gauge lines were already in position, from the main-line sidings up to the old South Tyne and other drifts near the Low Mill, with a branch into the gasworks.

A 1920s parade on Castle Hill showing the quarry/colliery line bridge. The men leading the parade are pit rescue brigadesmen with breathing apparatus. (M Henderson)

Earthworks required to provide a separate track for the quarry line involved: widening the existing colliery battery near the Manor Mill and up past the gas works; and alterations to the river bridge near Oakwell Terrace and to the road bridge over Castle

Castle Hill from the east; South Tyne Colliery screens on left, quarry/colliery bridge centre and Musgrave Tower on right. (I Hunter)

Castle Hill and Mill Lane from Castle Banks. The quarry and colliery lines can be clearly seen between Oakwell Terrace and Castle Hill. On the far right is the top half of Shepherd Terrace; the bottom half being built several years later. (S Blackburn)

A Cawfields Quarry engine crossing one of the ramshackle-looking bridges. (J Keen)

Stone abutments for colliery lines on the right and quarry line on the left at remains of former bridge No. 2 near Oakwell Terrace. (D Hunter)

Hill. Much of the formation further upstream was widened up to the Low Mill area by building stone walls on the burnside and filling up behind to track level.

The next length up to High Mill didn't need much excavation, but beyond the mill a bridge was required for crossing the burn to the west side. The bridges were of rather light construction, being made up of small-section steel girders decked over with wood planking and supported by steel frames concreted into the river bed.

From the High Mill bridge, the track bed was formed alongside the existing levelled area used as access road to Lees Hall or Herdman's Quarry.

Unusually large stone steps at the entrance to Haltwhistle Church Hall came from this quarry; the

A very substantial doorstep at the Church Hall: the bottom stone is about nine inches thick. These blocks came from Herdman's Lees Hall Quarry and are a fairly permanent example of local skills. Fitted about 1906, even today they show very little edge wear, other than the western end of the base stone. (D Hunter)

heaviest one caused a wooden cart wheel to collapse on the rough road opposite Rudstone Cottages. This cart stood for a few days, loaded with the massive bottom step, on wooden blocks and the three remaining wheels until the fourth one was repaired.

Hugh Edgar remembered making a detour to view this 'three-legged cart' on his way home from school to Redpath Farm in about 1905.

From the Herdman's Quarry access road, the track bed was formed up into the Burn Gorge. Extensive wall-building was required on the burnside; a short length of the hillside had to be removed to widen out this area.

Beyond that there was a gradual rise to the high crags (G.708653) below Lees Hall Farm. Some rock was removed and a short, steep cutting was formed, together with an embankment across a wide corner of the burn, after diverting the water and building more retaining walls.

An early view of Central Place; the building to the left of the Church Hall was demolished to widen Lanty's Lonnen. (S Blackburn)

Cawfields steam loco and trucks near Fell Chimney and Lees Hall lime kiln, midway between Military Road and Burn Gorge. Driver John Elliot, brakeman J Coulson. (R Bainbridge)

The track bed only needed 'squaring out' on the sloping burnside up to the next bridge position. This was of similar construction to High Mill Bridge and carried the track over into the Fell Chimney area.

With very little earthwork required past the mine, the next bridge was reached, and constructed as before. Just beyond the bridge there was a short distance where the slope required levelling, then the track bed was formed across the fairly flat Sunnyside fields to the Military Road.

Here another steel and plank railway bridge was erected over the burn and under the roadway (G.714660), with just enough headroom for locos.

The last gently rising section from the bridge to the quarry past the Roman camp sites needed very little excavation and forming.

It seems that this line was constructed with horse-working in mind; it sloped evenly most of the way but as with many similar schemes, the quarry company realised that horse power would never keep up with increasing output and locos would have to be used. Many times we walked up this track bed to Cawfields after the lines were removed but the building of a new bridge on the Military Road altered the direct route by removing access over what remained of the railway bridge under the old road bridge, thus blocking the footpath at rail level.

I know of two steam and two petrol locos that were used on the line in the 1930s; the heavier steamer was the main loco for long distance work in the early years; the small steamer shunted trucks at Haltwhistle Town Foot.

After the larger steam loco was retired the American petrol loco took over long-distance running; the other ex-army petrol loco remained at Town Foot, working alongside the smaller Kerr Stewart steam loco.

Usually stone was carried in sets of ten side-tipping trucks, although much longer trains were said to have run on the line.

I heard of only one accident, involving a loco which derailed and dropped into the burn near Herding Hill crags (G.709652). There was no mention of damage to men or machinery so it can be assumed that it would only need pulling back out and putting back to work.

The locos, particularly the later American version, travelled at a consistently fast pace, especially with the returning empty trains, which made a continuous racket on the way back up to the quarry. No hooters were required and people were not concerned about noise in the 1930s. Latterly the line was neglected and run down, however the trucks kept on the rails remarkably well.

Walltown Quarry at Greenhead, a place I visited many times, solved some of their transport problems by erecting an aerial flight, similar to the arrangement at Birkshaw Colliery, Bardon Mill. This stretched from the quarry yard, over Carvoran Moss and downhill to Greenhead railway station. Skips suspended from the rope were loaded under hoppers at the quarry and sent out on the moving steel rope down to the station. This system was in use until superseded by road transport in the 1930s, after which it stood idle for some years.

During wartime petrol shortages, the flight was used again for a time to carry stone to the railway; when fuel shortages eased it was dismantled.

An ingenious plumber, Mattie Reay, living adjacent to Carvoran Farm (G.667658), saved one of these aerial skips, and fitted overhead steel girders in a line through his farm buildings and out to the manure heap, making the farm barrow redundant. These farm buildings, minus track and skip, are now part of the Roman Army Museum.

The Greenhead aerial flight was not the last installation of this kind of mechanism; a cousin and

I constructed a 'plant' in Haltwhistle in the late 1930s which, apart from a few minor mishaps, worked for us. I inspected the Walltown flight and could imagine something similar from my bedroom window to the top clothes line post in our sloping back garden. This was a distance of almost 20 yards and I thought it would be a great place to try it out. Fortunately I had a Meccano set with which we made a 'wind-up' haulage machine to screw down to the top of a table I used as a workbench against the bedroom window. An old alarm clock with the balance-wheel escapement removed made an adequate driving motor. We found a length of good strong cord and made a skip to run along this, down to garden level. Another long length of cord acted as a hauler rope to pull the loaded skip up to the bedroom tipping point - on the table.

A few 'wind-ups' were necessary and sometimes some manual help for the alarm clock but it worked all right so long as the support rope stayed in one piece; over-ambitious loading by Bobby in the garden broke the cord more than once. We planned that the next machine would have a length of steel fencing wire for a support but we never found time to construct mark two.

About thirty years later, while dismantling at a Lakeland slate quarry at Hodge Close, one of the items scrapped was a rope haulage system on the same principle as our back-garden gadget as I pointed out, but the Hodge Close mechanism had been in use long before our effort. The Lakeland hauler was a Blondin lift; its main support rope stretched a few hundred yards across an 80 feet deep quarry for lifting the clogs of slate up to the surface. At two inches diameter, the main steel rope would have made a grand parade ground for the famous Blondin tightrope walker. It was disappointing in a way because we had thought we were pioneers, although a snag not encountered by Hodge Close emerged in our bedroom - garden system: the bedroom window wouldn't close at night without dismantling everything. In the 1970s I was intrigued

Erecting the aerial flight at Greenhead station to carry stone from Walltown Quarry. (R Bainbridge)

to find our then eleven-year-old son working on a similar construction, which ran - or walked: it moved slowly - from his bedside table, downstairs and out of the front door, the whole thing powered by a redundant wind-up gramophone motor. It was intended to carry hoppers of corn to the waiting hens, to avoid having to get up early to feed them, but he encountered the same snag that we did: the front door couldn't be closed.

Initial quarrying operations at Walltown (referred to locally as Greenhead Quarry) began in the 1870s near the position of the present carpark gateway and progressed eastwards for about a 100 yards, sloping down to approximately 20 feet below the Old Shields road level. A crushing and screening plant was erected against the quarry face and a new higher quarry level started, eastwards from the crusher loading point. The floor was near the 750 feet above sea-level mark

and when I was taken to the quarry in 1935, the north-south line of the high face was estimated at 250 yards from the crusher.

Many locals maintained that the westerly part of this now-removed crag was much higher than the existing Roman Wall and that much more of the Solway Firth could be seen from the top in those days than is possible today. The Wall takes a north-south detour at this point above the old quarry face, where a new blasting system was tried out in the late 1950s.

With advice from explosives experts, a tunnel was driven into the face at floor level for about 30 feet, a chamber opened out, then packed with explosives. When this was detonated, a huge area of the quarry face and the hill shuddered, rose slightly, then thousands of tons of rock slumped down, assuming a more sloping shape than before.

An early view of Walltown Quarry. (R Bainbridge)

Many onlookers were disappointed, having expected rocks flying through the air; others were heard to say: "And that … Wall is still there", having assumed that the exhibition was intended to remove this obstruction to quarrying progress.

In the main quarry, narrow-gauge rail trucks were used to move stone to the crusher, with horses providing the pulling power, with hoof protectors for safe walking on the sharp whin stones. Locos took over as the face was worked further away from the crushers.

I never saw any steam engines at Walltown but there would be some in the earlier years. The working locos that I saw were petrol-powered and made by Simplex and Austro-Daimler in the 1930s. Even then rubber-tyred vehicles in the form of Muirhill

Two of Walltown Quarry's Simplex locos. (E & MS Watson)

Narrow-gauge lines leading to the Walltown Quarry face. (E & MS Watson)

dumpers were hauling stone from the quarry to the crusher; the locos and rail trucks worked to their full capacity, but improved crushers needed greater quantities of stone, which could only be supplied by extra dumpers.

Some heavier Hunslet locos were used in the last years of the rail system in the late 1940s. After the rails and locos were scrapped, a motley collection of old lorries carried the stone to the crushers, most of them having been retired, or banned, from road haulage. During the 1940s the quarry employed women loco drivers and some of the internal quarry lorries were also driven by women; they managed it quite well but said that they couldn't get used to sitting on a cab-less loco in the frosts of a Walltown winter - and never would. At an exposed 750 feet above sea level, winters could be quite Arctic.

However, stone had to be quarried for wartime aerodromes, etc., regardless of the weather; only deep snow put a stop to operations.

The works expanded eastwards to a new quarry (G.675665), some distance to the north-east, where most of the Roman Wall had been removed, presumably to build the nearby Walltown farmhouse and building. An embankment was formed along the north side of Walltown Crags; the rails were laid from the new quarry to join the unloading loop of the older system. This new track was on a rising gradient to the quarry and being partly alongside trees, wet leaves in Autumn caused some trouble.

Often a loaded train left the quarry and skidded most of the way to the crushers and the driver couldn't do anything other than to hang on until something

115

Walltown Quarry workers next to the aerial flight; screens in the background. Front left is Bob Batey, who played football for Carlisle and Preston; middle row: far right, Billy Mitchinson; middle, John Johnston; far right, Walter Foster. (P Howe)

Mr Carrs (manager), Billy Nicholson (receiving long service presentation) and Mr Marshall (from head office); 1966. (E & MS Watson)

gripped. These northside lines were, generally, on a gradient of about 1 in 20 but some short lengths were more severe. Kenneth Lattimer told me of an incident involving skidding trains that happened when he was a loco driver in the 1930s. He was on the far quarry run one day when, as often happened after rain and with leaves on the track, the loco could not grip the rails to hold back the loaded trucks and away they went. Ken was not unduly alarmed about this; it had happened often enough in the past and he could only sit there and wait until the train slowed back to normal. Mr Carrs, the manager, had never objected to this speed-up in production.

What did cause some alarm was the fact that some clown had reversed his lorry on to the tracks, down near the crusher - and seemed to be shovelling chippings on to it. Ken was still a long way from this obstruction and expected it to move before he got there; he gave a few warning blasts on the

A view of the quarry looking eastwards after its being partly filled in to form a wildlife park. (D Hunter)

crossing at the College Farm and up the field footpath to Walltown.

Father thought I might be safer with Percy Mitchinson in the blacksmith's shop so I spent an interesting morning among the flying sparks, poking into all the gear they had lying about; unfortunately I nipped my finger under the big vice handle and split the skin open so Father was sent for to wrap my finger with some sticky tape. Then he thought I had better come with him into the quarry to help him rather than fiddle with Percy's work tools. That suited me, I had been wondering how I could get

whistle. Ken could hardly believe what he saw when the man ran to the front of the lorry to start his engine with the starting handle: 'He must have switched it off - he'll never get it moved in time. Do I jump off now - it might be safer - there'll be some firewood flying through the air when the engine hits that lorry body - I can't do anything on the loco, anyway'; such were his thoughts as the train clattered towards the lorry.

The driver got his lorry off the track and with only an inch or two to spare, engine and trucks shot past and came to a stand almost at the crusher tipping point. The manager had been walking to the quarry face when he saw this little drama unfolding. He could only stand and watch; he held his breath until the loco missed the lorry, shook his head and then carried on walking into the quarry.

My first visit to Walltown was during a school holiday when for some reason there was nobody at home at Redpath and I would have been left on my own all day. I could manage that all right; there were all these becks that needed seeing to, but Father asked if I fancied a day's work at the quarry. Great! I was up at crack of dawn and bait-bags on shoulders, we set out along the Carlisle road, over the railway

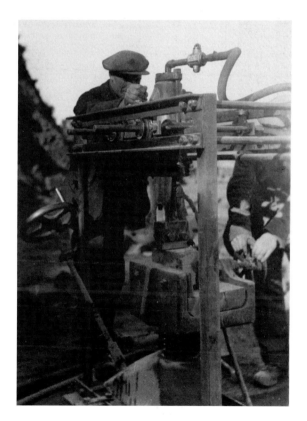

Walltown Quarry workers. (E & MS Watson)

117

nearer the locos and trucks and this was my first time into the quarry.

What a hive of activity at the face, men with huge hammers reducing great rocks into pieces small enough to be lifted into the trucks, others sorting out stones that they took to Father for him to dress into square-sided blocks; another man shook about violently as he hung over a pointed gadget with a rubber air pipe fixed to it; Father explained that he was drilling shot holes ready for blasting and later we would hear the bangs.

Kenneth Lattimer was working with his train sets while I watched all the manoeuvres of taking out full trucks and leaving empties; I would try to do the same with my trucks in the back yard at Redpath; passengers were not allowed so I didn't get a ride on Ken's loco.

When home-time came I was disappointed that there were no bangs as promised, but before we were out on to the road the shots went off when everyone was out of the quarry except the two shotfirers.

The next time I helped Father, his work place was much further away from the quarry face; he had a steel shelter propped up so that he didn't need to stop work when they were firing shots; in the old position he had to leave the quarry each time they fired and because he was paid by results, that didn't suit him.

His workshed was in a row of shelters for use in very bad weather; these were covered with wooden railway sleepers to prevent flying stones from the blasting going through the roof. Now I could watch the shots going off; a long length of flame and some smoke jumped up from the rocks followed by a loud bang; the stone was then ready for the hammermen. Father kept going in his open-air work position with his steel brattish for protection, and being rather deaf seemed not to notice when stones crashed on to the metal plate.

My contribution was moving some of his chippings with a shovel about three sizes too big for me and stacking some of the finished setts. The hammers wouldn't go straight for me so I didn't do any squaring out of blocks, but it was all very interesting.

Father had to pay from his own earnings the man who brought him the roughly-squared-out blocks and I believe the 'knocker-up' got something; it was all part of the agreement with the quarry company.

There was no sign of Kenneth's skidding trains when I was there - in fact the far quarry started operations after my visits, which was just as well.

On the two-mile-long Cawfields Quarry line a brakeman was employed to put drags in the wheels on the steepest sections. At Greenhead evidently it was thought unnecessary, so the loco just - skidded.

When quarrying reached the eastern boundary, a lower level quarry was started nearer the west end and to the south of the crushers; this was worked eastwards. In the 1950s and 60s stone-breaking was done by massive iron balls, lifted and crashed down by drag-line excavators. A more powerful crusher, which could break down much larger rocks, was installed. As one low-level quarry worked out a deeper quarry was started.

In the final thirty years, quarried stone was loaded by machine on to dump trucks; in the previous seventy years, stone had been filled by hand on to sledges, and later, on to rail trucks and dumpers. Sore hands were part of the job and quarrymen often cut pieces of lorry inner-tube to fit each hand; modern gloves might have lasted an hour but not much longer on the abrasive whinstone. A Haltwhistle chemist, Willie Milligan, made up a special mixture, Summer and Winter Fluid, for the quarrymen's hands and it was very effective. Glycerine was one of the ingredients but what the others were, only Willie knew. Mr Bell, the other chemist, also produced his own mixture.

Walltown Quarry

Top left: knocking up (centre) and drilling (right). (E & MS Watson)
Top right: filling shot holes. (E & MS Watson)
Bottom left: roughly-squared-out blocks (a waiting horse and cart can just be seen in the background). (E & MS Watson)
Bottom right: face-workers. (E & MS Watson)

Installing the new Walltown crusher in the 1950s. A Coles crane lowers the crusher into position; buses in centre background were the workers' transport. (E & MS Watson)

Part of the quarry work up to the late 1940s was making squared-up paving setts for town streets. Sett-makers were part of a team supplied with stone by a 'blocker-out' man in the quarry; he picked suitable stone and broke it into blocks that could be handled by the sett-maker. Another member of the team, the 'knocker-up', reduced the largest rocks, blasted down from the face, and the 'blocker-out' then picked the best of this for his sett maker; the rest went to the crusher.

Most of the men were paid by results and a smooth line from quarry face to sett maker 'made money'. The knocker-up and the blocker-out both broke stone with sett-making in mind because the rate per ton produced was so much higher, possibly five times the rate paid for crushing quality stone.

Knockers-up had a hard and heavy job, swinging the massive hammers, but if they were good at breaking, every shot with the hammer counted.

I remember hearing of a Silver Top quarryman going on holiday to a far-off part of the country where he spotted a quarry which he just had to go and look over. Apparently he noticed two knockers-up walloping away at some rocks so he went across to watch. As he said: "Aa cudn't bide to watch them any langer so Aa gat hod o' the hammer and asked if Aa cud try".

They warned him that the hammers were very heavy and it was a very skilled job etc., so Ivan, in his Sunday-best suit and polished tea-drinker's shoes, raised the hammer and started whacking rocks. Every shot was accurate and he had a mass of broken stone in a very short time, handed the hammer back and said it was much easier than he had thought it would be, then he walked away. The two would-be knockers-up never answered, and as Ivan glanced back, they were just gazing at the stone-heap.

Sett-making was revived at Walltown for a time in the 1960s but only until a special order was fulfilled. Local contractor John Lennox learned the sett-making trade at that time. Many of Carlisle's streets are still paved with whinstone setts which seem to be everlasting. Some were tarmacadamed over with a smooth top which enabled traffic to increase speed; bumps were then fitted to slow it down. Whin setts did that in the first place so the tar was removed in some parts.

One Sunday in 1937 father announced that we were all going for a walk round by Walltown Quarry, so that he could show us the marvellous Iron Man. What images this provoked. Our inventive minds had the Iron Man with arms and legs bolted on to a metal body, breaking rocks with his mighty fists.

The machine turned out to be even better than we expected: a real Ruston Bucyrus excavator on tracks with a large-face shovel bucket, festooned with steel ropes running over umpteen pulley wheels. It was a RB10 - possibly the first in the district and here it was at Walltown, digging out the almost eight-feet-thick overburden above the smooth-topped whinstone.

Ruston Bucyrus excavator at Threlkeld Quarry and Mine Museum, very similar to the machine the author's father described as the 'Iron Man' in the 1930s. (J Parker, jnr)

It worked eastward parallel with Walltown Farm road, along the bottom of the south-facing slope. Starting at the bottom proved to be a mistake. When digging was attempted uphill, instead of the bucket digging into the overburden, the whole machine on its metal tracks slipped downwards on the smooth whinstone surface. To overcome this, some debris was returned on to the whinstone and the machine carried on digging, leaving a layer of soil and stones

for adhesion. Much later, an old Caterpillar bulldozer was used on the quarry top to push the overburden down to the bottom of the slope. The conjunction of hard whinstone surface and metal tracks produced some spectacular side slips and the Caterpillar was a rather dangerous machine to drive.

Walltown Quarry bought one of the first all-hydraulic loading shovels in about 1953. This was made by Bray Loaders and was built over a Fordson Major tractor. As the quarry was at a high altitude, a petrol tractor was acquired for easy starting in winter; the Bray could then tow the other diesel machines to start them if necessary. This machine replaced the old wire-rope-worked Chaseside loader, which was built over the older standard Fordson tractor. The Bray, now diesel-engined, still exists but has not run recently; hard work at a local colliery since its quarry days has rather worn it out.

From the 1930s, concrete blocks were manufactured at the quarry and these were used countrywide for building work; they were slightly porous but at eighteen inches long were quickly assembled.

The first all-hydraulic loader of about 1953 at Walltown; a Bray machine fitted to the new model of petrol Fordson Major tractor; petrol type chosen for easier starting in winter at the high-altitude quarry.

Kerbstones and paving slabs were made and supplied for the streets and roads of the district; in the early days, these were vibrated during manufacture but as the surface layer was liable to shell off in severe frosts, they were then hydraulically pressed, which seemed to cure this fault.

The concrete products were grey except for some mock stone blocks and wall cappings which were made by mixing in red sand from the Brampton area; these tended to be softer than the grey whinstone mix.

The concrete plant was often laid off in severe frosty weather, which didn't suit the operators, because the only alternative work available was clearing overburden, or similar labouring, on the quarry top, and at 800 feet above sea-level it could be quite nippy.

After more than 100 years, the quarry closed in 1979.

Deep quarrying excavations have since been partly filled, mainly with surplus material from the construction of the Greenhead by-pass road, and grassed over, together with the creation of wild-life ponds, tree-planting and car parks.

I was disappointed when the Haltwhistle to Cawfields Railway closed in 1938, but as road transport was then thought to be more economical this was inevitable.

The public discovered that the track bed made an excellent, easy-going footpath from Haltwhistle to the Military Road.

Two quarrymen brothers from near High Mill regularly cycled down home from Cawfields on the old track bed and presumably biked up in the mornings; I occasionally repaired their bikes. There have been greater transport disasters since the Cawfields closure. The Haltwhistle to Alston standard-gauge railway closed in 1976; construction of the narrow-gauge line from Alston will, it is hoped, bring back locos as we remember them at Cawfields.

Because of its proximity to a Roman mile castle, Cawfields main quarry closed earlier than did Walltown. At Cawfields a lower-level area was excavated, the trucks and lines were scrapped, and dumpers used to carry stone to the crushers. The 30-feet-deep hole kept the quarry going for many years but the cost of pumping water out reduced profitability. Following closure, this quarry also has been partly filled and now forms a pleasant lake and picnic area.

Cawfields Quarry showing the remaining face of the earlier working and the flooded lower level of the final quarry. (D Hunter)

Chapter Six

Haltwhistle from the east about 1900. Henry Clark's sawmill and joiner's shop is the building on the right-hand side of the photo. The station footbridge can be seen because the original signalbox was situated over what were the Alston platform tracks; the later signalbox blocks the view of the bridge and some of the station-house from this position.

Back in Haltwhistle, Henry Clark's sawmill and joiner's shop, built in the late 1800s on railway land and demolished in the 1950s or 60s, was situated on the north side of the River Tyne, but without a waterwheel as might have been expected.

When I first knew of it, the sawmill was powered by a town gas engine which produced odd sound effects: put, put, bang, put, put, bang, and so on.

Whenever we youngsters heard it running and

popping, we looked through the engine room window to watch the flywheel spinning and to wonder about the heap of spent matches under the cylinder - it must have been tricky to light, like Joe Bowes' pipe.

Joe Bowes was Haltwhistle's intrepid fireman of long ago. His two-wheeled hand cart carried hand pumps for pumping to the long hoses; other equipment was stored in the box. Ladders were carried on top; the crew ran to any fires, pushing the barrow in front of them.

Joe ran with the cart to a fire at Gilsland Convalescent Home at one time but some of the local lads took over part way along the seven-mile race. They reckoned Joe 'conked out' and arrived at the fire much later. Afterwards, Joe boasted that the fire was so big that as he hurried through Greenhead he caught a hot spark out of the air and stuffed it in the infamous pipe and it went like a rocket after that.

The Fire Station then was a small lean-to hut on the gable end of Ernie Carrick's fruit shop in Westgate, now part of the Co-op Stores. The cement fillet where the shed roof fitted to the stone gable wall was still there in 1996 but the 'station' is long gone and the narrow site has been levelled and the tarmac road extended up to the gable end.

The only time I saw Joe in action was when the Working Men's Club in Aesica Road caught fire. Joe officiated; the pumps were worked by anyone he could grab out of the crowd of onlookers. These 'volunteers' enjoyed the drama and afterwards were to be heard telling sensational stories. As there was mains water supply in Haltwhistle, I was puzzled as to why they had hand pumps but apparently, these were used to suck out all the nearby rain barrels, etc. when the mains water pipes were too far from the fires, or were too small to supply enough water. Hand pumps would create more pressure, anyway.

Henry Clark and Sons moved in the late 1940s from the riverside premises up to the joiner's shop and sawmill, between Greencroft and Greystonedale, which previously had been used for many years by Issac Hetherington and Son. I wonder what became of Clarks' home-made puzzles. Harry Clark senior often produced them to amuse inquisitive boys visiting his Tyneside workshop - were they taken up to the Greencroft workshop? I remember puzzling over two pieces of two-inch square timber joined together with a dovetail joint on all four sides - an impossibility at first glance but these pieces were

slipped together diagonally and glued and took a bit of solving.

John Johnson, who owned a shop at the West End, had built the Greencroft workshop as a warehouse and cornmill, just over the western boundary of Greencroft Park in the 1920s, but after a few years, moved back and started a more convenient warehouse and mill opposite his shop.

Isaac Hetherington extended the building in the 1930s to house a sawmill and a timber-drying shed with a large garage between. Arthur Laidlow rented the garage for his lorries and as a repair workshop.

The sawmill was driven by a 15hp 3-phase electric motor, controlled by very suspect ex-Plenmeller Colliery switch gear. This switch gear aroused suspicions when it was noticed that the handles were wrapped with rubber from old car inner tubes. The big saw seemed to perform quite well but the rubber coverings were never tampered with.

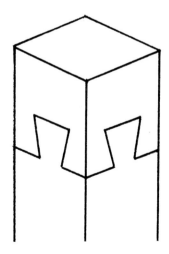

A sketch of one of Henry Clark's tricky pieces; a dovetail joint showing on all four sides, appeared to be impossible but Henry found a way as explained in the text.

The former Isaac Hetherington workshop, later used by Henry Clark & Son. The right-hand building was the joiner's shop converted from John Johnson's Corn and Meal Mill. The central building was added by I Hetherington and rented out to Arthur Laidlow as a garage for his lorries. The left-hand shed was finally added as a timber-drying storage and was also used for Billy Jackson's firewood depot; the sawmill was at the rear. Fronts and roofs have been renewed since Isaac's days. (D Hunter)

Norman Renwick fitted the motor and switch gear for Isaac and he had some trouble trying to get the motor to run; it only buzzed. He was employed at Midgeholme Quarry as electrician/fitter at that time, by Isaac's brother Joe Hetherington. I remember him travelling from Haltwhistle via Redpath bank, wearing a massive top coat with his cap back-to-front, riding an old square-tanked, girder-forked motor bike. Unlike many motor-cyclists of the 1930s, I don't remember him ever being stuck on Redpath Bank.

Apparently, though, he was stuck with Isaac's motor and switch gear, so the motor manufacturer was informed and their mechanic found the fault fairly quickly. During manufacture one of the terminal bolts had been over-tightened and broke off inside the insulation block - out of sight. The makers said the motor was tested at the works and they wanted

to blame Norman for the fault but somehow he proved them wrong. Isaac calmed down eventually and commenced sawing with his new 'toy'.

Later, during the war, the circular saw was used to cut logs suitable for household fires to save coal and gas; these were bagged and delivered round the town on a two-wheeled hand-cart by elderly Billy Jackson. It was amazing how he managed to push or pull loads of logs over streets that were far from level; he was very short, so if we saw the loaded barrow from the rear while he pulled from the front, all we could see of Billy was his two legs paddling along, the rest of him hidden by the load. On the rough road down from the sawmill with a badly loaded barrow, he was often lifted off the ground by the handles; but he kept on delivering for many years.

Billy Jackson and a friend decided that on one of their rare days off, they would go for a walk and picnic up the fell footpath to Warren House, past the end of the old Plenmeller pit yard; this yard then being used as a munitions storage area. Billy and pal walked past the wired-in compounds full of shells and bombs and continued up to higher ground near Warren House, which they decided would be a nice place to picnic on this lovely day. They opened

Laidlow's Thames 4D outside Henry Clark's workshop, where the wooden lorry backs were built. (A Burns)

their sandwich packs and after eating, leaned back and dozed off.

Billy was awakened by a shout from his friend and stared up into the barrels of army rifles held by stern-looking soldiers who grinned when they realised they were not spies reading maps, as they had thought, but two old boys picnicking. They apologised but Billy was not amused and jumped up and stamped off as fast as his short legs could carry him home.

Just behind Isaac's place there was another sawmill with a shorter rack bench but with a much larger circular saw blade.

I first met Bob Kennedy years before, among the old lorries at West End Garage, and now he had built this rack bench and he and brother Tom felled trees in the woods, brought them in and cut them up. He didn't have an electric driving motor but had what was known as an old Halley.

This was a type of motor vehicle chassis-and-cab, which had a large flat driving pulley behind the gearbox, next to the prop-shaft, which must have been intended to drive a machine mounted on the rear of the chassis. The machine appeared to be related to those old wagons Bob and Tom used at West End, and it resembled army vehicles from the 1914-18 war, or even earlier.

The driving-belt from the pulley to the circular saw was required to drive out of the side of this machine to the saw-spindle pulley, so one side was jacked up until the belt could drive from the gearbox pulley under the chassis, without scraping any parts of the vehicle.

This amazing outfit looked and sounded bizarre, the entire machine shaking, with a 35-degree list to starboard, resting on two right-hand wheels, the engine roaring, belts and sawdust flying and the saw howling - but it worked and was fairly economical on fuel.

The much-rebuilt left-hand shed was Bob Kennedy's sawmill where the old Halley stood in front and drove the saw by a long belt stretching through the doorway. The right-hand building originally housed butcher Willie Norman's vans and meat preparation department. (D Hunter)

If they had found a slightly larger pulley, the belt could have gone above and below the chassis, with the vehicle left standing on all four wheels, but they used their patent for years - tilted. Bob eventually fitted a more powerful electric motor and the old Halley was retired and finally scrapped.

Another of these old Halleys was used by Joe Foster (Jack's brother) at Gilsland, to haul and drive one of his travelling threshing machines in the early 1940s; it often worked in the Haltwhistle area. As may be imagined, setting that Halley in position to drive a threshing machine caused some headaches, especially on wet ground, but it was managed well enough by George Henderson from Henshaw, who seemed to know a thing or two about engines and used it until tractors were available once more.

Some time after Bob Kennedy scrapped his Halley, he tried growing tomatoes in two long greenhouses, just behind his sawmill. To heat the glass houses he found an old mobile steam boiler, threaded steam pipes through among the plants and fired it up with waste wood.

It worked very well but unfortunately the greenhouses were situated alongside the eight 3000-gallon-capacity, open-topped vats at Greystonedale Works (G.700640); all filled with a Prussian Blue liquid. One night a howling gale sprang up and swirled blue dye up into the air and over Bob's greenhouses.

Next morning the glass was dark Prussian Blue and to make matters worse, a 'helper' started to wash this off with a high pressure hose coupled to the works supply and scattered most of the glass from the north side of one of the glass houses. The story goes that Bob had blue tomatoes that year.

He grew no more tomatoes after a gale from a different angle blew the rest of the glass out and it was just left on the ground; it is probably still there under the grass.

Back at the riverside, Kilfrost Ltd now use the site of Clark's original sawmill and joiner's shop as the office car park.

Further east, on the site of Kilfrost's works, stood the buildings taken over by the Gelata Products Company in about 1920 and known as the soap works, having been used originally for that purpose.

The Gelata Company acquired the works together with the soap manufacturing process. I remember finding and reading the formula for soap in the office there and a friend went one better and made some. Something went wrong somewhere because we couldn't hold the finished product. We came to the conclusion that we had misread the formula and

Haltwhistle looking west from the Alston Arches; soap works on the right. (S Blackburn)

added twice the stated amount of caustic. It certainly livened up hand-washing.

As far as I remember there was no other product made here other than Gelata, or Rosin Size as it was known.

The process involved melting solid resin in a steel tank which had steam heating cavities, or 'jackets', all round. Resin was delivered in wooden barrels and to release it, the steel hoops were removed and the wooden barrel staves dismantled; these staves were chopped up and sold to local householders as excellent firelighters.

The solid block of resin was then broken into the heating tank. To this was added a lesser quantity of broken-up solid caustic. This 'hot stuff' came in 40-gallon steel barrels, and the method of breaking them was to lie each barrel on its side and strike it with a sledge hammer along a line from end to end, then roll the barrel over and repeat the battering. One of the ends was then rather crudely removed with a hammer and chisel. We always planned to make an outsize tin-opener and splitter for this job but never found time to do it.

A measured amount of caustic and water was added to the resin and the tank lid sealed; the steam was then turned on to the heating cavity at about 40 pounds pressure, for two or three days. The finished liquid was forced out by steam into a large open-topped tank and filled into barrels for dispatch to paper mills.

These barrels were rolled up a ramp on to one of Laidlows' lorries, often the Commer, and Sam Mitchell delivered them to customers. He sometimes returned with a load of coal from Tyneside for the boiler but it was usually of poorer quality than local 'duff'. We never discovered where he found it but he would have to shovel it on by hand and then it had to be thrown into the boiler house coal store, again by hand. Tippers were still rare on long-wheel-base lorries at that time; most had fixed flatbacks.

Steam for the Gelata process was supplied by an upright boiler which raised enough steam on the lowest grade of coal, or 'duff', for the three-day boiling, the fire being 'banked up' through the night to sustain the heat.

The chimney from the boiler had a lid adjustable from the boiler house to conserve heat during the overnight shutdown but it often crashed to the ground in a gale or was sometimes removed by exploding gas from the boiler fire. It always reminded me of the small steel works' cupolas with their rusty pull-wires and chimney lids.

This was a one-man factory. The late Alec Watkins worked this factory for many years even though he had a partially disabled leg. Our crew often helped him to fire the boiler and generally looked after the place if he had to go up into the town.

One day he explained to us how to start up the steam pump to fill the boiler if the water got too low in the gauge-glass, then left us to it. As Alec was away for a long time, we thought we had better make sure the water level was kept up, and besides, we wanted to be able to brag that we had 'driven' this machine, so we turned on the steam valve.

After sundry rattles and bangs, the slide bars and links just fell off the pump on to the floor, then all was silent apart from the gentle 'singing' in the boiler.

We expected the boiler would be damaged if it ran out of water and to make matters worse, Alec arrived back just then - and confirmed this. What a panic: "Bring us this, and bring us that, and bring the tool kit." That was easy; as far as we could see, the tool set consisted of three spanners and a hammer. It only needed four nuts turning slightly and the rods fitting together again but we were not cheeky enough - then - to say that we could have had it done if he had kept out of the way.

While Alec was mechanicing he kept bawling: "Keep an eye on the water gauge else we'll all be

A 1920-30s aerial view of Haltwhistle. (C Keen)

blown up." We forgot to tell him that it hadn't needed water anyway - it was still showing in the bottom of the glass gauge tube. In half an hour all was peace and calm once more.

A few days later we noticed a valve well up on the boiler side with an arrow pointing into the boiler; we traced the pipe to the water mains. When asked, Alec said that he hadn't known about this valve... Gelata Co. would have had to pay for mains water whereas the boiler pump sucked it out of the Tyne for 'nowt'. Alec's panic could have been brought on by guilt at leaving us bairns in charge. It struck me much later that with the water mains at over 60 pounds per square inch pressure, water would run

in as required against the boiler pressure of 40 pounds.

In the early 1940s there were some very severe frosts which caused trouble with frozen pipes. We were on holiday, it was cold, so we decided to help Alec with his boiler, but as we ran to the factory, it looked as if the boiler finally had blown up. Steam issued, hissing, from every door and window. We dashed round to the boiler house door but the fire seemed to be going well even though it was partly obscured by clouds of steam. The noise was loudest in the main factory building then suddenly it stopped, to be followed by the sound of running water.

A grinning Alec appeared at the door carrying the end of a large rubber pipe wrapped with sacking,

Steam boiler at Oakland Nurseries, Melkridge, similar to Gelata Products Company's installation. (K Rickerby)

which, coupled to the boiler steam-pipe had thawed the frozen pipes. It was much quicker and safer than a blowlamp. Alec sometimes had to carry hot water in a bucket to thaw the frozen pump suction-pipe showing between the 'strum-end' in the river and the river banking. Reaching out from the frozen riverbank to pour hot water over the pipes was a precarious occupation. Alec never slipped into the Tyne as far as we knew but he likely wouldn't have mentioned it if he had done. Fortunately the boiler

water-feed pump was fixed right up against the boiler and the heat kept it free from frost.

Some years later, the Oakland Nurseries at Melkridge installed a steam boiler of a similar type to the Gelata upright model, for heating the many greenhouses.

The Gelata process and works were taken over by Kilfrost Ltd. in 1945 and Alec apparently left and took to coal-mining at Ventners Hall pit, even though Messrs Kilfrost Ltd. wanted him to carry on making the Rosin Size. A director of Gelata Products, Mrs Scrivinger of Gosforth, arranged that conscientious Alec should have a job there for life, whoever owned the works, but Alec seemed determined and went mining, had an accident at the pit and was off sick for months.

This was not Alec's first accident. The story goes that his disabled leg was caused by two lights. In his younger days he and others often biked to Hexham for a night out and then biked back again much later.

On the return journey, Alec noticed what he thought was a wide vehicle approaching with its sidelights on, so he dismounted and stood off the road until it passed. It seemed too quiet to be a car and he saw through the gloom that it was two bikes.

Alec remounted and continued homeward until another two lights appeared. Well, he didn't intend to get off for these two and thought he would give them a fright by racing between them. Unfortunately, these two lights were fitted to a stationary car. This account came from Alec's mates who were with him at the time...

At the renamed Albion Works, Gelata was still made and supplied by the new firm, as required, but their main product was, and still is, the well-known antifreeze solutions used worldwide.

This firm came to Haltwhistle from the London area in the early 1940s and was allocated space in the works of Smith & Walton Ltd., then moved to the 'Soap Works' when the Gelata factory became available.

Antifreeze treatment of engine cooling systems, particularly on aircraft, was the main purpose of their products in the early days, with later variations for all water-cooled engines. Developments progressed as the firm expanded into aircraft surface and blade de-icing. I well remember the large blades spinning round in a framework, driven by a petrol engine for test purposes; a rather surprising sight in the factory.

One of Geoff Lamb's creations, this contraption had various names: many of them unofficial. De-icing products for railway sliding points and surfaces of electric conductor rails in Southern Region were manufactured at Haltwhistle. Compressed-air icing problems are also dealt with and cured by using one of Kilfrost's products.

Much of the output from the works is exported throughout the world but it is unlikely that their products will travel much further away from home than the antifreeze they sent to the South Polar expedition many years ago. There is still space exploration, I suppose.

In the 1960s and 70s Kilfrost Ltd. and others formed the TKS Company to expand the aircraft de-icing side of the business. I remember the fitting of a Ward capstan lathe which had been converted to work automatically.

This was one of the earliest 'computer-controlled' lathes, on which a programme could be set up by inserting pegs in a pattern across a pegboard-faced control panel. A relatively crude and slow system compared to modern machines, yet it worked. This was the nearest I had seen to a robot at that time and it did the job well enough, performing the many operations in the making of pipeline fittings used to convey antifreeze liquids from a central onboard pump to the leading edges of the aircraft wings.

A modern Kilfrost office block and laboratory. The higher right-hand factory building is situated approximately on the position of the original soap works and later Gelata Products works; the left-hand office and central laboratory buildings were erected on a 'green field' site between the soap works and Clark's sawmill. (D Hunter)

Pumps were assembled and tested in the works and some time later the leading edges themselves were machined and finished at Haltwhistle.

I believe this was the system used on the magnificent sleek Concorde and by many other long-haul airlines, and if used with the proper antifreeze solutions, it is much superior to other systems.

Various antifreeze mixtures which were applied while the aircraft was on the ground were adequate for up to four hour flights, but for longer flights there was only one make available then and that came from Kilfrost's works.

Another installation at Kilfrost's was that of a 'very cold room'. This was designed and constructed to freeze down to a temperature of 36 degrees below, if I remember rightly, to test some of the products. Surprisingly, it was not as cold as anticipated although I was in for a short time only — with the door ajar.

Kilfrost Park. (S Blackburn)

Over the years Kilfrost Ltd. transformed into a pleasant walk and lawned area what was previously an overgrown dump on the stretch of riverside land between the works and the Tyne. This had been one of our main playgrounds at one time and our gang dug out, transported and dumped loads of cinders and soil with our large-scale model lorries.

Much of this riverside land had been an ash tip, used by the soap works and the Railway Company when they owned this land. We moved our model lorry-tipping operations to the other side of the river where there was a good sandy area, much cleaner to work with than the old ashes on the soap works side. When it was home time, we buried our models in the deep sand to save carrying them home and marked the secret hides; we always found them again.

The local council used the field east of the Alston Arches on the north side of the river as an open-air sewerage outflow from the town, until the disposal works were built at Seldom Seen. This wasn't as bad as it sounds, because flush lavatories were still unknown in Haltwhistle and the outflow would be mainly washing water and rainwater; in fact the drains themselves needed flushing out, and to achieve this, large underground tanks were constructed at various 'high points' throughout the town. Some of these were of about 400-gallon capacity and were fitted with large syphon pipes into the drain. Water from the mains was regulated by a valve to fill these tanks slowly; when the water level reached the top of the syphon, the whole tankful was flushed down the drain in a matter of minutes. As modern plumbing methods were introduced the tanks became obsolete but most of them will still be there.

There was one at the end of Sycamore Street near the doctor's house and a large one which was reckoned to be about 600-gallon capacity, under the Market Place. There were other tanks at the head of the drains in various parts of the old town but being out of sight, these locations most probably have been forgotten about. I believe there were usually two heavy manhole covers quite close together near to these tanks.

Subsequently, the outflow field was used as a tip for the town rubbish; simultaneously, it provided a useful practice ground for the wartime AFS when the rubbish caught fire.

The firemen all had full-time jobs so they often carried out their tip fire-fighting on long winter evenings in the blackout, which made things difficult for them but which provided the rest of us with the nearest we got to fireworks displays during the war. The surface fires gave adequate light to set up the trailer water-pump on the edge of the river and arrange the hoses, but once these fires were extinguished, only intermittent bursts of red-hot ashes flew up into the air from the main body of the tip.

It always amazed me that glowing cinders could be shot up by high-pressure water jets without being quenched; however, there was nothing burning when we saw the tip in daylight the next day.

The firemen did well to gather up all the hoses, hitch the pump on, etc., in the dark and to drain the water from the hoses hooked to a very tall pole at the fire-station, which was at the bottom of St James Lane in the early 1940s.

All this activity in the darkness was often accompanied by the cry of the ARP warden: "Put that light out!" Even with the tip ablaze he still bellowed: "Get that light out!" - and often got quaint replies out of the darkness.

During the Gelata Products era, the riverside road was a rough stone and ash track but this was greatly improved by Kilfrost. Jake Johnson finally made a good job of it by laying tarmac from the factory and through the end arch of the railway viaduct to join the hard surface near the paint factory. Apparently it took Jake several months to start work there as he was tarmacing his way from Dumfries.

Fortunately for me, Jake was short-handed when he did this work and he asked if I could spare the time to steam-roll the tarmac as they spread it with the Barber Green machine.

Could I spare the time? That was a daft question. The last roadwork I had done there was with model lorries in among the bushes on the ash heaps.

It reminded me of my first turn on No. 27 Bedford lorry at Ventners Hall nearly 30 years earlier and it was every bit as enjoyable - a new toy. The roller was fairly new, as rollers go, and was built in Newcastle in 1947 by Vickers Armstrong but had been slightly redesigned by Jake himself who fitted

Terras, the steam-roller which the author used to roll the tarmac at Kilfrost works. Now in a much cleaner condition, it attends rallies in the North East. Jake Johnson's footbrake appears to have been removed from the roller but it now sports rear-view mirrors and hauls an almost new living van. (I Seymour)

his own invention, a Johnson foot brake, which was a great help on short rolls. I was a bit fierce with this brake on the soft tarmac and left a few minor depressions but Jake said nowt; many years later it was still a good road to drive on.

It was better to drive the machine than to watch how George Rutherford did the job, from my seat in the coal bunker on his roller. The thought did pass through my mind that promotion was very slow in the steam-roller world. From watching George to driving Jake's machine must have taken about 40 years.

The Vickers roller was still attending rallies from its base on Tyneside a year or so ago and is still a treat to see - and hear - and to handle.

The riverside area beyond the Arches was bulldozed flat when the refuse tip was relocated, and then used as playing fields, but much of it had yet another change of use as part of the latest town by-pass route.

There are more changes now between Albion Works and the river. On a recent visit to the works, I rather thought that the rocket-testing towers from Spadeadam had been reincarnated and erected on Kilfrost Park, but I have been assured that these structures are very docile compared to Spadeadam towers. They are two loading points for transferring bulk liquids between the works storage tanks and the massive road tankers that now ply between the works and many parts of this country and Europe. The towers are more efficient than the old system of transferring between tanker and the works via various pipe connections through the factory wall. There is more tarmac now and it looks as if my rolled tar has been buried without trace. These latest installations are very tidy and most interesting, and do not detract from what is still a pleasant riverside walk.

The author, Mike Neville and Jake Johnson on 'Jenny' at Corbridge Steam Rally in the early 1970s.

Chapter Seven

John Smith & Son's works van at Greystonedale. (A Burns)

It wasn't only the Sunday School garden party in Greystonedale House grounds that lured me to the West End one day in the 1930s. I had my eye on a very interesting set of buildings and a tall chimney stack to the rear of the house - the tall chimney I had seen from Redpath and earmarked to be investigated. My sources told me how John Smith & Son, the paint and varnish manufacturers,were at Greystonedale works from the mid 1800s and used a steam-powered generating plant initially for

lighting the factory and office, although I recall seeing on subsequent visits an extractor fan in the wall of the old spray shop which was still 'freewheeling' on windy days in 1956, about thirty years after it was last used for fume-extraction; the bearings still appeared as good as new after all that time.

Originally the fan was driven by belt from an electric motor which had been disconnected and was

John Smith & Son's workforce outside the Greystonedale offices; Douglas Smith is standing on the far right.

missing. I had hoped to find out the voltage of the electricity generated, by reading the metal label on the motor; other parts of the old system appeared to have been 110 volts.

The walls and floor of the spray department had various coatings of paint and much of it was difficult to remove with a hammer and chisel. Evidently they made some special 'everlasting' paint in those days, which was about the time John Smith and Son merged with Hoyle, Robson & Company of Newcastle in the early 1920s. The two firms worked together for some time until the new directors decided to close the Haltwhistle factory and transfer all production to Newcastle, including the well-known John Smith's Varnish and Tyne White Enamel paint.

This was totally unexpected and with two local pits about to close, it would have been devastating for Haltwhistle. There had been a varnish works at Greystonedale since the mid-1800s and Smiths determined that Haltwhistle was not going to be without this industry because of boardroom manoeuvres on Tyneside.

Smiths had lost the Tyne White Enamel and John Smith's Varnish with the merger and had no further control over their manufacture but decided that they could start again - only better.

The new Smith & Walton company was formed and in about 1929 building of the present Hadrian Works started. Smith & Walton were very fortunate to entice such a 'bash on' man as the late Gavin

This 1930s photo taken from Whitchester Tunnel top towards Haltwhistle shows a much smaller building complex on the paint factory site than exists today. (S Blackburn)

Sherrick from Hoyle, Robson & Co., to get the factory going.

Isaac Hetherington, a local contractor, was in at the start to erect much of the first factory, mainly of timber and steel girder framing with asbestos sheets; the side cladding was replaced by brickwork as the works expanded; many of the bricks were reclaimed from demolished buildings at Baron House Colliery near Greenhead.

When the news spread through the town that Isaac had been awarded the building work, a long queue of unemployed men formed from his back door at number 7, East View, along the street and into Park Road. For Isaac the hardest part of the whole job was telling some of the hopefuls that there was no work for them; many of those he did start used to say how grateful they were to have a pay packet again. They were the lucky ones: Isaac had to wait almost ten years before he was finally paid. A reluctant, interest-free shareholder?

Gavin Sherrick sorted out where the machines were required and soon got things moving, with men eager to work and available on the unemployment register. Like the Smiths, Gavin strongly believed in using everything from local sources, to boost employment. He even employed men to dig out old metal bed ends etc. from the adjacent public tip, to use as reinforcement in his 'concrete adventures'. Very resourceful was Gavin.

Mechanical engineering for the new works was in the capable hands of Jack Birkett and helpers. Jack worked at Plenmeller Colliery and Greystonedale before coming to Smith & Walton's and was a great innovator and a clever engineer. I did have the opportunity, as a schoolboy, to glimpse inside these works while delivering messages to various people working there and I made the most of it, something that wouldn't be allowed nowadays.

Line shafting was used for driving the machinery but instead of the power from steam engines and boilers that Jack had been involved with at Greystonedale and Plenmeller, the shafting and generators were driven by Ruston Hornsby, horizontal-cylinder, diesel engines with massive flywheels.

There were three engines running in the early days; the beats of those exhausts were part of Haltwhistle to us young'uns. I often remembered them and imagined I could hear them years later, when far away from Haltwhistle.

The original layout of driving the shafting involved one engine driving a long length stretching to the west end of the works from the engine house, which was situated about a third of the way down the main building; this was the first part of the factory. A second engine was installed alongside the first one for driving a length of shafting from the engine house to the later, eastern part of the factory. A third engine was coupled to a generator. More engines were added as the works expanded but power transmission was mainly through cables from generators coupled to these later engines.

In one part of the switch house, a large rectifier was installed to convert the power for some of the electrical equipment, and I remember Matty Hetherington coming home one evening with a marvellous tan except for a small area round his eyes. Some asked if he had been to the sunny 'Ry-vera', but Matty replied that he had been working all day in the engine house near this rectifier and had been told to wear dark glasses.

I remember the strange-shaped rectifier valves in the cellar at Westgate Picture House and another in the old generator house at the Gem Cinema; they were housed in steel cabinets, which didn't prevent an eerie light flashing across the walls, accompanied by a loud buzzing sound. These valves were referred to as 'Martians' by the managers and probably helped to keep some of the young-uns away from the electrics.

The valves converted the mains 440 volt AC electricity to 110 volt DC to work the American pattern projectors and equipment; it was more economical to fit them, than to change the machines to suit our mains supply.

Prior to the mains electricity supply, Lawrence Rushton had a 110 volt generator at the Gem and used this DC power direct and also through batteries to the equipment.

Horizontal engine at the Threlkeld Quarry and Mine Museum very similar to the Ruston Hornsby engines at Smith & Waltons, although the factory engines were on a much larger scale. (J Parker, jnr)

The Smith & Walton paint factory with Enid Hargreaves and Margaret Bell. (C Keen)

The Smith & Walton Synflat works: Angus Henderson and Edward Robson working. (C Keen)

Aerial photo of Smith & Waltons in the late 1930s: the storage-and-packing house is in the centre of the photo; the tall building on the right is the Alkide plant, behind this is the varnish 'kitchen'. Work has started on the first Haltwhistle by-pass (top left). Remains of the South Tyne Colliery sidings can also be seen heading north-east from Haltwhistle East signal box. (C Keen)

I read somewhere that the 120hp models of the Ruston Hornsby engines used at Hadrian Works were assumed by some engineers to be a copy of those used in German U-boats of the 1914-18 war.

As so many of the older stationary engines were very much alike with only slight variations, it is questionable who was copying whom, but in any case, if the German engines were covered by patent, this could well have been confiscated as reparations of war and sold to Ruston Hornsby by the British Government.

If the engines were in fact copied from U-boats they must have been greatly scaled-down versions. The 1906 built 'U 1' of 240-ton surface displacement had a 450hp, vertical-cylindered, petroleum engine and two 200hp electric motors for driving on batteries, but by 1914 the U-boats had more torpedo space, so engines would, presumably, need to be more powerful.

Submarines would have been very poor performers with a 120hp Ruston engine fitted but Smith & Walton found these to be satisfactory machines for their purposes.

While the main factory building was being extended to a point almost opposite the now demolished Haltwhistle East railway signal box, Gavin got to work on two large buildings that predictably he wanted up immediately. One was the storage-and-packing house, the other a separate varnish 'kitchen'.

These buildings were doubtlessly designed by Gavin and any plans would be in a notebook in his back pocket. Apart from wooden doors and window frames in the packing house, and steel doors and frames in the varnish end, these constructions were of concrete, concrete and more concrete. Gavin and 'Concrete Bob' McAlpine would have got on well together.

All the old doors, boards and planks of the district were collected and set up as shuttering for the concrete walls. Loads of stone chippings and whin dust from local quarries were mixed with cement to make 'Sherrick's puddings' and tipped in between the wall shuttering. This was where all the old bed-ends and anything steel was put to good use as reinforcement in the concrete.

Much of this cement was mixed by hand and Gavin was not averse to wielding the shovel himself if it

George Reed in Smith & Walton's boiler room. (B & J Reed)

wasn't going fast enough for him. When the walls were up to their required height the builders kept on mixing and went on to form the roof with concrete. A mechanical platform hoist was a great help in lifting barrows, filled with concrete, up to roof level. Unfortunately, Dick Lamb was badly hurt when this machine, loaded with concrete, crashed to the ground, but he recovered and worked in the factory for many years, in addition to wartime service in the RAF.

When high rows of shelving were needed in the storage areas of the packing house, the same method was used: shuttering up and concrete poured in. There would be no woodworm problems and of course the concrete was fireproof, but it must have imposed a tremendous weight on the packing house site.

A newer method in the manufacture of coatings came in when the 'alkide plant' was built next to the varnish kitchen. This department had an unusual Cochran upright boiler filled with a heating liquid which I believe was called 'dowtherm'. Liquid overflow from this process was so corrosive that it had to be carried in glass pipes. A fire in the 1960s reduced the alkide plant to rubble and scrap iron, as was also the fate of Gavin's concrete varnish kitchen and packing house, but at different times.

His varnish kitchen had two 'kettles' at one time, heated by pressure burners. These burners were on a lower floor level, about three feet below the yard surface. This may have been foresight on Gavin's part. When the varnish caught fire and boiled over it poured into this lower level and was contained in the building, thus preventing liquid fire-spread to the rest of the factory. When the ground-level packing house caught fire, burning liquid ran from the building, carrying the fire along with it; the biggest problem was keeping it away from other departments.

When clearing up started after the fires, hundreds of damaged tins of paint were shovelled on to lorries then dumped and covered over at Plenmeller Tip and Crindledykes Quarry. Shattered concrete from the demolished buildings helped to fill Plenmeller pit shafts. Multi-coloured paint leaking out of damaged tins and under lorry side boards decorated the road between factory and tip for weeks afterwards.

Reading this, some people will conclude that paint works are high fire risks - and they can be, but the Hadrian Works had a very good record compared to paint firms further down the Tyne. Many Newcastle area manufacturers seemed to have frequent blazes at one time but stricter regulations now seem to have reduced these risks.

None of the S&W buildings of the late 1930s had the line shaft system as fitted in the original factory; machinery and burners were supplied with electricity from the generators or the later mains supply.

On one occasion, the electric supply company started checking power requirements with a view to installing mains supply to all departments, but gave up part of the way through, saying that they couldn't compete with the low-cost Ruston Hornsby diesel-engined generators and line shafting.

One of the enginemen, a Mr Walton from Melkridge, who had previously driven one of Laidlow Bros' Bedford lorries, successfully looked after these Ruston engines and kept them running smoothly for many years.

Inevitably, the engines became overloaded and because replacement machinery was not being made for line-shaft driving in any case, the national electricity suppliers took over and eventually provided all of the power. One of the redundant engines and a generator were sold to Mr Shepherd for use at one of the Alston mines but it is not clear what happened to the others. There was a great demand for this type of engine from overseas, so they were probably exported.

At least one of the oil engines always ran a generator and in later years all of them were hard-worked continuously. If any of them had to be stopped and then started up again, there was a compressed air system coupled into the engines to turn them over; this made starting much easier than the old manual method. This could well have been another Jack Birkett idea and installation.

Matty Hetherington started work an hour earlier on Mondays, to ensure that the engines were all running before the main work force arrived; he was always pleased to see that air hadn't leaked out of the reservoir during the weekend; they needed it for easy starting. Matty lost that extra hour when the engines were retired but I don't think he objected to a later start.

Jack Birkett and Matty Hetherington, both very industrious, could also be jokers if the opportunity arose, such as the day when they were working alongside some of the other men, carrying out alterations to part of the factory.

The workmen were all members of the Home Guard and familiar with small arms. Suddenly Jack shouted and appeared to pick up a hand grenade from the floor of the trench in which they were standing and

The most dramatic of Smith & Walton's fires, 4th August 1966. The fire started in the Alkide plant then spread to the rest of the buildings. (G Banks)

The fire started at around 2am and burned for nearly 20 hours; ten fire engines attended, some from as far away as Newcastle and Gateshead. (G Banks)

Smith & Walton fitters: l-r, back row: Tom Bell, John Mitchison, Jack Birkett, John Bell, Colin Keen, Alan Burns; front row: Michael Little, Mattie Hetherington, Nigel Smith, Terry Pattinson, Terry Spark, Alan Watson. (C Keen)

everybody gathered round, wondering how it had got into the factory. Jack was fiddling about with the missile when the pin fell out and the metal grip shot up into the air.

He reckoned nobody had ever moved as fast at Smith & Waltons as his curious workmates did that day. When the bomb failed to explode, the vanished ones slowly returned to see Jack and Matty still examining the grenade; holding it up as if trying to see through

it. Jack said that he had better take it to the stores for safe keeping in case it went off. Afterwards, Matty mentioned that Jack had carried the missile in his pocket for most of the day and it was highly unlikely to go off without a detonator…

The fact that Jack Birkett engineered at Plenmeller Colliery makes me wonder if he had something to do with a belief still held by ex-miners years after the pit closed.

This concerned the flooding and 'drowning out' of a pump electric motor near the bottom of the shaft. Engineer Dickinson and, I suspect, Jack Birkett wired a multitude of electric lamps in series with the windings of the motor, the resistance in the motor and lamps creating heat in the windings and so - ingeniously - drying the motor out. Years later some of the old chaps would say how amazed they were that heat from the lamps, passing through the motor, had soon dried it out - it would have been amazing if not impossible. On another occasion at Hadrian Works, although Jack and Matty were there, no joke was intended - they said. When fitting in a new machine it was found that a brick partition was needed underneath; the builder thought it would be better to build this single-brick wall first and then fit the machine so he quickly put the wall up to five feet high and eight feet long.

Just then somebody came looking for the bricklayer and was informed by Matty or Jack that he was just at the other side of the wall. Instead of going round about, the seeker leaned over the top of the still soft-cemented wall and sent the whole lot over. The brickie, who had been kneeling down pointing the wall, appeared to rise up through a mountain of bricks as they fell over him. Then he started raving in what Matty thought was a foreign language.

Matty and Father, being neighbours and gardeners, often compared notes over the fence about their various vegetables, and one day Father complained about the poor crop of peas. Matty reckoned he

BRICKY'S PILE

PUSSY PEA EATER

needed lime or some better kind of fertiliser when he next sowed them but Father shook his head, "No, no, nowt to do with the soil - it's that damned cat of oors, it chews the young pods so we only get the peas it canna reach".

Matty had a cure. As a member of the Home Guard he had access to various explosives so he brought home one or two of these crackers and told us to let him know the next time the cat was at the peas. We hadn't long to wait and ran next door to tell him, whereupon Matty crept up his garden and lobbed a Thunderflash in among the neat rows of peas.

Immediately the cat raced down the garden path and was indoors when a mighty bang was heard from the garden and when the smoke cleared, the rows of peas were completely flattened. People hanging out of their windows asked if the invasion had started. Matty reckoned there were different grades of Thunderflashes and he had, unfortunately, picked the most powerful. To cap it all, within an hour the cat was chewing peas among the debris - ready podded.

Another large building with potential for a much longer future than the partition wall was the grand Olympic Hall built at Hadrian Works in the 1930s.

The Olympic Hall during the August 1966 fire. (G Banks)

Contractor Isaac Hetherington was again involved on the work, which comprised concrete foundations, steel upright girders later encased in masonry, and deep horizontal steel beams to carry the upper floor.

I remember girders being raised by hand-winch and fitted into position. Each girder was laid alongside the foundations with its base plate end near its finally fitted position. A two-man winch was anchored in the small field which is now the works car park. From the winch, a wire rope went up and through a pulley at the top of a sturdy, tall pole, well 'guy-roped' in all directions. The hook-end of the winch rope was fastened to the top end of the girder which was then hauled up to its upright position and fixed.

To me, watching all this building going on was much more educational than school work.

I wouldn't have seen this operation but luckily I had yet another accident near our school one morning which resulted in a few repairs to my forehead at the hospital. As a treat I was taken by an uncle to see the Hall being put up, and learned that one of the winch men had been struck by the turning handle that morning and also taken to hospital.

The floors of the Olympic Hall all received 'Sherrick's pudding' treatment via the concrete mixers. Most of the doors, fittings, wall-panelling and the wide stairs were salvaged from S.S.Olympic, a sister ship to the Titanic. The Hall was named after the ship from which came so many of the fittings and materials used in the building.

SS Olympic was broken up just prior to the building of the hall and provided reasonably priced material for the fitting out. Many of the stateroom lights and large ceiling panels were utilised and the floor was covered with parquet wood blocks.

The hall was used for dances and Sunday evening concerts for troops stationed in Haltwhistle, during the second World War; currently, the works canteen is on the ground floor; the upper floor at the top of the grand staircase has always been used as offices.

Some infilling has been carried out between the Olympic Hall and the works to provide more office space. A new building was erected to the east of Gavin's varnish kitchen, to accommodate a new rubber process, but the 'bottom end' has also been used for printing, wallpaper and paint storage in recent years.

It would be impossible to repeat the only work I ever did in the 'bottom end' area, during the war. Then, the paint factory boundary was much further west and Dav Kennedy farmed the - now non-existent - four acre field between the works and Haltwhistle Burn. A crop of oats was grown for the war effort, and teenager Sid Wanless, during his

The Smith & Walton's fleet of wagons: l-r: John Grant, Hugh Haston, Jimmy Henderson, Billy Bushby, Leslie Bell, Jackie Archer/Armstrong, Jake Strong. (A Burns)

*Pre-war Fordson tractor and binder near Bardon Mill.
(A Burns)*

holidays, started harvesting the corn with a binder pulled by a hired iron-wheeled Fordson tractor.

Owing to delays caused by the weather, his holidays ran out and he asked me to complete the cutting during the rest of my holidays. After finishing the binding, I fitted the road travelling blocks, between the spade lugs on the tractor rear wheels, and trundled off with the tractor, up the infamous Castle Hill, without mishap. The clatter of metal wheels on tarmac startled passers-by; heads turned to watch our progress across Fair Hill but finally I delivered the machine into the care of mechanic Ronnie Henderson at the grand-titled 'War Agricultural Executive Committee Depot', then situated behind Liddell's workshops in Aesica Road. Dav stooked and stacked his crop, later to be threshed by Joe Foster's machine, which was probably powered by the old Halley attended by George Henderson.

Fumes from the works and the tip fires, filtered through the crop, would add an extra dimension to the nation's porridge…

Hadrian Works does not sound the same nowadays. The Ruston exhaust beats are missing; the line shafting is just a memory now.

Fortunately, there was not much trouble with subsidence at the factory even though the South Tyne Colliery workings are underneath, albeit a long way down. A solid pillar of coal was left under the railway alongside the works but directly below the fields of Kirkholmedale; the NCC yard; the Mill Bridge and under the Hadrian Works area, plus the Alston Line embankment and the viaduct, were all mined out about 1928, just prior to the building of the factory.

The coal seam is at a depth of over 600 feet in this part and as far as I know, there has been no sign of serious subsidence on the surface since 1930; it was normal mining practice to leave adequate pillars of coal to support the mine roof, so they must be satisfactory.

An extensive coal pillar was left under the centre of Haltwhistle as it existed in the 1920s; this continues under the railway and Kilfrost's works and across the river about 50 yards upstream from the railway arches. Perhaps this support was meant to be under the arches.

Some movement did occur in the bridge stonework; to monitor this, thin strips of glass were cemented across the joints between the large spandrel stones, each one being dated in the cement bedding. Any small movement and the glass broke; I saw a lot of cracked pieces of glass.

Presumably this has now settled down; the bridge was built on large wooden raft-type foundations which were laid on the first shallow rock formation encountered by the railway contractors; these circumstances, rather than mining, may be the reason for faults in the bridge. Excavations in 1996 have revealed better quality rock at a depth of about 70 feet which will provide a good base for the new by-pass road bridge.

Our gang discovered a rather curious hole at the Haltwhistle end of the Alston Railway Arches in the early 1940s. The hole was a three-feet-square shaft sunk into the embankment about 15 feet from the end of the bridge and perhaps eight feet west of the running rail; it had been lined out with timber and cross-braced. We often sneaked across this bridge as a shortcut and generally walked down the east side embankment, but this day we decided to go down the west side and so found the hole, which was hidden under short planks and turf.

If this was supposed to be secret, they had made a poor job of it and we easily moved the turf to lift the wood covers and there was the shaft, but for what purpose? We kept a watchful eye on that embankment but never saw anyone near the hole and we assumed that it would be dug for planting explosives to blow up the bridge if we were invaded. What else? Because of the war we regarded anything unusual as the work of saboteurs or spies, but I doubt if they were responsible for digging the shaft; more likely to be our lot. A recently mobilised search party failed to pinpoint the shaft, which was probably filled in when the war ended.

Another wartime puzzle for our gang was how a steam loco managed to crash into the buffers, during the night, at Haltwhistle East signal box. We assumed that the loco had set out from Haltwhistle station in the Newcastle direction and was speeding up on the long north siding instead of on the main line, then crashed into and scattered the buffers, flattened a plate-layer's cabin and came to rest against the signal-box wall.

When we first saw the mess from the old South Tyne pit sidings area we thought the engine had done well to move so much buffer metal and cabin walls, it being only a tank loco and lighter than the express engines. There was nobody about. It was suggested that we have a look in the cab; bikes were jettisoned and we raced to the engine. Nobody was injured in that rush to grab the driver's position but only one of us was sucessful so the others were appointed as fireman and lookout; the driver shouted for more steam, the fireman shovelled coal through the fire hole and the lookout kept watch.

Ancient and modern. Almost 150 years separate the building of the two bridges; the six-arch stone bridge for the Alston railway line in 1850 and the Haltwhistle by-pass road bridge of 1997. (D Hunter)

When we all changed positions, the activities were repeated until the fireman could get no more coal through the fire hole because it was full to overflowing. How fortunate it was that the fire was out or we would have had steam flying everywhere; that would have alerted them up at the station. As far as we knew nobody spotted the industrious three in the engine but I bet they knew we had been there when they had to clear all of that coal out of the firebox. The loco was rerailed on the following Sunday and towed away to Blaydon sheds; unfortunately, I missed the cranes working on that job, being confined to the house for some misdeed or other.

Larger paint-making machines used in the original J.Smith & Son's Greystonedale Works were belt-driven from the steam-powered line-shafting on the ground floor of the factory. Other line shafts on the upper floor were driven from the main shafting by belts passing up through slots in the concrete first floor.

In the 1950s, whenever alterations to pipelines or machinery involved drilling through the upper concrete floor in this building, it was thought that

Gavin must have been mixing here also; it was just as hard and tough as his concrete at Hadrian Works.

Nichol Birkett assured me that their firm had laid the concrete but they hadn't used whin dust and chippings as Gavin did; they just went down to the river and dug out sand and gravel as they needed it.

Chimney stack used in John Smith's varnish factory at Greystonedale Works. The taller chimney which was situated behind the camera position has now been demolished. (D Hunter)

This was the method used by the builder of Greencroft housing scheme, in the 1930s. The foundations were laid with waterside sand and gravel with plenty of big cobbles mixed in, plus a few 'spoonfuls' of cement, and they seem to have stood the test of time. I believe Wallace Laidlow with his horse and cart carried some of the gravel from the riverside to the housing site - competing with his brother Arthur with his WL Bedford wagon.

At Greystonedale, yet another unusual feature for this district was the large louvre-sided condenser, situated high up above the boiler-house water tanks. Jack Birkett remembered that this apparatus was constructed in position, with what seemed like a mile of steel pipe and loads of screwed fittings. I remember looking up at this high structure from the garden party at Greystonedale and there was no steam or smoke issuing from it, so the party was probably held when the factory was closed for a few years.

All the exhaust steam from generator and shaft-driving engines was directed through this condenser and the resulting water injected back into the steam boiler.

Initially, water for the boiler came from a tank set down into the field drainage system at the rear of the works and was unreliable in dry weather; hence the condensing system, and as Jack said: "Once the condenser was built it cost nowt to run."

An extra bonus was the reduction in scale build-up inside the boiler by using this 'steam water', thereby increasing the efficiency of the steam-raising process.

In about 1938, the amalgamated paint firms on Tyneside, trading under the name of J Damphney & Company, and quite separate from Smith & Walton, decided to re-open the works, which had been closed for some years. The Hydrate of Alumina manufacturing process was moved to Haltwhistle from Guyzance Mill (G.205029) near Alnwick and

A distant view of north-west Haltwhistle with J Smith & Son's Greystonedale Works. The large condenser can be seen near the tallest chimney. (C Keen)

the boiler put back into use for process heating and drying ovens.

The wooden vats, which had to be used because of the corrosive liquids in this process, were invariably manufactured and erected by McNichol Brothers of Pollockshaw Road in Glasgow. This firm specialised in supplying vats to the Scottish whisky industry and consequently their products were extremely accurate, well-made and finished.

Pine planks, three inches thick, were clamped together and cut into a disc shape of eight feet diameter for the vat base. The upright staves, cut out to fit on the edge of the base timbers, were such a good fit that they were self-supporting even before steel hoops were fitted. When these bands had been hammered down the tapering sides to tighten the joints, each stave was hammered in or out as required until the whole side presented a smooth finish.

Latterly, vats were tightened by 1-inch-diameter, circular-section steel rod hoops with threaded ends and nuts. The round-rod system enabled the hoops to be made in two halves, and these were much easier to handle and transport on the railway from Glasgow to Haltwhistle. Eight-feet-diameter flat steel hoops were often too large to go through some of the factory doorways and had to be made up inside the buildings.

Both methods of tightening worked very efficiently and I never saw any leaks after craftsman J McNichol pronounced that the work was complete. Jock often said we could look for leaks and if we located any, he would buy us a whisky for each one

151

we found. Knowing Jock, he was either very sure of himself or he knew that we didn't drink whisky, but in any case we never found leaks in his vats.

Whisky distillers, McNichols' usual employers, would have held an inquest if any of their products had leaked from the vats so they had to be near perfect - and they were.

During his frequent visits to distilleries, Jock spent quite a time on inspections inside the whisky vats - empty ones... He didn't object to the fumes given off from the vat walls; he said it saved buying whisky; it was often difficult for him to keep on an even keel, but he put up with it. His only regret was that the euphoria faded soon after he came into the fresh air. There was nothing intoxicating about the fumes given off by Greystonedale vats.

The Hydrate of Alumina process involved dissolving several sacks of solid alum in 1000 gallons of water in a wooden vat of 3000 gallons capacity. Dissolving was accelerated by a four-feet-long square oak blade, shaped like a propeller and bolted to a revolving upright post, fitted at its top end to a crown wheel and pinion mechanism driven from a line shaft. There were about fourteen of these 3000-gallon alum vats in the works, in addition to eight soda vats of 1500-gallon capacity.

Over a period of an hour, one thousand gallons of steam-heated and well-stirred soda ash, prepared in a higher-level steel vat, was run into the dissolved alum. Water was then added to this mixture in the vat up to the 3000-gallons mark, where the stirring action ceased and the fine particles were allowed to settle.

After a few hours the clear acidic water was drawn off, the tank refilled and stirred again. After the final drawing-off of the clear acidy water, the remaining white liquid was pumped at high pressure through special filters to separate the water from the solids.

Various piston pumps were used on this filtering system, and owing to the acid nature of the liquids they required constant maintenance. One vertical single-cylinder pump, made by Tangye, regularly squirted the white liquid up to the roof, 30 feet above, when the cylinder-packing burst out under pressure; this was quite spectacular. The other cylinder pumps could also be quite entertaining as they wore out.

Then a D10D Mono pump with stainless steel parts was fitted and found to be very satisfactory for this operation. After working for a year it was dismantled and appeared to be almost 'as new' inside, which was amazing; Bardon Mill Colliery fitters usually had to fit new parts monthly and sometimes fortnightly in their Monos.

Two further Mono pumps were fitted in the other departments, all of them continuing to pump up to 120 pounds pressure and above for some years, without having any new parts fitted while they worked at Greystonedale. Unlike the NCB 24-hour running of their Monos, the Greystonedale pumps ran for a few hours only, five days per week, and had no stones and grit in the liquid to go through the pumps as happens in the mines. The absence of this makerash would be the main reason for their trouble-free running at Greystonedale.

Pumping problems seemed to be solved for a while but more trouble was still to come.

After filling of the filters to the limit, the semi-solid material was then removed and spread over drying trays in steam-heated ovens.

When dried out, the trays were emptied into a high-speed pulveriser and the resulting 166 formula powder dispatched in paper sacks to printing ink firms throughout this country and also exported, some as far as Australia.

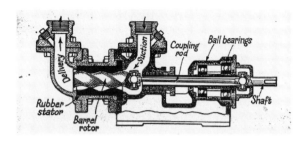

D10 Mono pump similar to Greystonedale D10D type.

Another variation of this Hydrate of Alumina, the 1808 formula, had Barium added for certain customers with their own special processes.

A later Prussian Blue process involved mixing yellow prussiate of soda, green copperas, acid and water, the final dried-out material being ground in a revolving stone mill in the same way as corn was ground a century earlier, at Manor Mill on the burn side.

The acidic liquid drained off during this Prussian Blue process gradually eroded the cement filling between the whin chippings in any concrete it splashed on to, and yet it was not apparently, regarded as being too dangerous to be allowed to drain into the river at the end of a half-mile-long pipeline under the town. I suspect that other drains added to and diluted this liquid by the time it flowed into the Tyne; water from the drain is fairly clean nowadays.

The blue liquid was also pumped through a filter press as in the Hydrate of Alumina process. The first pump I saw in the blue department was constructed almost entirely of lead; unfortunately, the vanes on the impeller tended to wear off fairly quickly owing to the corrosive nature of the liquid and regularly needed building up. This pump was replaced by a stainless steel centrifugal type made by a French firm, I think LaBore; possibly the first pump of this

kind to be made by them. The firm regularly enquired about the pump's performance and within a year they asked if somebody could dismantle it to see how it was resisting the acid liquid; they would pay for the necessary work involved. When opened up, this pump was found to be like the stainless steel Monos: as new, with no signs of wear on the impeller or casings. Lower working pressures in the blue system would help to minimise wear.

J Damphney & Co. had no need to generate electricity or drive the machinery by steam as John Smith & Son had done. By the 1930s, mains electricity had arrived and a transformer to serve the works and the West End of Haltwhistle was installed in the factory.

This increased the cost of production well above what it had been at their previous premises at Guyzance Mill.

There the machinery was driven from a turbine on the side of the River Coquet via a long drive shaft under the yard and into the mill. A dam across the river diverted water down a race about six feet wide and seven feet deep, into the turbine which had been manufactured and installed in the early 1900s by the well known engineering firm of Gilbert, Gilkes & Gordon of Kendal.

I believe this installation was originally for the Duke of Northumberland's Corn Mill, and was adapted later for the Hydrate of Alumina process, which continued to use the turbine power-source.

Dynamos were driven from the shafting to generate electricity for lighting and these ancient generators came from Guyzance to Greystonedale in 1938 but lay unused for 20 years, then mistakenly went for scrap instead of to a museum.

The turbine and everything belonging to it had 'disappeared' from Guyzance before 1950 but had been in working order when J Damphney & Co. left there in 1938.

At Greystonedale there was a shortage of water for the works. At Guyzance, a pipe out into the adjacent River Coquet had sucked up all the water they needed, but even with the mains water connected there was still a serious lack of water at Haltwhistle.

It was decided to sink a bore hole in the factory yard and this was drilled down to a depth of 300 feet, well below the level where the experts said there would be all the water they could ever need.

After a disappointing capacity test, the well was drilled further to a depth of 530 feet, which then supplied more water, on test, than the intended pump could raise.

A Sumo 10hp electric submersible pump was suspended on the end of a four-inch-diameter steel water pipe down the well, at the 300 feet mark, and restricted by a lockable valve to supply about 120 gallons a minute, more than enough for the rate of flow required.

The water was not fit to drink without treatment. This was not unexpected. With the well sump at 530 feet and the seam in the closed South Tyne pit at about the same depth, water would come from the old mine workings, which pass under this part of Haltwhistle into the Birchfieldgate area.

The solid pillar left under the town centre extended as far west as Dale Street or Lorne Street; a similar support was left under Greystonedale House, the older factory buildings and the taller chimney, but this did not extend to the smaller chimney or the north side building.

If the pump was unused for a few days and then restarted, water from Greystonedale borehole often reeked of sulphur, very like Gilsland or Haydon Spa wells. When used for boiler feed water it left a scale sparkling with mica inside the boiler. The main thing was that it speeded up production and the water cost only about a quarter of the mains water price.

The borehole pump electrics burned out at one time and the 300-feet pipeline had to be raised up from the well to remove the underwater pump motor, just when we thought pump problems were behind us.

Once the pipe was clear of the well, the reflection of the sky on the water's surface could be seen clearly, down the steel-lined hole. This water surface depth was measured and it was calculated that at 45 feet down, it approximately matched up with the water level in the closed South Tyne Colliery shaft, confirming our theory. After the factory's closure, the pump and the pipe were removed and the well has not been used since the late 1950s. One man attempted to fill up the borehole as a safety measure; he tired of this when all his filling disappeared under the water; nobody had told him it was over five hundred feet deep. In the end, he capped it.

The last steam boiler at Greystonedale, similar to the 16-feet long boiler at South Tyne Colliery, was a Davy Paxman, coal-fired, horizontal twin-firebox type. It was installed in 1922, according to the insurance certificate, and built into the boiler house.

It appears that this boiler was fitted new about the time of the amalgamation between J Smith & Son and Hoyle Robson & Co.; perhaps the renewal of the boiler was part of the deal. Heat from the two fireboxes in the lower half of the boiler passed into a brick-built, tapered, combustion chamber at the back of the boiler and returned through about 80 smoke tubes, two-and-a-half-inches diameter, fitted through the boiler above the fireboxes, to a smoke box on the front of the boiler, then round the sides into more brick-built chambers along the full length of the boiler and down under into the smoke tunnel leading to the chimney; a most efficient installation.

Birketts were involved in this design and building project; it saved a considerable amount of fuel in 30 years of use. Steam could be raised to a high pressure in a very short time with this system, although care had to be taken to prevent it rising too quickly from cold.

In the 1950s it was found that of the local mines, the coal from Ramshawfield pit (G.753647) near Bardon Mill was the most efficient for this boiler. The coal was fairly soft and rust-coloured but the heat output was ahead of coal from other mines, perhaps because of its clean, stone-free nature.

The boiler had been designed to have a large steam super-heater but this was never fitted.

When the works closed and the boiler was cut up in the 1950s, the scrap men said that it could have been used safely for another fifty years, it was in such good condition - easy enough to say that after they had cut it beyond the point of no return.

The major part of the steam output from this boiler was used for heating the drying ovens when Hydrate of Alumina was manufactured here.

The heaters in the larger 20-feet-long ovens had rectangular steel base tanks, into the top of which were welded 80 or so steel tubes of one-inch diameter and five feet long, in a vertical manner with the top ends either blanked off or another tank welded on to them. Others had ten-feet-long pipes bent in the form of a 'U' with both ends welded into the bottom tank. A steam trap was added to drain out condensation.

Steam was directed into the lower tank at up to 120 pounds pressure and a 5hp fan circulated the heated air through the oven which maintained the temperature at 150 degrees; the heater pipes themselves were much hotter than this; I once had to find a steam leak in one of them; the radiating heat was endurable for a short time only and was so intense that no steam was visible. However, the leak could be heard and when it was located finally, the hole could be seen, with only a

The 'new' building at Greystonedale Works, originally used for paint manufacture, now a motor body repair firm. (D Hunter)

few drops of condensation blasting out and no sign of white steam in that high temperature.

It was discovered that during the building of the oven, a large nail had been driven through asbestos coverings, missing the timber and penetrating the heater pipe, in which it was a steam-tight fit for many years. Eventually, it had rusted away until only the hole was left, which was quite easily welded by removing the remains of the nail from the asbestos sheeting, drilling a larger hole and threading the welding electrode through it, right into the leak hole and then welding. Steam leaks in the ovens had to be repaired immediately or the resultant damp circulating air retarded the drying process.

The taller chimney at the works was built in the 1920s, about the same time as the newer main building, by the local builders, James Birkett & Sons. Nichol Birkett, one of the sons, and brother of engineer Jack, remembered that he was serving his time as a builder when the chimney was constructed.

He had forgotten how high it was but remembered that it took 38,000 bricks. Later the height was measured off the yard level with a 45 degree bevel and found to be 80 feet high.

After measuring this chimney, I always used it as a guide for estimating the heights of other structures in the district.

The smaller chimney stack at the east end of the works, about 40 feet high, was used in conjunction with J Smith's varnish manufacture.

The electricity generated in the works was extended in the 1920s to the new offices in the west field, probably via the 'glass house', originally a vinery and now demolished.

One of the last brick buildings erected at Greystonedale is situated on the north side of the works; from 1938 it housed wooden vats and agitating machinery. The tanks had a combined capacity of over 20,000 gallons, weighed approximately 90 tons plus machinery, and were set up on girders.

The building gradually tilted, in one piece, towards magnetic north; this happened shortly after it was built but it appears to be stable now.

Like Pisa's leaning tower, part of Greystonedale is also off the vertical.

The builders probably had not calculated or allowed for the vibrating machinery that was used on these tanks but it is interesting to note that this building is just off the edge of an underground pillar far below in South Tyne Colliery, as mentioned elsewhere.

A smaller storage building, now demolished, also leaned to the North so there must have been more unstable areas on the site.

Smith & Walton maintenance men (possibly Wilf Teasdale on the left) loading a Dennis lorry on the site of the new laboratories. (A Burns)

Chapter Eight

Replacing the main winding rope at South Tyne Colliery. (E Coates)

While searching for evidence of electric generators, I gathered that Plenmeller colliery had a standby diesel generating plant, in addition to the main steam generators, to work the 240hp Koepe electrically powered winding gear and the ventilating fan, in the event of a total steam shut-down.

At South Tyne, with a 20-inch-diameter, twin-cylinder, 48-inch-stroke steam winding-engine, boilers had to be up to at least 60 pounds pressure to work the shaft cages, so the miners would have had to walk out by the fan drift in the unlikely event of all boilers being off at the same time.

Some described this alternative outlet as "like climmin up a hoos end" and it likely seemed longer than it was to men coming off shift.

In fact, the only time the cages were unavailable was when work was needed on the winding gear, ropes and cages, rather than when there was a total boiler shutdown. High pressure steam was needed at all times, to generate electricity for the mine ventilating fan and the boiler chimney draught booster fan.

Normal boiler pressure was well over 100 pounds for generators, reduced to 60 pounds for the shaft winding-engine. One job at South Tyne I would not have cared for would be riding up the shaft on top of the cage periodically to lubricate the metal guide rails, while hanging on to the cage lift chains. One ex-miner told me all about it; he had done the job in the past.

The shaft-top arrangement at South Tyne was unusual in that the tubs were landed at ground level although at other pit heads generally the tubs were landed on to gantries 20 feet or more above ground, for tipping on to the screening plant; this was not needed at South Tyne pit, where loaded tubs were run into a long shed and made up into sets, then clamped to the continuously moving endless rope for dispatching to Town Foot.

This rope was powered by a 48-inch-diameter driving drum near the winding-engine house (G.709646) and stretched down to the return wheel at Town Foot screens (G.713641) in the form of a loop about half a mile long. This was made up by splicing together over one mile of steel rope.

An uncle of mine was rope-splicer at South Tyne pit almost up to the closure and then moved to the gas works as a stoker. Splicing skills never left him and I can remember at Manor Mill Farm, watching him splicing, rather than knotting, one of Isaac Tallentyre's broken hay-bogie ropes, which was in such a state that nowadays it would have been discarded.

Isaac was a man who firmly believed that things should last for ever when other folk thought they were done. Chains eventually replaced these ropes

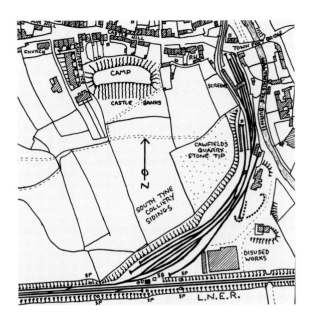

Plan of South Tyne screens at Town Foot. (R Hunter)

for pulling hay pikes on to bogies. Isaac's hemp rope must have been one of the last in the district.

Later that day, uncle gave me a piece of old clothes line to practice splicing, which I found was more complicated to do than he made it seem; mine was more like a very rough Chinese pigtail. He said he thought it was 'platted' not spliced. There was no nod of approval that day, but I think he would have passed the splices I made many years later in the steel ropes used for timber hauling. His instructions were that there mustn't be any difference in thickness in the whole of the rope length after splicing, and that a critical passer-by shouldn't be able to see the join.

With practice it wasn't such a difficult job, although I can still feel the painful steel prickles that appeared. I always blamed those 'spelks' on wartime ropes which seemed to be poor quality, but perhaps most of the ropes were just past their best.

On the pit rolleyway, the full tubs travelled down to the screens on one track, passing the returning empty tubs clamped to the other half of the rope loop on the other track.

On arrival at the screens the tubs were put through an automatic tub-weighing machine then into a power-driven tippler. I wonder what kind of chaos was caused when the tub with a solid block of coal fitted tightly into it got into the tippler. This had been loaded down the pit by tipping the tub on its side, sliding the coal block in and then uprighting it; some loose coals were put on top and the lot sent to bank. There had been complaints about too much duff coming out of the pit so I suppose the solid block was a subtle hint to fettle any more complaints about small coal.

According to miners, the most important job was to unhook the metal token out of the tub because they were paid by the tub load and they each had their own numbered tokens. Whether there was a token in the tub with that solid block of coal was never revealed. From the tippler, the coal spread over a 25-feet-long screen, or 'jigger', and was graded into hoppers above the railway sidings.

One of the two standard-gauge steam shunting locos brought up the empty railway trucks for loading under the hoppers, then hauled the full trucks away after weighing, to make them up into trains for dispatch by the Newcastle & Carlisle main line.

One of the engines was built by Kerr Stuart in 1919 and with 14-inch-diameter cylinders and 160 pounds boiler pressure, easily handled the railway wagons. The other older Barclay engine sometimes struggled, having only ten-inch-diameter cylinders at 110 pounds boiler pressure. At the colliery closure sale

Building of foundation blocks for crushing plant, looking south, at South Tyne sidings, Town Foot; Marshall Coulson, builder; John Teasdale, labourer; Mr Sample, engineer - plus dog. Signals on Newcastle and Carlisle Railway in left background.

Sliding crusher into position and erecting timber-framed building at Town Foot. Looking north, the former cloth mill is in the background.

these engines made £90 & £50 respectively; they were good buys, the Kerr Stuart having been sent to Hawthorn Leslie's at Newcastle only two years earlier for a complete overhaul. The other engine had been overhauled about six years previously.

At one time any stone or slag removed from the screening plant was sent directly over the tip, but in later years it was put through a newer crushing and grading plant and the resulting small coal dispatched, if I heard correctly, to Ireland.

I remember in the 1930s seeing the large tippler for loading coal into ships, at Silloth docks, and realised that South Tyne coal would have passed through it.

I would have liked to see the tipping operation but as it was Sunday nothing was happening apart from a ship delivering Canadian wheat into Carr's flour mill.

A timber-framed building for the grading machinery was erected by the joiners, down the yard from the screens and almost opposite, over the burn, from the old cloth mill at Town Foot. Marshall Coulson and John Teasdale appear to have done the masonry and foundation work involved.

West of this siding area, Cawfields Quarry loading dock was situated, alongside the standard-gauge track. Narrow-gauge rails were laid along the top of this dock, over a bridge and up the slope past the end of the screening building and on to the quarry, two miles distant.

Further west a blast furnace and buildings had existed but were dismantled by the end of the 1800s.

On the east side there were coke ovens and to the south a brick and fireclay works, the same works that William Reay left in 1878 to start his own manufacturing at Bardon Mill. Both of these Town Foot factories were closed by the 1920s.

The Plenmeller tub-landing gantry was about 22 feet above ground level; tubs were given a similar turnround to that at South Tyne Colliery, except for the trip on the endless rope.

Coal was screened over the railway-siding hoppers, and rail trucks shunted about by what Mr. Teasdale, a winder at the pit, described as 'leaky old kettles' - or did he say 'reeky'?

He evidently didn't think much of the locos, although I doubt if a winder would have anything to do with shunting, but he might have seen something wrong from his 'upstairs' winding-engine room.

Town Foot industries: l-r; woollen mill, South Tyne Works and old brewery yard with line of mineral wagons and Haltwhistle East signal box behind. (S & R Sim)

Plenmeller screening plant: pitheadgear almost complete in this view looking south-east. Slot in winding-tower cladding left open until 11-feet-diameter wheels fitted. The lower part of winding tower still to be covered with steel sheeting. Steam crane and loco in left-hand sidings near weighbridge. The back stays of No. 2 upcast shaft can be seen above the fan building and below the right-hand corner of the screen building. (R Bainbridge)

More than once I was told about the rough shunting at this pit and also about a train of wagons that 'escaped' out on to the Alston line without a loco and ran down to Haltwhistle. There are no official notes available about this but many older people have assured me that it happened.

With the loading sidings on the west side, the winders would often get clouds of steam blasted to them 'upstairs'. With a west wind blowing, some steam and smoke would be sucked down the shaft from the adjacent sidings. In recent years it only took one fool to park his lorry, with its engine running, near a surface air intake for a mine to be 'gassed out'; it often happened at Wrytree but with the air flow now exhausting from the drift, this is no longer the case.

During the 16-year or so life of the Plenmeller seam at 775 feet, the north shaft was the main working access; the twin south shaft was there as a return

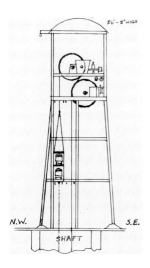

Sketch of Plenmeller pitheadgear looking north-east and showing loaded cage at 'bank' level, 22 feet above ground; guide wheel and control position at 56'6" level; driving wheel, motor and brakes on 66'6" floor.

Screen and winding tower looking south-west, with the lower cladding completed. Spiral stairs can be seen, giving access to driving position situated behind the lower windows in the tower. The driving wheel, gearbox and motor were on the higher floor behind the top windows. The tower was about 80 feet high, almost the same height as Greystonedale main chimney. Steam crane on the left seems to be blowing steam through the drain cocks to clear condensation from cylinders. (R Bainbridge)

airway and as an alternative way out. Ventilation was downcast north and upcast south, but the air circulation could have been reversed by manipulating the air doors in the top cross suction tunnel between the two shafts.

These doors were still in the tunnel many years after the colliery closed and were discovered on one of our exploratory trips to the old pit yard.

Brick walls had been built up round the shafts for safety, although we managed to look over the top and down to the water surface far below. Then we discovered a way through the old fan building and down a dark steel staircase to the level cross-tunnel; we could go to either end and look up or down the shafts from there.

We crawled to the edges of the shafts and just glimpsed over. The reasons for crawling were: no handrails and old Charlie Scott.

Charlie, a retired tub-onsetter, who worked at South Tyne shaft bottom and later as a joiner's labourer at Isaac Hetherington's, often tried to shock us with blood-curdling tales of the coal mines - and of anywhere else he could think of.

When I was a young lad I watched George Renwick, a new starter in Isaac's sawmill, 'taking off' short lengths of boarding at the rear of the circular saw, as they were cut from the timber, when mistakenly he put his finger between the riving knife and the spinning saw blade and lost part of his finger. Charlie said he was no first aid man and the others looked away so I, with my long experience of suchlike, wrapped his finger with a bandage in 'scout fashion' and he went off to hospital.

Presently, Charlie came out of the sawmill with the removed part and announced: "It's not so bad, there's no bone in this fleshy bit." Nobody was really upset until then.

One of the tales he told us was of the time he had to gather up the remains of a man who fell down the shaft at South Tyne pit.

This definitely happened and there were all kinds of stories about how the man, named Mitchinson, came to fall down the shaft. Charlie reckoned that Mitchinson had been pushing an empty tub up to the safety gate ready to return it down the mine in the cage, but the gate had been stuck open, and with the cage still down the shaft, the tub went over and he probably tried to stop it and went over with it. This gate had been known to stay up on rare occasions, after the cage was lowered back down the shaft.

Another way that it might have happened was if the cage 'over-wound' and went past the onset level, lifting the safety gate as it went up and leaving a gaping hole into the shaft if the closing mechanism failed.

Over-winding happened at South Tyne more often than it should have done. One pony handler was travelling up in the cage with his steed when the cage kept on going and crashed into the safety kepps and stuck there until the fitters got the winding gear back into order.

The pony handler was Willie 'Plonk' West, who worked there as a boy and evidently he was soaked to the skin in the rainstorm, having to stay with the pony, Bess, while the cage dangled below the pit-head wheels.

Charlie then went on to tell us of some advice he was given years before: keep away from unfenced edges by at least two-thirds of your height so that if you do happen to trip, you have a chance of staying on the top without overbalancing; otherwise, crawl, if you have to go near the edge. I remembered his advice in the cross-tunnel - and crawled.

Looking at the air doors, situated halfway along this cross-tunnel between the two shafts and opposite the suction-tunnel, which was at a right angle up to the fan, we realised that the air could be sucked out of the mine by the north shaft, but to do this it would have meant fitting more cladding around the main working shaft, to prevent a 'short circuit' of air to the suction fan, which was why the south shaft was kept covered.

Although the doors in the tunnel were adjustable, the ventilation was probably never reversed, but if an underground fire had broken out, a reversed air circuit could have been very helpful in certain circumstances.

An example of an upcast air flow in the main working shaft can be found at the Florence Iron Ore Mine (G.018103), near Egremont, West Cumberland.

There, the pit-head gear, landing deck & winding house are all enclosed; the suction fan was designed to draw air up the 1400-feet-deep shaft and out through an opening in the side, just below the shaft-collar level.

In this mine fresh air came down an older shaft, a mile or more distant and then through the workings to the newer shaft. The arrangements here have now been changed; workings below 200 feet are flooded and used as a water reservoir for BNFL at Calder Hall. Ore-mining carried on at the 200-feet depth and above for some time but having lost their main customer in East Germany, following the reunification of the East and West of that country, Britain's last iron-ore mine has ceased regular production and the surface installations are all part of a mining museum.

I was interested in the power of the winding-motor at Florence Mine: 350hp, the same as the £20 'bargain' motor at South Tyne Colliery sale, so perhaps the South Tyne Co. had intended changing the steam winder to electric drive.

Some iron ore was mined in the Haltwhistle area from workings on Cawfields Fell (G.720664), Melkridge Bog (G.730665) and other locations. These appear to have been mainly open-cast but some are marked on plans as levels; ore was won from below and above the coal seams in some early mines. During the 1800s, ore from these operations was processed in the Town Foot and other Tyneside blast furnaces.

164

At Plenmeller, with the shaft being the main access, the Koepe winding gear had to be available at all times, hence the diesel stand-by generators.

I was told of the time when a diesel engine refused to start, even though the fitters had tried everything they knew to coax this new kind of power into life. Then Willy Postma came along and said that if they would step outside he would start it up for them, and he did, although he wouldn't tell them how he had done it.

This was in the 1920s when diesel mechanics were rare. Air in the fuel system was a problem in the old engines mainly because most manufacturers didn't make it easy to bleed the air out; seemingly Willy Postma knew about air problems and how to cure them.

Some older residents might remember Mr Postma, who walked with a very pronounced limp after an accident with machinery. I was told he came originally from Holland but had worked in the Krupp works in Essen and was injured while working near revolving line-shafting. He reckoned he was lucky to be alive and grateful for the 'bonus' years after the accident.

Fortunately, most of the potentially dangerous shafting and belts are gone now but they were quite safe if properly guarded - and if operators would leave them in place.

The late Mr Teasdale of West Tynedale Terrace, Haltwhistle, one of my informants and ex-winding-engine-man at Plenmeller Colliery, liked to talk about 'his' Koepe winding gear, and as I was very interested in this machinery, I learned a lot from him in the 1950s.

He was gifted with a marvellous memory and talked as if he had just come off shift yesterday, not 20 years before.

The Plenmeller Koepe system was basically two cages, one fixed to each end of an 800-feet long

A view of Plenmeller Colliery about 1911 with boilers in position, some framework erected for shaft sinking, buildings in course of construction and the chimney, 'the capple', built some 28 years before the author reached the top. The chimney was felled in about 1940 when the army took over the yard. (R Bainbridge)

steel rope with a breaking strain of about 90 to a 100 tons so, of the ropes available at that time, it must have been about one-and-a-half inches diameter.

This was balanced over a large driving-wheel fitted with wooden blocks to grip the rope and situated straight above the shaft. A flat balance rope which he called a steel belt, of the same length and weight, was fixed under one cage and allowed to hang as a loose loop down to the shaft sump and up to the bottom of the other cage; the two ropes alone weighed almost one-and-a-half tons.

Another large guide-wheel, the same diameter as the driving-wheel and fitted just below it, pushed the rope over to keep the two ropes the correct distance apart, to suit the centres of the cages hanging in the shaft.

The guide-pulley was also geared to the depth indicators and controlled the automatic accelerating and retarding arrangement.

Mr Teasdale reckoned that the automatic nature of the winding system at Plenmeller made one engineman as good as another. "You just pushed the lever to one end and the mechanism automatically accelerated up to full speed as the empty cage went down and automatically retarded the speed as the other full cage came to the top".

I heard from another source that the pit manager could time the arrival of the cages at the landings and knew whether Teasdale was driving; he was just a bit quicker than the others.

As the cages had two decks of three tubs each, carrying about two and a half tons of coal, I think he must have been more skilled than the other drivers at the move between deck levels. A quick turn-round would also be greatly influenced by the speed at which his tub-onsetters could do their work.

There was an emergency lever for the operator to override the automatic system and it is possible that Mr Teasdale brought this into play before the end of the cage-travel. It was used with the control lever for the move between decking levels.

Another way in which he could have scored was in judging the stretch in the winding-rope. After some use the rope became slightly longer, with the result that the loaded cage might not reach the top 'in balance' if the other cage landed on kepps at the shaft bottom.

The best cure was to keep the rope adjusted, but if the driver knew how much stretch or over-length there was, he could be prepared to override the auto and 'lift' the loaded cage enough, relying on the grip of the rope in the wood blocks of the driving wheel.

The weight of the other cage would be lost when it rested on the bottom kepps and wouldn't help the rope to grip, but it was reckoned there was always about 15 tons weight on the driving wheel with the cages, tubs, coal and ropes, so it would grip so far, even without the three tons or so of the one empty cage.

Mr Teasdale never revealed any tricks he had for hanging on to his speed record.

To adjust the rope stretch, a RH/LH screwed bar of three-inch diameter was fitted between the rope-end and the lift chains on the cage, and after adjustment, special chain links were fitted in parallel with the screw to take the weight.

Mr Teasdale had a strange name for this screw but I failed to write it down at the time and probably wouldn't recognise it now.

Parallel links were required because the Coal Mines Acts forbid the fitting of solid lifting-rods, as the screw would have been classified. The same Acts brought in the ruling that all cage ropes had to be 'capped' every six months, that is, a short piece removed from the ends, to check the condition of the rope.

These Acts came in after the contract was started for the Koepe or the system might never have appeared at Plenmeller, but fortunately, the stretch in the rope was about the same as the eight inches they capped off each end of the rope. None of these details was mentioned in teacher Miss Keenleyside's 'Coal and the Miner' book.

Eight inches seems to be very short for a capping and wouldn't do nowadays, but Mr Teasdale reckoned there was no wear on the Koepe because the rope ran in the wood block slots and never touched metal wheels or drums. There was always rope vibration on those 'ordinary' drum winders; this hardened the ropes and might make them liable to break at the sockets.

I found out later that by 'rope vibration' he meant the wave motion which can be felt in hauler ropes under tension; the motion always stops at the rope sockets, which explains why the ropes are prone to hardening and breakage near the ends.

Even though the rope on the Koepe was under tension he reckoned that for some reason the vibration was not there, although he said he had only felt the rope when it was running fairly slowly off the driving-wheel; he had been assured that the vibration was absent if the loaded cage-rope was felt with a long cane at the shaft-collar level.

It seems that a lot of poking into things went on; Mr Teasdale said there was never anything wrong with the ends of the rope when they were capped, so he must have been into that as well.

After all this information from Mr Teasdale I was beginning to think he was a Koepe enthusiast, and he converted me at the time, to what was then a new system invented by Koepe in Westphalia, a few years before Plenmeller started.

However, after some research, I found that a machine with the same balance principle, and relying on the rope gripping the driving pulley, was built by Frost and Strut in this country in 1835, about 75 years before Plenmeller ordered the Koepe.

This sort of situation appears to have occurred before, the Stephenson/Davy safety lamp controversy being a case in point. No doubt Stephenson invented the lamp but was too busy to take it further, and Mr Davy and his committee claimed it as their invention. It appears that Frost and Strut had other interests and Koepe came along some time later and developed the system. A difference at Plenmeller was in the electrical variable voltage control, and according to Mr Teasdale the name British Westinghouse was on the electrical equipment, so it appears that was also British-made. I learned later that the main contract for the pithead winding installation was awarded to the British Westinghouse Co. who manufactured all the electrical equipment and sublet the structural steelworks to Teesside Bridge and Engineering Ltd. at Middlesbrough and the mechanical equipment to Cowans, Sheldon & Co. Carlisle, so it is only the name of the system that sounds foreign.

The system used a 600 volt AC driving-motor and DC generator at 350 volt output at constant speed, and by varying the strength of the generator field, the output voltage to the cage-rope driving-motor was also varied for different speeds. It gave a smooth and precise control when automatically operated by the depth-position indicator.

This type of electrical control, known as the Ward-Leonard control, was tested initially in 1898, on lifts and elevators in buildings, but was not used extensively until the 1920s.

It is possible that Plenmeller was the first mine to have this type of control fitted to a double-cage mine-shaft; it was inspected quite often by the makers while Mr Teasdale worked there.

I thought the Koepe was a great idea at the time, but today's capping regulations, requiring much more rope to be removed, would have caused problems for the Koepe systems. I can't imagine there would be much gain in having a system that doesn't wear out the rope, if frequent cappings mean that the rope must be renewed in a short time to make up the length lost by the capping.

Mr Teasdale remembered that on night shift, from his driving platform, he could see through a gap in the floor down to the bottom of the shaft, 800 feet below, and occasionally see a glimmer of light, probably from the onsetter's lamp.

Not a position I would care to be in now. I never mentioned to him that in the 1930s, long after the pit closed, I had looked down that same awful hole from the cross-tunnel, although it was well filled with water by that time and consequently, it didn't appear to me to be all that deep.

When asked if he knew the highest speed that the cage could reach, Mr Teasdale reckoned it seemed like 30mph judging by the spinning driving-wheel. We couldn't agree on that figure so we worked it out with a pencil on one of the corner bricks of his house and we got it to almost 15mph maximum.

Even that was fairly fast but as the full speed was controlled automatically and each cage ran smoothly on four guide ropes, it would be designed for that speed.

I could see that Mr Teasdale disagreed with this figure; I am sure he did some checking of his own later on. What he meant was probably the closing speed of the two cages as they passed in the shaft, which was approximately 30mph at the highest automatic speed.

We wondered what it would be like travelling at 15mph in a South Tyne cage guided by uneven metal skid rails. He said that it would likely "rattle ees teeth oot".

Often, we lads looked over the wall surrounding the South Tyne shaft and noticed the heavy timber division across the centre, extending down to the water level and presumably to the bottom of the shaft. The uneven skids he talked about were fixed to these timbers on one side of the cage and fixed to the shaft lining on the other.

Another interesting thing was that the kepps and the release levers were still on the shaft-top behind the wall and will perhaps still be there under the filling.

Plenmeller shaft had no timber division across the centres and looked very plain compared to that at South Tyne. The two Plenmeller shafts were filled and capped in the 1970s; by the 1950s South Tyne shaft was filled with ash and reject pipes from Tyne Fireclay Co.

Our gang investigated another mine installation near Melkridge which had a shaft (G.738649) with a small cage and skid rails, and which was used to raise coal from the north side of the Blackett Colliery seam, near Common House Farm.

This had a steam-driven winder and an upright boiler for steam-raising. The cage in this shaft was the smallest I had ever seen and appeared to be made to take one coal tub only, although a second deck could have been below out of our sight, under the landing platform which covered the whole of the shaft-top.

Pitheap at site of shaft near Common House Farm, Melkridge, the only obvious slag heap left in the district. The depression near the centre appears to be the shaft position. (D Hunter)

Evidently the shaft was not required as an air circulation inlet; its whole width was covered over but there was no sign of any swinging hatch covers for closing the gap when the cage went down to the bottom. The lower parts on the wooden uprights of the pit head gear were boarded over and doors fitted across the tramway at the edge of the shaft, making it difficult to distinguish details and, no doubt, to keep adventurous boys out.

There was no evidence of a ventilation fan near this site; underground ways would be connected to other shafts and outcrop drifts higher up the hill behind Bayldon Farm.

I never saw the Melkridge winder at work; it was dismantled and the shaft capped in the 1940s. The shaft is marked on 1860 maps and was sunk 165 feet to a 25-inch-thick coal seam; the pit heap is still there, but on my last visit to Common House there was no sign of the three-feet-high shaft capping. The shaft must be filled up now.

The Blackett Colliery (G.744638) at Melkridge, associated with South Tyne Colliery at Haltwhistle,

Head of the pumping borehole from Blackett Colliery, Melkridge. The coal seam was just over 100 feet from the surface; the pumps were in the lowest east dip of the mine directly below this point. (D Hunter)

Water still runs from Blackett via the pump borehole, concrete ducting and earthenware pipes into the River Tyne. (D Hunter)

was entered by a drift which passed under the main road to the east of the Three Horse Shoes Inn and worked northside coal on a north-west rise.

This mine had the old type furnace shaft, often used in the mid-1800s, to suck out the foul air, replacement fresh air coming in by the working drift.

The Blackett furnace shaft (G.744643) came to the surface on the hill behind Horse Close, north of Melkridge, like a massive chimney sticking out of the field with a very small wheel fitted to two beams across the top. It was in fact a chimney; a stoker kept the fire blazing; 'putter' lads kept him supplied with coal, loaded on tubs and pushed along the track to the underground furnace.

Many new starters at the pit were put on this furnace road to get used to pushing tubs. As usual on the first day, they were shown the way round before starting their regular job, some of the older men telling them that they would soon see the Devil in Hades.

Of course, the lads didn't believe that, until they saw the stoker silhouetted against the bright glare from the furnace, giving him the appearance of a skeleton moving about. Many a lad bolted out of the place and took some convincing that 'it' wasn't really the Devil.

At a later date, a shaft (G.745638) was sunk near the railway at Blackett but was used only as an access for the endless haulage-ropes and pump-pipes for a considerable time, before eventually drawing coal.

The shaft was only about 80 feet deep and according to one of my uncles, workmen shouted any messages between the surface and the bottom. The rising main from the pumps on the low side was well over 100 feet deep.

This pump-pipe surfaced (G.749636) in a riverside field below Woodhall Farm. One pump usually kept the water down with another as standby. These pumps were situated at the end of a fairly low and narrow driving, mined out as quickly as possible, to connect up with the borehole drilled from the surface.

Pumps were installed and connected to the borehole, the intention being to widen the area out soon afterwards, although apparently this widening never happened; perhaps roof conditions allowed only a parallel driving which was made to the pump area. On one occasion, when one pump was dismantled for repair, the spare one also broke down. Owing to a very small sump area water quickly rose up in the small tunnel so the fitter had to splash out through rising floods and leave the pumps.

Earlier pump stations had been abandoned for the newer, lower borehole position so there were no spare pumps capable of clearing the water flooding into the low side workings.

It was decided to close the low side of the mine because of the flooding and the diminishing coal reserves left under the River Tyne up to the whin dyke on the Shankfoot side.

The drift under the main highway was still open in the late 1930s so we made good use of it as we rode in an old Austin Seven car abandoned in the pit yard. The yard sloped down to the drift mouth making a good runway; we jumped into the Austin and careered down to the dark opening.

We were lucky that this drift wasn't on a steep slope and was almost level inside, or we might have gone underground earlier than intended. Some soft ground just within the drift stopped the car anyway, and thinking back, this was probably the safest part for freewheeling; had we taken the opposite, more precipitous route, we would have ended up in the back lane of Kittlebelly Row at a much lower level.

In 1940 the Henshaw Drift (G.774645), or as most people called it, Bardon Mill Pit, was put down from the end of the old Birkshaw aerial-flight tipping point, at the railway sidings near Bardon Mill. This was to win the low-side coal in the seam worked by Blackett to the west and Ramshawfield and old Henshaw drift near Low Fogridge, to the north.

Using tubs and tramways, the new mine was worked east and west from the drift bottom and to the high side. In later years under the NCB it became the first pit in the north to have conveyor belts from coal face to surface.

The south-east dip on the east side was driven under the Tyne towards Partridge Nest Farm (G.779641); another south dip passed under Redburn and to the Haughs area (G.763640).

Coal between these two dips was mined out in the 1950s and 60s, by using the long-wall mining methods, where large areas of roof were allowed to fall, causing much subsidence damage up on the surface to houses and to the railway. Most older mines used the bord-and-pillar method whereby adequate pillars of coal were left in position at regular intervals to support the roof. Modern machines and conveyor belts work more efficiently on long-wall faces, so apart from a few small mines,

Bardon Mill pit mechanics beside the drift conveyor: l-r: Clive Dixon, Derek Wheadon, Percy Mitchinson and George Pape. (C Dixon)

the bord-and-pillar system is no longer used. Much of Haltwhistle is supported on South Tyne Colliery coal pillars.

Main pumps, situated in the south-east dip, forced water up about 300 feet through two boreholes to deliver at a riverside position (G.777645). Note: On some maps Bardon Mill Station is shown on this grid position but the Station is actually at G.779645.

I remember looking up these boreholes from the mine, shortly after they were drilled down to the seam, and it was noticeable that one drill had veered off the vertical for some reason. On the surface a few feet separated the holes but down below they were some yards apart.

Water became a big problem at this pit and although it had been planned to develop eastwards at one time, under the Strand Farm (G.788647) and towards Morwood (G.796674), the final areas of activity were on the south-east side towards Beltingham and to the west side under Stone Hall Farm (G.758645), where the seam was thinner and the coal had much further to travel on rather worn-out conveyor belts.

When closure came, the underground machinery, apart from a small amount of electrical equipment, was just left where it stood, this being NCB policy by that time, unlike at Ventners Hall in 1958 when it took about six months to salvage underground material.

The cost of pumping out water during that six months probably cost more than the salvaged material was worth to the NCB.

On the surface at Bardon Mill, empty railway trucks were pushed into the NCB sidings from the Newcastle to Carlisle line by a main line loco. From that lower end, trucks were then pushed up to the top end past the screens by a steam shunter. I recall a Barclay 0-4-0 loco with Jackie Irving at the controls bringing the trucks up three at a time, and it amazed me how the wheels stayed on the rails.

The lines moved up and down as well as sideways when the loco ran over them but the train struggled to the top - with occasional mishaps.

This photo of Bardon Mill pit shows miners rushing to the shower room for the very last time. (C Seal)

Work for the loco was finished for the day when all of the trucks had been moved up. The yard sloped down under the screens, enabling trucks, using their own brakes, to be filled and weighed and formed into a full train, usually destined for Carlisle Power Station.

Main-line locos were not allowed far into the colliery yard but on one occasion a J39 came well on to the NCB rails, which, being in a poorer state than the main line, spread out under the weight and derailed the loco. With the help of a lot of wood blocks, lifting jacks and the colliery staff, the loco was re-railed.

Whether the derailment was reported or not, it would be a difficult situation for the driver, who shouldn't have passed the warning sign.

Jackie Irving also had some fun with his loco, which could be unpredictable at times. It ran with at least one broken spring for a long time and one day, but not with Jackie driving, it went into the engine shed, through the brick gable end and stopped against the deputies' cabin. The deputies moved to another cabin after that trespass.

One clear February morning I arranged to film Jackie and locomotive performing, but the engine had only moved a few feet through the shed doorway when the firebox fusible plug melted and damped the fire down. The fire had to be emptied and left to cool before a new plug could be fitted. A few hours later when steam was up to pressure again, we managed to take a good film. It was the only time I have been fortunate enough to film pure white steam going almost straight up and condensation pouring back out of the steam column like rain.

We were just in time to film the loco. The NCB fitted a hauler to pull the trucks up the yard and scrapped the loco very soon afterwards.

Many Haltwhistle-and-district miners travelled to Bardon Mill by the pit bus but I was told of another way they devised to get home on Saturdays, when the bus was not available: by train of course, which sounds normal enough, but not the way they did it.

They noticed that a long goods train pulled into the passing siding at Bardon Mill every Saturday morning, to allow the faster passenger train to overtake on its way to Carlisle. The miners jumped up on to the buffers of the goods train trucks - and hung on.

At Haltwhistle the goods train pulled into the passing siding to allow the next all-stations passenger train to pass, and the buffer riders jumped off, very pleased at having saved both time and fares.

This worked well until one Saturday, as the train approached Haltwhistle, they realised by the amount of steam flying, that it was speeding up and not slowing down to stop. They could see that the mainline signal was 'off'; and that the left-hand siding board was 'on'. The driver also had seen this and opened the throttle. This train was going straight on towards Carlisle. The miners jumped off somewhere east of Smith & Walton's paint factory, into what they reckoned were the strongest stinging nettles and bramble clumps in the district.

To make matters worse, the guard leaned out of his brake van, laughing and pointing. It turned out that the second passenger train was cancelled, so his train was not siding off that day.

This painful episode put a stop to the ever-innovative miners' version of riding the rods. In later years there was a further diversion on the railway, concerning the two-carriage diesel DMU train used for passengers on the Alston Line. The train stood idle at Haltwhistle for long periods between trips on the branch line and was sometimes used for shunting, to save bringing in a loco from Blaydon just to move a truck.

These activities were extended to removing empty trucks off the coal drops and shunting them up through the station into the west sidings, then

Barclay 0-4-0 steam loco at Bardon Mill Colliery. (J Carrick)

collecting more full trucks and placing these over the drops.

Judging by their expressions, driver and guard seemed to enjoy these sorties, as if they were reliving their goods train days. Alan Kent had not lost the art of coupling up with a shunting-pole.

Unfortunately someone 'higher up the tree' did not approve, so the practice was stopped.

On one occasion in the early 1940s I witnessed what I thought was a very unusual occurrence, but one which was probably fairly general on branch lines.

The screeching of locomotive brakes alerted me in time to see a long eastbound train of empty trucks coming to a halt, just short of the West Lodge crossing, two miles west of Haltwhistle. At the same time I noticed a white cardboard box on top of the wall between the railway and a house garden. A hand stretched out from the loco cab and collected the box; at the same time a fair amount of nice 'roundy coals' disappeared over the garden wall with the help of a long shovel. Then the train, with a grand display of slipping wheels and exhaust steam, sped off on its way to Newcastle. This operation took less than a minute and I never saw a face, only arms and shovel.

It turned out that the box was a signal for the driver to pull up and load surplus fresh-laid hen eggs into the cab. The coals would be in payment, courtesy of the Railway Company, no doubt. I wonder whether the guard got a share of these wartime scarcities… At the back end of the train he was over a quarter-of-a-mile away from the transaction at the front end, but he likely knew what was going on.

Many years later at West Lodge crossing Mr Bowran, stationmaster at Haltwhistle, and myself were standing near the roadside gates looking across the tracks at the 'Train on Line' indicators fixed to the large stone gate-post. He thought there was something odd about the dials and after waiting while a train went past, we crossed over and discovered that they had been wrongly set up and showed 'train on line' when no trains were anywhere near the crossing and showed 'line clear' when a train was approaching. Residents in the nearby lodge said that they took no notice of the dials anyway but they agreed that strangers would be confused by them.

Back on West Tynedale in Haltwhistle, Mr Teasdale never again questioned Plenmeller cage travel speed, so most likely he agreed with the reckoning. I wonder if our sums are still on the house wall after more than forty years?

We were interested to find later that the Co.Durham Koepe winder was working at Murton Colliery and I managed to get details of the output. These cages travelled at a higher speed of 21mph as against 14mph at Plenmeller. Murton raised four tons of coal each run compared with two and a half tons; had a 750hp winding motor compared to 230hp, and travelled 1224 feet in 52 seconds compared with 800 feet winding depth in 45 seconds at Plenmeller. Murton, with four deck cages, managed 36 trips per hour but Plenmeller could put in over 50 owing to the quicker decking time with only two deck cages and with a shorter distance to run.

When Mr Teasdale heard about the Murton winder he was keen to know if any of his suggestions for speeding up the output of the Koepe had been taken up. Some improvements had been made to the Plenmeller system before the Murton installation and presumably were noted by the engineers fitting the Murton head-gear. One great difference between Murton and Plenmeller was the lifetime of the Koepe winders. Plenmeller ran for approximately 15 years before the seam became uneconomic, whereas Murton was in use for about 70 years with a much higher output - and according to many miners should still have been going yet - and I wish it were. I had long planned to inspect the Murton system to see

how the capping of the rope was managed but now the Durham mines have been swept away, so I missed the only working Koepe winder in that area. These winders are used much more in Europe, so perhaps I will be able to visit them some day and see how they cope with the ropes.

Both Koepe installations seem to have been capable of handling adequately the outputs from underground, but Murton had a higher cage speed. Plenmeller equipment was quite capable of this speed but it wasn't recommended. These speeds were for coal-winding; cages on man-carrying trips were supposed to travel at about 4mph in those days.

We worked out one statistic that pleased Mr Teasdale: the total distance that a Plenmeller cage might travel at full output was 60 miles in an eight hour shift. He reckoned that that put the South Tyne miners a long way down the league with their 'ordinary winder'. Not wishing to upset Mr Teasdale, I didn't mention that Murton had 'ordinary' winding shafts in addition to the Koepe. Plenmeller coal output was minute compared to Murton.

South Tyne Colliery: Gertie Lee/Haswell (centre), Harry Nancarrow (top left), George Bradford and Tom Bowman (top right), Jack Bowman (middle row left). (M Henderson)

Chapter Nine

An early view of Plenmeller Colliery. (R Bainbridge)

A landmark estimated to be 120 feet high, which stood for 30 years at Plenmeller pit, was the brick chimney stack. Because of the good steel ladder built into the inside brickwork, as lads we had to class the climbing of it as a 'capple' or an 'I'm better than you' challenge.

There were not many takers, only one or two at that particular time, and yet it wasn't difficult to climb.

Only steel ladder rungs and brickwork were to be seen in front and there was no sensation of height, but when I reached the top and stuck my head above the brickwork… I threw my stone over the top to prove I had reached it, had a quick look round, and got back down. I can feel pains behind my knees even now, just thinking about that exploit.

The ground felt good after that climb. I only saw one other person climb to the top and that was Eddy

Bowes of Central Drive, but there would be more that I didn't hear about.

I believe it was Eddy who forgot to take a stone up so he threw an old penny over the top and although the onlookers heard and saw it, nobody could say exactly where it landed. The story goes that Eddy spent the next few days looking for it but from that height, had it landed on edge, it would likely be several inches down into the ash heaps. I often wondered if one of the onlookers found and pocketed it before Eddy got back down to search for it.

The chimney was toppled on behalf of the army when they took the site for a munitions dump in the 1940s.

One former Plenmeller miner who knew it was to be brought down at a certain time was anxious to see the landmark drop. He leaned against the railway wall at the Metal Bridge, from where he could see the top part of the brick chimney showing above the hill behind Bellister Castle - and waited.

Then somebody came along and distracted him and when he looked across to Plenmeller - no chimney. Herby seemed upset at missing the vital moment and I heard that the intruder, a Mr Isaac Brown, got his 'Sunday name'.

When some of the ammunition sheds were removed in 1950, we walked over the old chimney site and couldn't find even one brick; only ashes and pit waste.

We didn't see Eddy's penny either.

It would be interesting to know what happened to the bricks. If Nichol Birkett reckoned on 38,000 bricks in his Greystonedale chimney, there would be at least 60,000 at Plenmeller. Perhaps the army shovelled them down the disused shafts or used them to extend the yard area towards Gowk Hill.

The story goes that Plenmeller chimney was put up by builders from Holland and that each course of bricks came in separate numbered crates, each course being slightly less than the one before to account for tapering in the circular chimney, and that it was built in just over six weeks.

The separate crates detail seems a bit far-fetched. A good bricklayer can easily cope with tapering in a chimney with normal-sized bricks. According to Nichol Birkett chimney stacks were quite easy to put up; it was the working height that put me off doing them.

I haven't seen an official record of the chimney building, and although the story came from many different sources, the account may have been exaggerated, but the chimney builders lodged at a house in the West End; for six weeks.

There seemed to be a touch of class about all of the buildings at Plenmeller Colliery and the chimney was no exception. The bottom 20 feet of the stack was octagon-shaped and had many 'stepped out' courses up to about the 15 feet mark, where the brickwork was gradually corbelled out some nine inches and capped back in 12 inches, then straight up for about 18 inches and again capped in to where the circular part of the stack started, after which it would be a matter of piling the bricks one on top of the other and holding on.

This appears to have been the quickest building job at the pit, unlike the shafts which took about five years to complete; the Koepe pit-head gear was ordered in 1910 when shaft-sinking began and it was May 1916 before the complete system was in operation; difficulties in the shaft sinking were blamed for the delay. Actual sinking probably took four years, then the temporary wooden pithead gear would have to be removed to make way for the permanent steel structure, commenced in June 1914 by the Teesside Bridge Co. It certainly would take a long time to lay the three-quarters-of-a-million bricks required, if the linings of the two shafts were

A view of the Plenmeller shaft-sinking in progress about 1913. Both shafts are fitted with the temporary headgear and drum winders which remained until shafts were completed. The right-hand framework over the downcast shaft was then removed in 1915 and the Koepe winding tower and screens erected ready for coaling operations in 1916. (Mr Teasdale)

two-brick thick - they could have been four-brick thick and more, in some parts of the strata - a massive stack of bricks.

It was thought by some folk that reinforced concrete was used in the shaft lining, but as far as could be seen down to the water level in both shafts - perhaps 60 feet - it was brick-lined and the ends of the bricks showed at regular intervals in the heading courses, therefore it must have been at least two bricks thick but was more likely to be four bricks wide nearer the top. It is possible that the lower parts were shuttered and built with concrete, similar to the entire 1400-feet shaft at Beckermet Iron Ore Mine, which, however, had no reinforcement throughout the whole depth; it was not thought to be necessary, and so it proved.

At Plenmeller, some miners thought that the surrounding ground was 'frozen', a process used to solidify the area round the shafts to prevent water flooding into the working area while the sinking and lining was in progress.

Mr Teasdale's photo of the sinking of the shafts shows the two temporary pit-head gears but no signs of the ammonia plant required for freezing operations, no drilling rigs for boring round the shafts if a full length freezing operation was needed, and no concrete mixers or reinforcing bars.

Unfortunately we cannot give an exact date for the photo but as the fan building, power house, blacksmiths', joiners' and fitting shops are shown to be complete, the photograph could have been taken in 1913 when the shaft-sinking was well advanced. Building materials visible are bricks; perhaps, as surmised, the only linings to be used in the shafts.

Concerning the chimney stacks, I should think it would have taken Nichol and his gang a bit longer to build the Greystonedale chimney than it was supposed to have done at Plenmeller, although he always maintained that the difficulty was not so much in the actual bricklaying but in the raising of the materials as work progressed.

The original square chimney for South Tyne Colliery boilers, later modified for fireclay purposes but now redundant. (J Parker, jnr)

I climbed up the inside of the Greystonedale chimney many years after the Plenmeller adventure but it was quite different.

It wasn't so high, was square-flued and was much dirtier, having been used regularly, whereas the disused round-flued Plenmeller chimney had been washed down by about eight years of rain, so it was fairly clean. Better still was the fact that I was being paid to climb this later one and was fully insured.

Nichol Birkett would have been very put out had he gone up to Greystonedale in recent years and seen that the tall chimney was no more. All factory chimney stacks were highly rated by local councils, which is perhaps why so few are left.

The original square chimney at South Tyne Colliery was adapted in the late 30s to take flues from two long kilns for firing fireclay pipes, also flues from a large drying flat converted from the old power-house.

A new building was added between the colliery workshops and the old power-house, then a fireclay grinder, clay-mixer and pipe-press were installed.

When this mill was working, solid fireclay was fed into the edge runner/rolling crusher and forced down through fine holes in the heavy metal base plates and on to a bucket conveyor. The crushed clay was then carried by the conveyor up to a screener and a hopper, from where it was fed into a mixer and water added, to create the right condition of plasticity for pressing through the pipe machine.

This press forced the clay out through dies to form the pipes as required; these were then hardened off in the drying flat, heated by under-floor coal fires, after which the pipes were taken to the kilns and stacked ready for firing, with pipe-fittings placed on the top of the pipes.

Great skill was needed in loading these kilns and if badly stacked the whole load could collapse during firing, resulting in a great waste of clay, coal and labour.

The door opening was bricked up to seal the kiln, which was then fired up using the rows of fire grates on each side.

A pipe was built into the sealed doorway so that the three sega clay test-sticks, with slightly different melting points, could be seen, set up on the stack of pipes in the kiln.

At a predetermined heat the first stick melted over. A close watch, as a guide to firing, was then kept on the remaining two sticks as the temperature increased to the maximum required. Salt was added near the end of the firing cycle to glaze the surfaces of the pipes.

After firing ceased, the kiln doorway bricking was partly removed to facilitate cooling, before removing the finished product.

These were the South Tyne Fireclay Company methods; perhaps normal but not necessarily the best.

Fireclay was mined in the old South Tyne workings via the fan-drift up the burnside from the works. Three-phase power was once again carried on poles up to the former fan drift and used for the underground operations. Clay was carried in narrow-gauge tubs and drawn by a pony to the crusher position. Later it was found that the clay was much better to process if it was stockpiled for six months, but this was rather difficult to arrange. Mr Little of Park Road, Haltwhistle was in charge of the underground operations.

Ventilating the clay drift was not so difficult. It was found that there was a free flow of air through, on most days, up to the Fell drift about 1000 yards to the north, so to improve the flow, a duct was fitted from the nearby Fell Chimney stack into the old drift and its mouth sealed. This worked well enough to clear the foul air and fumes from the workings.

The clay mine was closed after a few years and clay was later bought in from the Milkwell, Corbridge clay works and the NCB open-cast mines near Throckley.

Coal for kiln firing came mainly from Ramshawfield mine, near Bardon Mill; a load of sea coal was tried at one time, but was found to be a poor substitute for maintaining the temperature; some firemen managed it better than others.

A much older and lower chimney than the Plenmeller stack is this preserved chimney up the Haltwhistle Burn, sometimes known as the Fell Chimney. The brick extension was added to increase draughting for the steam boiler. The brick-built engine beds still have steel bolts showing; the bolts on the left held an endless rope hauler in line with the drift to the right of the picture. The drift was used as an air vent by Tyne Fireclay Co. with ducting into the chimney; this free circulation saved the cost of running fans in the clay mine some 1000 yards downstream. (D Hunter)

An early view of Fell Chimney. I was told that the boilers were horse-drawn along the Military Road (not much more than a track in those days), uncoupled, then rolled down the bank from the road and the horses re-harnessed to bring them to their final destination. (S & R Sim)

Another chimney stack and two round kilns were built later, on the site of the old colliery tub dispatch shed, at the south-east side of the shaft.

With the advent of PVC pipes for drainage, demand for fireclay pipes dropped and this firm ran into difficulties. They tried making field-drain tiles with the excellent clay which had been cast aside at the iron ore workings on Cawfields Fell, but it was too late and the firm was forced to close.

The newer round kilns and chimney were dismantled but the former colliery buildings were left standing.

The original machinery for the fireclay works was installed at South Tyne in 1939 together with the building of the two long kilns, flues and drying flats; owing to the war this expensive equipment remained idle for some years and was a big financial loss to the company.

When manpower was available again, production started but it was thought that the firm had a long way to go before their products matched the quality of those at Bardon Mill; I do not think they ever did.

Errington Reay had over 60 years experience of manufacturing fireclay products before Tyne Fireclay started, so they were experts in the trade. Observation showed that the Bardon Mill men understood heat and how to control it, and were much more precise in all the processes: grinding, moulding, loading and firing, through to the finished article. Tyne Fireclay did not seem to be in the same league; although there were some first-class men, often they were let down by others.

It is normal practice to recycle faulty or broken pipes through the crusher but there is a limit to how much can be mixed into the new clay to improve it.

There were so many rejects at Haltwhistle that they were tipped down the old colliery shaft in the yard, presumably to get them out of sight. This waste, mixed with ash from kiln fires, quickly filled the shaft up over 500 feet to the top.

Following the Fireclay Company closure the buildings were used as workshops for manufacturing industrial high-pressure washers and also as a builder's yard.

On the east side, an area was cleared and used as a coal merchant's yard, together with a storage depot for traction engines, steam-rollers and other interesting machinery.

The old colliery chimney, which appears to be about 60 feet high, still stands; I do not intend to climb this one.

My highest local climb, over 300 feet up a steel ladder, was to the top of the original Hopealone TV mast (G.735718). The day was clear, the view from this high 'seat' was outstanding and extensive, at approximately 1300 feet above sea-level.

Consett Iron Works in Co.Durham, the Solway Firth, the hills of Southern Scotland and the English Lake District, all seemed very close.

When I'm asked now why I climbed away up there, I usually say, like the mountaineers: "because it was there", but the clear day and the prospect of a long-distance view had much to do with it; I believe the latest mast is under 300 feet.

Hopealone TV mast, just under 300 feet high, replaced an earlier steel framework mast of about six feet square section with ladder inside and slightly more than 300 feet high; a great view from the top. (D Hunter)

Looking more fully into the history of electricity in the locality it appears that apart from Greystonedale, one of the first Haltwhistle houses to be illuminated by electricity was on the Comb Hill.

A cable was laid underground from South Tyne pit, over the Burn, up the hill and across the fields of

181

South Tyne Colliery: l-r from back; Tom Bowman, Mr AB Hare (Manager), Albert Lee, Harry Nancarrow. (M Henderson)

Comb Hill Farm to Hill House, sometimes called Woodbine Cottage (G.703644) then the home of Mr Hare, the pit manager.

Foster Kennedy and Jackie Burn after him often ploughed up parts of this 800-yard length of cable in their turnip and potato fields but much of the cable will still be there. Digging the trench, shallow though it was, would be a mammoth task for men with spades.

It would be interesting to know the cross-sectional area of the conductor, as the volt-drop on that length must have been considerable; perhaps there were no regulations on depth in those days - unless they were simply ignored. I have not seen any of this cable but I wouldn't be surprised if it was only a telephone cable from pit to manager's house.

In Plenmeller village the first houses at the west end were built for Mr Dickinson, the colliery engineer, and other officials and were connected to the pit electricity supply and by private phone for emergencies.

I haven't heard of any Plenmeller farmers ploughing up cables; presumably they were overhead wires and fitted later than the South Tyne underground cable.

I remember that an unusual visitor to Plenmeller Colliery site in 1940, when the army took over the yard and started clearing it, was a Caterpillar D8 bulldozer and trailing grader.

This machine travelled via Lanty's Lonnen and through the River Tyne near the Alston Arches, from the second stage of the new Bardon Mill to Haltwhistle trunk road scheme; the first stage was begun in the early 1930s near Redburn, Bardon Mill, completing a long straight length of road up to near Stone Hall within a year or two.

The second-stage earthworks between this new road and Haltwhistle were started just prior to the 1939 war, and this is when the Caterpillar came to the district.

The Cat seemed to be the ultimate in power, its wire-rope-worked blade and grader transformed green fields into roadbed formation in a very short time, except for the solid rock encountered near How Burn (G.720640).

Moving this vast quantity of stone necessitated weeks of blasting when work resumed after the war. Earlier, in the late 1930s, when some of the overburden was moved to the How Burn valley, it looked rather like the rebirth of the Cawfields railway. Narrow-gauge lines were laid from the east end of this rock formation and a diesel loco was used to haul trucks of spoil to How Burn top, to fill the deep ravine up to the new road level. A 10RB or similar excavator loaded the rail trucks with the soil and clay.

Large precast concrete pipes were laid along the valley floor to take water flowing from the Oakey

Knowe area. Local lads discovered that by dropping into a manhole in the How Burn bottom, near the old main road, they could run through the dark concrete tunnel and out into Oakey Knowe valley. This was not attempted during floods.

We always thought that the D8 could have bulldozed the spoil over the edge in a fraction of the time taken by the loco and trucks, but the Cat was not available then, having been requisitioned for Plenmeller munitions dump.

The road works were classed as non-essential and eventually stopped for the duration of the war; the concrete pipes in the How Burn remained uncovered and most of the rock lay undisturbed until the late 40s when work restarted; the D8's final work in the district was at Plenmeller, to level out the pit heap up on Gowk Hill, near the pit reservoirs (G.707626).

The pit heap was burning when I first saw it from Redpath in the 1930s, so it would have to be made safe when the wartime ammunition store was

The author inspects a Caterpillar D7 without its bulldozer blade, at Threlkeld Quarry and Mining Museum, similar to the 1930s D8 machine that worked on the How Burn road and at Plenmeller. (J Parker, jnr)

The burning pit heap from Shield Hill. The Plenmeller chimney is just visible to the right of the heap. (S Blackburn)

extended from the pit yard into this area. The heap was still hot in 1939, years after the pit closed.

Evidently the fire had burned hollow under the surface; the bulldozer sank into this and had to be dug out by the few labourers who were still working on the new road site. Many hours of overtime were put in to retrieve D8, and we had thought such a vast machine would never come to grief.

This pit heap was later added to the ammunition storage area, so they evidently thought the fire was out by then, and safe. Most of the colliery yard was used for munitions and many low buildings were erected, some almost covered over with earth where loading and unloading of ammunition was carried out; the earth covering was presumably to contain any explosions that might occur and as protection from enemy aircraft.

The ammunition was stacked in small craters dug into the yard and after the war, when these munitions were no longer required, they were transported up to the old pit-heap site where the explosive was burnt off. Some Haltwhistle residents were startled to find their south-facing rooms brilliantly illuminated during the day from the burning cordite. Youngsters seemed to be attracted to it - although it was much too bright to look at with the naked eye.

In later years, the reservoirs and pit-heap site were covered with Haltwhistle town refuse; it is now a green field.

The army buildings were sold and the land cleared, except for the old colliery buildings; then in the 1950s two large government storage buildings were erected at the east end and filled with various emergency supplies.

G. Ridley carried out washing and sorting of fluorspar minerals and stored mining supplies and equipment at the top end of the yard near the original blacksmith's shop.

Jackson's Timber firm moved into the old mine-fan building and erected a sawmill near the two mine-shafts. They discarded their sawdust down the shafts until a market built up for sawdust as cattle - and poultry - house bedding, etc.

When one of the government buildings became available in the late 1950s, Cascelloid Ltd of Leicester took it over and started the plastic bottle production which has provided employment for hundreds of Haltwhistle people over the years.

The rear of the original power-house at Plenmeller pit with workshops beyond; all now used as lorry repair depot and offices by Crawfords Transport. (D Hunter)

Construction of the Plenmeller workshops: joiners', blacksmiths', electricians', fitters' shops. (R Bainbridge)

I was interested to see this name in the north because I had fitted some Cascalite roof light sheets in Haltwhistle in about 1954; these were made by Cascelloid of Leicester. Over forty years later these sheets were still fitted to the roof: evidently good material.

Within a few years the other emergency stores were cleared and Cascelloid took over the second building.

Output of the well-known plastic containers has increased over the years, although there have been ups and downs in demand; still those hissing, squirting machines continue to produce endless rows of bottles; long may they hiss. Cascelloid became part of the BP Group.

The sawmill and the railway sidings used for ammunition transportation were cleared away; car parks were formed and roads were built to Crawford's transport depots at the top end of the yard.

Many changes have been made since the colliery days, the first big upheaval being made in the early war years by the D8, which eventually disappeared from the district - no doubt, to some more essential war work.

In the 1940s other Caterpillars were brought to the district for wartime forestry work; a D6 and a D2 worked in the Featherstone area together with a later International TD14, two older TD9s and a TD6, a fleet of American crawler tractors plus many British-made Fordson four-wheeled winch tractors.

Mechanisation had certainly come to the forests but 'Darling', a Clydesdale horse, and Nelly Bell, her handler, were still indispensable for awkward places; they often moved more timber in a day than some of the tractors managed.

Most of the largest trees were loaded on to an ERF tractor unit and pole wagon and delivered to West Hartlepool by driver Hughie Burns, brother of

Kitchener. These huge loads travelled up Pinkins Cleugh and over Redpath, because of the weight limit of three tons on Haltwhistle Tyne Bridge, although I remember a load of 11 tons crossing this bridge at one time.

Some of the empty lorries surreptitiously crept over on their return journey, whether they were over three tons or otherwise; others followed the diversion. Loaded timber lorries had to be helped up Pinkins Cleugh, or the Stone Bridge, usually by the D6 Caterpillar tractor - not the best machine for towing, with its metal tracks, but they managed, one track running on the permanently flattened roadside verge for extra grip.

Following the tow up Pinkins, Hughie was on his own to Hartlepool, sometimes with a bit of drama at Haydon Bridge. Long loads were driven into Church Street and reversed over the bridge to avoid damage to the corner buildings from the overhanging trees, as happened sometimes when lorries tried to turn on to the bridge from the west. Some drivers said that it was easier to reverse over the bridge and up Allendale road then forward to Hexham, than to try to drive directly on to the bridge. Of course, all traffic was stopped during this manoeuvre; the chaos that would have ensued these days can only be imagined.

Later a limit was imposed on overhangs so that lorries could drive straight on to the old bridge; better still, traffic lights were fitted, to be followed by a new bridge in the late 1960s.

A doctor's daughter from Blyth, 17-year-old Margaret, drove an Austin timber-pole lorry between Featherstone and Hartlepool during the war years, and with no power steering to help her, she did well to manage what was regarded as a strenuous as well as a skilful job.

It was unheard of for a girl aged under 21 years to drive an articulated vehicle with perhaps ten or twelve tons of trees on board; nowadays she would require an HGV license.

In wartime, many restrictions were ignored. After a week or so of training, if people could manage the work, they carried on. This included driving Caterpillars as well as wheeled tractors, although 14-year-olds were kept off the large circular saw benches, so I never got the chance to try those noisy machines at the Stone Bridge sawmill.

Featherstone had its own narrow-gauge railway about half-a-mile long, for moving timber from the Park Burn Wood (G.686616) across the parks to the roadside at Hallbankhead (G.678608), near Featherstone Station. A twin cylinder Ruston Hornsby diesel loco with a few wood-framed trams was used to haul the timber.

Winch tractors pulled the trees up to the top of Park Burn Wood, where they were sawn to length, loaded and transported to stockpiles at the far end of the line. The loco and winch tractor were also driven by fourteen-year-olds if the usual drivers were not available, which happened quite often. I had always wanted to be an engine-driver but this was not quite what I had in mind. It was to be another five years before I got on to a real engine.

I had waved goodbye to teacher Mrs Walker at Haltwhistle Council School in the Spring of 1942 and was very attracted to all these Caterpillar and International tractors, so I started working at the Featherstone Stone Bridge sawmill run by the HGTP department of the Ministry of Supply (Home Grown Timber Production). At first the work was clearing the forest debris into heaps and firing these, just like November the Fifth, and it was some time before I got near the tractors.

For me the first job with the wheeled tractors was to pull the long winch ropes out, hitch them to the trees and walk back to the tractor while the driver hauled the tree up to the top of the hill with the tractor winch. Then I unhooked the rope from the tree, pulled it back down to the next tree and repeated the process. I covered miles in the first week of winching. We were never lucky enough to have a level winching job, the Caterpillars could reach those trees to haul them with their own chains.

We always worked on the steeper slopes, which were great for pulling the rope down and hooking on, it was the climb back up to the top to get the hook for the next tree that knocked the puff out of us. Sometimes we tied a piece of rope on to the tail of the hauled tree which pulled us up - that was a dangerous place to be if the rope snapped, as sometimes happened, but we still had to climb up the length of the tree at the top. Occasionally we took turns between rope pulling and driving, but usually youngsters pulled the rope, older men stayed on the tractor and they were quite welcome to it in hard frosty weather. On tractors without a cab (all of them at that time) drivers were really cold, whereas rope pullers were always warmed up with the exercise.

On one occasion, we asked if we could be on 'piecework' rates hauling the wood out, and a price was agreed. We worked like Trojans that first week, clearing a large area of the Crow Wood, and kept Gladys going with her measuring tape and note book, working out how many cubic feet we had pulled. Unfortunately, we were too successful. If we had been paid what we had made, they said it would amount to much more than an adult earned, so to avoid any labour troubles, they had to cancel the piece-work arrangement. I rather thought we had been done; they said we had to go much slower so we were back to the nineteen shillings and sixpence per week rate. What a 'lift' that would have been if we had been paid the piece rate. According to our measuring, it would have amounted to about five pounds, so if that had become known, the men would have been upset.

After winching we were often moved round to different jobs with various tractors, when I had a try on most of them, unofficially; we had to keep a look out for the manager and some big-headed fitters from Chopwell workshops who chased us young'uns off the driving seats, although sometimes nobody was available to drive the machines, so some of us occasionally did the men's jobs.

The loco at Hallbankhead was almost a shared machine. Whoever was nearest the engine, out of the three lads who were all under sixteen, jumped on to the seat and drove it. We tried piece-work with the train at one time. Jackey Bromley and myself, with a small D2 Caterpillar tractor, pulled a lot of trees up to the track side at the loading point. This we did on overtime one evening when the regular D2 driver had gone home and we made everything ready, we thought, for the next day — piece-work day. Unfortunately, the long length of the trees caused the trucks to overbalance and we had an awful job trying to get these trees to the top end of the line. We did get some timber up but when we reckoned up what we had made, somebody suggested it might be better to forget about piece-work or we might have to pay the firm, not the other way round.

The tracks for the loco and trucks were in a terrible state and derailments certainly held us back. Whoever laid the line must have thrown a few planks down as sleepers and nailed the rails to them. These were merely laid on the grass and no attempt at packing or levelling appeared to have been tried. The two-ton loco squashed the sparse sleepers and lines down into the soft, damp areas and we could only hope it stayed on the rails because when it derailed, the wheels invariably sank into the soft ground until the axles were resting on the rail tops. Then it was a matter of levers and blocks to get it back up again and on to the lines. After that sort of railway work I was not so sure I wanted to be an engine-driver, certainly not on narrow-gauge lines if they were all like this.

One foreign forestry worker said that he had worked on European railways and knew all about them, but what he knew best was how to derail a loco with all four wheels off and beyond the tracks. Normal practice on the line was to leave loco and trucks up at the top, or west end, of the line so that in the morning we could 'bump start' the diesel engine down the incline - if we were lucky. The starting handle was at an awkward height for us and was designed for adults to swing, and even then it was a two-man job; much easier to bump start it, if possible. To be sure of a good run-down, we raised the top, first lengths of rail off the ground on planks and sloped the second lengths down to the rails at field level. A little more power and speed was needed to get the loco up the slope and on to the more level length of rail where the loco was parked for the night; a length of plank across the track served as a buffer at the rail-ends.

On this particular day the work had been held up and if we had taken the loco up to the top end at finishing time, we would have been too late to catch our lift home but if we left it at the lower end we could go by the Park Burn Wood and catch our lift beyond the village. We were dreading the thought of trying to start the engine with the handle in the morning at the bottom end, when along came our foreign worker who offered to take the loco up as he was going that way. This was the man who previously was sent to align the curved rails into the wood and had canted the track the wrong way, causing the trucks and loco to derail.

We thought we would take a chance and allow him to take the loco. We explained how he would have to charge up the slope at the far end and how to stop the engine and park it for the night. We uncoupled the trucks in case he derailed them on the way and watched him go, then turned and ran to catch our lift from the Park Village road-end. The next morning we could hardly believe our eyes; the loco was beyond the rail ends with all four wheels dug into some planks lying in the grass; we could only guess what speed he must have been doing to clear the end of the line; it was at least a nine-inch drop to the planks.

We lowered the raised and inclined part of the track down to the field level and after re-railing the loco on temporary lines and an awkward handle start, we managed to get the engine back on to its working

A Simplex narrow-gauge loco at Threlkeld Quarry and Mine Museum, almost identical to the Featherstone Ruston Hornsby engine of the 1940s. (J Parker, jnr)

rails again. Apparently the foreign driver had charged up the slope, jumped on the sanding pedals, which he thought were foot brakes, and in the panic of the moment, completely forgot about the full throttle or about de-clutch. The plank across the rail-ends had not been designed to stop a two-ton loco at speed and had little effect; some of the other foreign workers thought he had only been a ticket-collector, anyway.

There was less bother with the short runs of rail at the sawmill, used for moving timber from the saw benches to the stockpiles, but they had no heavy loco to squash the rails into the ground; they were pushed by hand, although there was a steam engine in the mill, albeit a stationary one.

Circular saws on the two rack benches and some smaller benches were driven by a portable steam engine and boiler. When I first saw this outfit in the 1940s, it reminded me of the similar boiler and sawmill used at Wydoncleughside in the early 1930s. Set up near the roadside, it was used by Sproaty when he extracted timber from the Wydon Cleugh Wood.

Horses were used for pulling trees to the saw bench; when that job was done these same horses were employed to haul this portable steam engine and sawmill over to the Black Wood (G.678631) at Redpath.

At that time trees were extracted from the Tootup Wood by a recently acquired Fordson tractor and winch and across the fields by the horses to the sawmill in the Black Wood. A young Willie Hall, who lived nearby on Redpath Bank, started working for Mr Sproat at Tootup and he soon noticed that Sproaty, who had always worked with horses, was nervous of the 'new-fangled' tractor.

Willie laughed when he saw Sproaty moving the tractor and shouting "Whoa, Whoa" when he wanted his mechanical horse to stop, then he would jump off and the driverless tractor carried on. Willie would race after the tractor, bring it back and promptly be sacked by Sproaty.

In the beginning Willie set off homewards when this happened, but Sproaty would run after him and tell him to get back to work, as if nothing had happened. After a few days Willie took no notice when he got the sack, often twice a day, and just carried on. If anything went wrong Willie got the blame. He got so used to it that when ever he saw Sproaty trotting down Currys Hill towards him in Tootup Wood, he jumped off the tractor and ran towards him, knowing that something had gone wrong and he was about to get the sack - again. This action on Willie's part seemed to disconcert the advancing Sproaty and the sackings gradually tailed off.

Willie reckoned later that he must have been the most sacked man in the country and he rather missed these bizarre affairs when they ceased, but at least he kept his tractor job until the wood was finished.

The horses extracted the trees in the Black Wood to the sawmill until this wood was cleared, when the next move was to Painsdale Burn Wood (G.688641), behind the Spital Farm.

That was the first time I had seen 'slippers' used on steep hills. These irons, like shallow carriers, were laid on the road and the road wheels of the portable steam engine pushed or pulled on to them. The metal slippers were fixed to the framework of the machine by strong chains, so that the wheels couldn't overrun them, but had to remain on the slipper, and these skidded along the road carrying the load with them.

The horses dragged them downhill easily but were wise enough to stop, without being told, when they reached level ground. If they had four slippers, they acted as four-wheeled brakes and were essential on the steepest places, such as Redpath Bank.

I lost track of this most economical, mobile sawmill after that Painsdale job in 1936 but a few years later I saw a much more confident Mr Sproat on his tractor, at the site of the new maternity hospital in Haltwhistle. He had set up the winch tractor against the bowling-green wall and almost on the back lane of Banks Terrace; the long winch-rope was fastened up into the tall trees that had to be removed from the area. Once the roots were chopped through, the winch pulled the trees away from the general hospital building and into the gap between the hospital and the bowling-green wall. After cutting to length the trees were removed from the site and the builders moved in.

Cutting up trees in the form of bark slabs provided plenty of fuel for the portable steam-boilers, which kept up the steam pressure.

This method was used at Featherstone and it raised enough steam to run the saws and the later pendulum cross-cut saw that was added to the range, and run separately from a wooden pulley fitted to the steam-engine crankshaft.

Portable steam engine as used for glasshouse heating at Oakland Nurseries, Melkridge. Only the steam-raising boiler was needed at that time and as far as is known the engine part was not used. This engine was similar to Sproaty's and the Featherstone wood burners. (K Rickerby)

The pulley was made in a very short time by stacking 12 boards of one-inch thickness, in a laminated fashion, bolting them together then cutting the board-ends off to form a roughly circular block. This was bolted to the flywheel and with the steam engine going was turned out true, almost as good as turning on a wood-lathe. It only needed the belt fitting and the pendulum saw was complete and running.

The other saw benches were driven by belt from the opposite side flywheel pulley.

Using waterwheels, windmills, wood-fired boilers etc., always seems to me like living off the land; that, and the thought of getting something for nowt, gives a great feeling of satisfaction.

When the Featherstone timber job came to an end, the Caterpillars once more departed from the district, and the 'new road' D8 we remembered, as well as the requisitioned lorries from Haltwhistle, never came back after the war; perhaps they stayed in some corner of a foreign field...

I also moved on from Featherstone and had a spell learning more about joiner work at Isaac Hetherington's, a place where I had spent a lot of my spare time during my school days. After about six months, I returned to the Redpath farm that I had known since my earliest days but then I got itchy feet and moved to Cumberland doing similar work. From there I took a much bigger leap down the country to Shropshire, or Salop as they called it, where I managed to take on a job which officially was land work, together with another part-time job involving mechanical work, which I was most interested in at that time.

Labour was not available in the quantities most firms required then and they took on part-time workers where full-timers were not available. This suited me; I had my official address and land work for part of the time or as required and I could take any of the other part-time jobs that I fancied. They were long days but I gained experience in pipe-fitting, mechanics and electrics, and for a short spell at a Shrewsbury works, I formed thick copper steam pipes into a set shape and profile so often that I could do the job blindfolded, hence the short spell. At that time there was plenty of work for everybody.

An Elswick cycle, bought new at TP Bell's in Carlisle, was my local transport in those days, and after covering much of Cumberland with it, I took it with me on the train to Shropshire but didn't visit all the industrial sites and quarries that I had planned. Working long hours rather confined these trips to Sundays only and the few places I did visit, I had to imagine how they operated during the week. The Elswick covered many miles round sites and between different jobs; it was a very good buy.

After a while I got itchy feet again and moved to the South Leicestershire area, where I managed to get two jobs for a short time. Part of this work was an evening shift in a machine-tool works which really opened my eyes to what engineering was all about. It was certainly in a higher class to the mechanicing I had done up to that time. I was lucky enough to make the acquaintance of a man who worked with jet engines at Lutterworth. He showed me round these newfangled gadgets. From a soundproof room it was possible to see the engine working, but I would rather have watched the LNER steam pistons and connecting rods on the locos flashing past on the Great Central Railway. The jets seemed so simple and there was not much to see, only a spinning centre piece. Workers in the neighbouring factory often hoped that the jet would run out of fuel, so that they could have a quieter time with only their own hammering to listen to.

About that time, two of us began travelling into Leicester on Saturday evenings, but not on our bikes; it was much handier on the train and we did not have to leave Leicester Central until the last train at about 11pm. We always bought fish and chips on the way to the station and I thought it might be a good idea to wait where the loco pulled up when it came into the station from Nottingam. The smell of fish and chips was much appreciated by the driver and fireman and they reckoned they were the best they had ever tasted. Well, one thing led to another and we often bought extra suppers for the engine men and watched them eat them as we rode on the footplate to our station. They were not always the same men each time but they seemed to know about the free fish and chips. It was not the cleanest of places for our best clothes when the coal dust blew

The type of loco trespassed upon on the illicit Saturday night trips in the 1940s.

about on what I thought was a rather crude 'battleship' of an engine, although it was a great firebox for throwing chip-papers into. I always thought these late local trains were hauled by J39 locos, which were more suited to goods trains, but these could have been J38s; I didn't know the difference at the time. One thing I did find out was that I could hit the engine firebox with coal more accurately than I fired at those Haltwhistle gasworks retorts in my schooldays - and get a few sparks and hot cinders out of the chimney too, although this was allowed only on rainy nights, because of the danger of causing line-side fires.

The train ran through, past Rugby, and terminated at Woodford & Hinton shed, much further past our station than we thought when we had the mad notion of riding right through to Woodford. We found out later that after dodging past the staff at Woodford, we had a long walk back, and daylight came long before we got back to our lodge; it must have been almost 20 miles. Time still didn't mean much to me but I was beginning to think we must be mad - young and daft - to go on these one-way rail trips. We had been in three counties that night: Leicestershire, Warwickshire and Northamptonshire.

This long trek didn't cure my itchy feet and soon I was off to the Birmingham area, where I managed to do mechanicing, building, plumbing, electrical and even returned to the timber trade for a short time. I was trying to gain experience in as many different trades as possible, although I couldn't imagine at the time of what use well-boring would be to me, but drilling holes into Welsh hills was interesting enough while it lasted.

Some of the jobs were just plain money-making; a friend and I offered to do some night-time combine harvesting while the weather held fine, intending to work for a few hours, until the promised relief took over at midnight. We set off with the Massey-Harris harvester, one of us driving while the other bagged the grain. We took turns with the two jobs and worked with lights when darkness came and rather

lost track of time; neither of us had a watch but we would know it was home-time when the relief arrived.

Unfortunately, the sun was well above the leafy Warwickshire horizon when the relief finally appeared, having overslept. We had yet to sleep and eat and also go to work as normal. Mr Evans, the early rising farmer - grinned from ear to ear when he saw all these acres of wheat harvested - and gave us a generous tip; that certainly wakened us up but I never volunteered for all-night harvesting again. Eventually the call of home became too strong to resist and I returned to Haltwhistle in 1950.

The Elswick bike disappeared about six months before I left and was probably stolen and used by

Combine harvesting at a more sociable hour. (J Caldwell)

South Birmingham tearaways. I paid five pounds for a Sunbeam 350cc 1929-model motor bike which I used for two weeks for travelling to work, but I was often so frozen when I got there that I bought another pedal cycle for ten pounds, just to keep warm, and vowed I would never buy another motor-bike and I never have. With proper clothing I might not have been so cold, but at least I got my fiver back when I sold the Sunbeam. I left the latest push-bike with a friend and came back north with a suitcase only. There would be plenty of bikes available in Haltwhistle.

After a walk round the town and district, I saw that the How Burn valley had been filled up, the rock formation removed and the new road completed as far west as Town Foot; most of the surplus rock was spread out on the wide grass verge of the new road (G.727640) between How Burn and Melkridge.

After many years, a use was found for these large rocks. They were all carted to Plenmeller and dumped down the two pit shafts, on top of all the other various fillings that were put down there over the years; a waste of good rock filling. These shafts are now capped over below surface level with a very thick layer of reinforced concrete; which was all that was required in the first place, but the powers that be said the filling was there to support the capping. I would be surprised if over 700 feet of filling has not settled somewhat since the cap was fitted. There is now very little to indicate that the shafts ever existed.

The two 775-feet deep Plenmeller shafts are now concreted over under this yard area, which is about 460 feet above sea level. (D Hunter)

Chapter Ten

Underground at Morwood Colliery 1958: l-r: Alan Hewitson, Allen Cowan, Tommy Rogerson. (A Hewitson)

A great deal of pioneering work has been carried out in this district; new and interesting forms of working are still being created.

Few people could have envisaged the establishment of the Blue Streak rocket testing station near Spadeadam (G.615705), (G.596719) & (G.620744), just over the county boundary, which provided employment from the late 1950s for many Haltwhistle workers. They can look back on this period with satisfaction, knowing that the main Blue Streak stage worked when tested, which is more than can be said for many of the foreign stages of the launchings at Woomera, Australia.

In the last few years of the twentieth century, a system of mining on a large scale began, in the form of open-cast workings on Plenmeller Fell. New temporary mountains were formed and wide, deep holes excavated; never again will we see the sites

Opencast operations on Plenmeller Fell are over 500 feet higher than the earlier 1910 pityard and coal is transported by conveyor belt from left-hand building down to railside screening plant near Melkridge. (D Hunter)

Were it not for the conveyor belt fitted down the fell, and coal hoppers near the railway west of Melkridge, which will be gone by late 1999, a traveller along the Tyne Valley would not imagine that the area had any connection with coal mining. However, a person standing on the Beacon Top, as I did when I returned to the district in 1950, near the present-day Plenmeller open-cast site and looking northwards, could imagine what would be seen underground if a 'lid' could be lifted off the surrounding countryside.

The nearest mine, Plenmeller, at the bottom of the hill and to the west, was started in about 1910, with shafts sinking down 775 feet from the surface to 27 inches of coal at 340 feet below sea level. Underground operations did not start until 1916. A block of about ten acres of solid coal was left for support round the shafts with roadways cut through to the different working districts.

By 1918, on the east side, mining reached a point under the west end of Plenmeller village; a reduction of the seam to 25 inches was a disappointment, however, a rise of 60 feet in 800 yards from the

of the old Rockhouse Fell drifts or the Plainmellor pit of the 1850s, so often confused with the 1910 Plenmeller pit, down in the valley. The 1850s pit used water-power from a dam on the fell stream to work a pump some distance to the east from the main entrance and had an engine-house and pump to the south. These sites will be swallowed up by the open-cast mining area which includes most of the older pits on the fell.

Mechanical shovels used on the open-cast site put the old faithful 10RBs in the shade, although I believe that some 10RBs are still at work elsewhere on open-cast sites. The massive dump trucks working on Rockhouse probably could run over the old two-ton Bedford tippers without noticing them.

In the 1970s, a small open-cast site to the north of Melkridge won coal from the outcrop of the Blackett and Melkridge seam. Later, a Scottish firm, Leslie Duncan, opencasted the outcrop of the Ventners Hall and Wallshields seams; these sites were on a very much smaller scale than the RJ Budge Plenmeller Fell operation.

Conveyor belt and line-side screens near Melkridge. (D Hunter)

shaft by G.712632 helped the water drainage and avoided the need for pumping to the shaft sumps. The seam also rose 80 feet south-eastwards to Sandyford Rigg (G.710625) at 600 yards from the shaft. The southerly incline to Warren House rose 60 feet in 800 yards at G.706620.

To the south-west the seam dipped 30 feet in 500 yards in the direction of Coanwood. This inclination of the seam, dipping to the north-west, was opposed to the south-east dips in the mines on the north side of the whin dyke, except for the south-west part of South Tyne Colliery which tended to dip to the west, as in Plenmeller. By 1921 mining had progressed to the south-east, under the lower lake (G.712623) and the lake wood, to a fault of 21 feet almost under Hirst Top (G 718623), where the seam had reduced to 22 inches and was not advanced beyond the fault.

In a westerly direction the Wydon dip, which never progressed under Wydon land, won coal towards the whin dyke which passes under Bellister Castle, then along a line parallel with the dyke to Bellister Bank bottom (G.698628) and towards Broomhouse Farm (G.698626). The lowest point in this area was 75 feet below the shaft bottom in just over 900 yards and was abandoned in 1927. At about the same time mining had reached a point to the east (G.719625), under the first valley up the Whitfield road beyond the village, which carries the outflow from the bottom lake; here the seam had reduced in thickness to 21 inches and was abandoned.

By 1928 the most southerly point was reached at G.705611, 450 yards to the east of Park Burn waterfalls with a 160 feet rise in 1900 yards from the shaft. 1930 saw the operations stopped under the Broomhouse railway cutting (G.693622), 1500 yards from the shaft and at 110 feet below the shaft bottom. At 450 feet below sea level and about 930 feet below the LNER Alston Railway lines, this appears to have been the lowest point in the mine.

The final year, 1932, saw the last of the coal mined from Lynn Shield area (G.699615) at 1650 yards and 90 feet lower than the shaft. That year, beyond the block left under Plenmeller village, the coal was mined out under East Farm and just beyond to under G.717631, 1500 yards from the shaft, over 600 feet down from the surface and with a coal seam thickness of 22 inches. Underground operations were then halted and the mine closed.

The area of working covered approximately 450 acres in Plenmeller mine; had the Company driven through the whin dyke towards Haltwhistle, they could have mined a further 90 acres belonging to Unthank Estate; this was always assumed to be their original intention. The distance from the shaft bottom to the centre of the River Tyne near the present Kilfrost factory and the limit of the Unthank Estate was 1400 yards at the most and would have been a fairly level main haul across the inclined seam, through the dyke and to the shaft.

With the south-east dipping seam on the north of the whin dyke and the south-east rising seam on the south side, at a point 200 yards east of Bellister Castle (G.703630) and 750 feet below the surface, the two opposed slopes in the seams appear to be level with one another; the dyke could have been breached here for an easy haulage road. As it happened, these 90 acres were acquired by South Tyne Colliery and probably lengthened the life of that mine by three years.

Unfortunately this resulted in both mines closing about the same time and throwing hundreds of men and boys out of work. As can be imagined, this was a terrible disaster for the area. If these 90 acres could have been worked from Plenmeller it would have softened the unemployment blow by spreading the closures over five or six years.

Back on the Beacon Top, and looking to the north-east of Haltwhistle, the Burn Gorge can be seen twisting northwards towards the Roman Wall in the middle distance. It is in the lower part of this

Haltwhistle Area Coalfields

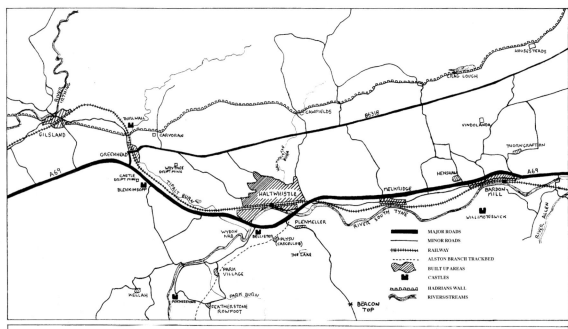

MAJOR ROADS
MINOR ROADS
RAILWAY
ALSTON BRANCH TRACKBED
BUILT UP AREAS
CASTLES
HADRIANS WALL
RIVERS/STREAMS

Key to Mine Workings

A - Plenmeller   H - Morwood
B - South Tyne   I - Castle
C - Bayldon   J - Wrytree
D - Blackett   K - Fell End
E - Ramshawfield   L - Byron
F - Bardon Mill   M - Gap Shields
G - Birkshaw   N - Roachburn

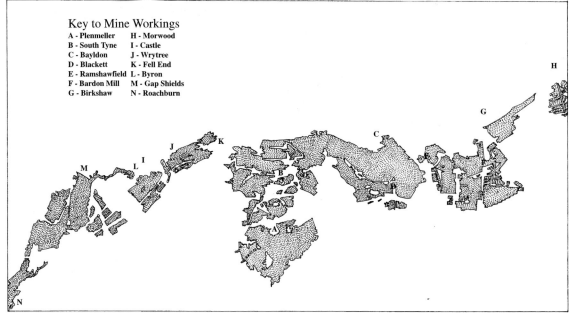

Haltwhistle Area Coalfields

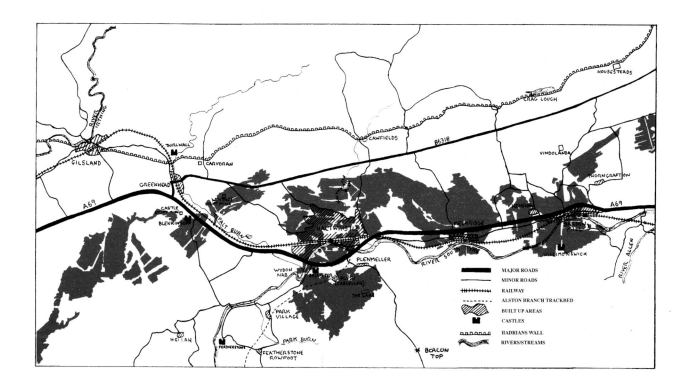

valley that the main shaft of the later South Tyne Colliery was sunk over 500 feet to the coal seam, mainly to win the coal in the low side areas. An appreciable amount of coal was won towards the outcrops on the north side.

Unlike Plenmeller, which didn't work through the faults to the fell-top mines, the South Tyne seam had been mined at the outcrops in several places, in the 1800s and earlier, but the mine at the Burn, or Fell Chimney (G.710657), and the drift lower down the burn (G.708648), had penetrated furthest into the lower part of the seam. After coal-drawing started from the shaft, the main winnings appear to have been to the west along the north side of Haltwhistle, south-east towards Town Foot, and north-east towards Folding Steads and Hollin Crags (G.716648) to join the older workings.

Under the Shield Hill area (G.714650) a long east-to-west pillar of coal was left in about 1908 for some unknown reason; strangely but fortunately this pillar is directly below the reservoir tank built over 60 years later for the town's water supply. By 1912 the coal had been mined to a fault on this east side and then progressed through into Hollin Crag area.

To the north-west, mining advanced towards Comb Hill and had reached G.696653, under a field to the south of Glendale by 1918 and further west to a limit at G.693653 by 1919.

Further progress was made towards the upper Comb Hill area during 1921, and the Hardriggs area limit at G.689648 was reached, 2100 yards from the shaft-foot and rising about 60 feet, and at the same time Birchfieldgate district was abandoned at G.691648, about 2000 yards inbye.

Across the Tyne in the Bellister Haughs area, coal formerly intended for Plenmeller was mined from 1925, and workings reached the whin dyke (G.708633) about 1929 and continued east to the Alston railway embankment (G.709633) and west to near Bellister Castle (G.700631) by 1930.

Coal under the paint works (G.700638) was removed by 1928; further south under the railway arches and into the corner of the target field (G.711635) the coal was mined out by 1931. Under the present-day Mill Bridge on the 1950s by-pass, coal was mined out in a south-east direction in 1929 and continued to a point under the present Seldom Seen caravan site and the river bed at G.719638, 1400 yards, and about 120 feet lower than the shaft bottom. This was about 200 feet below sea level, and was abandoned in 1931.

The most southerly point under Wydon Nab or the 'Sheep Hills' (G.696629) was also the furthest in-bye at 2300 yards and the lowest at 360 feet below the shaft bottom. This was about 450 feet below sea level and was worked out by 1930. Interestingly, the seam at this point is about the same level as the Plenmeller seam, through the whin dyke at this south-western end. Another driving in South Tyne pit was made to the north-west under the position of the199 Haltwhistle by-pass and bridge, between Tipalt Foot and River House at G.697632, but it too was abandoned in 1931; this part is about 800 feet below the surface.

To the north-east, workings were advanced up to a 21-feet fault towards Oakey Knowe (G.717644) and then abandoned in 1931. No further districts were developed after early 1931 and the mine closed. In the 1970s I heard of some borings taking place near Oakey Knowe, apparently intended to bore into the South Tyne seam at about 300 feet down. It is not known where they found their information but I reckoned the only coal they would find at that depth was the 12 inch or thereabouts of the small seam well above the South Tyne main seam. This 12 inches of coal was showing in the old fan-drift further up the burn from the South Tyne pit yard. When it was pointed out that South Tyne shaft was over 500 feet deep, and that the seam dipped away from the shaft bottom to under Oakey Knowe, which was situated on high ground and consequently they could expect to bore down about 700 feet or more before finding the thicker coal, the operation was abandoned.

Perhaps if they had bored further to the east, they could have drilled into the untouched block of coal between the Blackett west-side fault and the South Tyne east-side fault. This part of the seam should be nearer the surface but what fun any future developers would have with the Planning Department, trying to get that coal out.

Much of the north-eastern part of the South Tyne Colliery seam, which adjoined the Melkridge/ Blackett seam, was mined earlier, but South Tyne went as far as their eastern boundary under High Plantation beyond Hollin Crag at G.724653, and about 1800 yards from the shaft. It is interesting to note that apart from the 90 acres of coal mined out from the Bellister Haughs/Alston Arches area, South Tyne Colliery Co. avoided mining under Unthank Estate land on the north side of the Tyne, which includes the block of untouched coal stretching eastwards from Oakey Knowe to the Blackett area.

The whole area of the seam which included South Tyne workings, extended to about 1450 acres, covering a much larger area than did Plenmeller pit. South Tyne was worked for over a century, first by small mining concerns at the outcrops and by larger mechanised companies later on. I remember hearing about the old baskets and sledges found in old workings behind Moor Cottages (G.718659), and at the time it was thought these particular items were last used in the early 1800s. Coincidentally, an ex-Bevin Boy acquaintance was trained at a colliery in South Wales, where most of the coal was extracted from the low-seam faces in baskets, as late as the 1940s. I believe many of the 'boys' transferred to the armed forces for an easier life.

Looking again from the Beacon Top to the north and slightly to the east, a large strip down the south-facing side of the valley, over one-and-a-half miles wide with Melkridge at the centre bottom, has been almost completely mined out underground, apart from the usual coal pillars left for support.

A small pit heap (G.738649) south-west of Bayldon Farm (G.700653) is the only sign of any underground activity in this area.

Here again the outcrop was worked at an early date, but more modern concerns such as at the Bayldon Drift (G.740656) in 1899 and Melkridge top shaft (G.739655) mined to the fault on the east side and then south, avoiding Bayldon Farm, by 1900.

More drifting, including Dene House (G.733656) was carried out along the outcrop to the west and up to the South Tyne boundary from 1900 to 1905. The shaft at the small pit heap was sunk in about 1850 to a 25-inch-thick coal seam at a depth of 165 feet and had main roads away from the shaft bottom across the incline to the north-east and south-west for fairly level haulage. High-side coal was worked down to these main ways and raised in the cage to the surface.

Some 1400 yards lower down from the shaft, a water-level drift (G.743639) was put in under the old main highway about 1875, entering the coal seam under the Horse Close area at G.743643. A furnace shaft to the west of the drift foot at G.742643 was sunk for ventilation, and coal extraction was carried out on the rise to a south-east - north-west

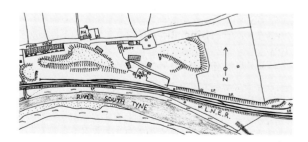

Plan of Blackett Colliery yard. (R Hunter)

fault on the west side and to a fault on the east side on a line from Hardriding up to the east of Bayldon Farm.

Most of this free-draining area was mined out by about 1908 and with the new low-level shaft at G.744638 sunk down to the seam and a main way driven uphill to the bottom of the furnace shaft area, the 32 inch thick coal either side of this new roadway could be won and the water pumped out at the new shaft.

Workings were extended east under Carrsgate (G.748640) 450 yards from the shaft by 1912 and to the fault against Hardriding new road cross-roads (G.753643) at about 1200 yards, terminating there in 1913.

To the west of the shaft, all the coal to the north of the railway line was mined out and by 1915 a point was reached just over the railway from the site of the plate-layer's cottage along Greengate Lane (G.732637). This is near the screening plant built for Plenmeller open-cast coal. To the north-west a large area was mined out up to 1917, about 400 yards wide and 1500 yards long, between a line from the plate-layer's cottage almost to Middle Plantation (G.724647) on the south-west side, and to the north-west fault running from the old drift-bottom area up to the outcrop.

Meanwhile, in 1912 drivings were made under the Tyne into the Shankfoot area, to work the coal up to the east - west whin dyke (G.743634). This area was worked until about 1916 but was abandoned when the main pumps in the low-side borehole at G.750636 failed and flooded these workings.

The mine was much reduced in output after that trouble but carried on high-side mining on a smaller scale. Although the low areas of the mine were flooded, most of the districts to the north of Melkridge were still self-draining, via the shaft overflow and the pump borehole outlet.

I was told of the explosive charges dropped down this borehole to split the pumps apart so that the water could rise up unrestricted and drain out into the river. This water ran out of the borehole continuously until about the 1960s when it suddenly dried up. Evidently, with workings in Bardon Mill progressing westward towards the Blackett, the water found its way through the strata, adding to Bardon Mill water problems, and had to be pumped via their boreholes.

The drift under the highway at Melkridge was still workable, and coal, probably gained by splitting pillars left in the earlier workings, was brought out until about 1927.

This area of coal from the valley bottom to the outcrop amounted to about 1100 acres.

To the east of Blackett workings and over the Hardriding fault, a small mine was started by the Nancarrows at Ramshawfield in the 1930s. The coal seam was, on average, about 22 inches thick; they had worked west to the Hardriding fault at G.752648, by 1944, and then worked east, avoiding the farm, to under G.755648 by 1954.

A new drift, on Shawhead Fell, was driven and screens erected at G.758654; from this drift the coal was worked west towards the outcrop at G.755654 in 1979 and a further westerly section was taken to G.754453 by 1980. The mine closed shortly after this. The thickness of coal varied but as far as I know was never more than 28 inches and was of very good quality.

The area of the next mine to the east would perhaps better be seen from another vantage-point such as the fell road above Penpeugh (G.766620) - what a grand name that is; I believe it means a sheep-fold near a quarry.

Looking north from this point and slightly to the right, the site of the Bardon Mill Colliery or the Henshaw Drift (G.774646) on the north side of the

River Tyne has now been landscaped and covered by a playing field.

George Pepperal & Co. put the drift down from the end of the redundant Birkshaw aerial rope-way terminal and utilised this building for his screening plant and hoppers. The coal was found at a depth of 300 feet under Brockalee Hill, and mining reached Cragside to the east (G.774649) by 1943 and Henshaw to the west (G.766646) by 1948.

Huntercrook (G.764652) to the north west was reached by 1951 and Shawhead Hill (G.759652) by 1954. Mining advanced northwards and almost to Low Fogridge, touched the smaller old Henshaw Colliery workings at G.772655 and to the east reached the Birkshaw fault (G.776655) by 1958. An old shaft on the west side of this point is 214 feet deep to 28 inches of coal.

A limit just north of Bardon Mill at G.780650 and up against the fault was abandoned by 1957. The seam here was reckoned to be about sea level.

The most easterly workings were under G.785640 between Partridge Nest Farm and Beltingham village. This was also about sea level and 1650 yards in a direct line from the drift bottom, though the actual travelling road was nearer 2400 yards. This did not proceed further after 1967 but some coal 25 inches thick, under the Tyne (G.784642) and directly in line with the river, was mined out during 1972 and 1973, then the district was abandoned.

To the south, the coal was worked off to the east-west whin dyke in a westerly direction almost to Haughstrother Wood at G.765635, 1800 yards from the drift, by 1970. A block of coal was left under Willimontswick Castle (G.770636).

West-side coal was worked out to the Hardriding fault, almost to Hardriding new road cross-roads (G.756744) and against Ramshawfield old workings, (G.756647) and was then abandoned in 1972. The mine was closed shortly afterwards. Bardon Mill was, in area, one of the smaller local mines but even so, it was double the size of Plenmeller at about 900 acres.

An interesting comparison between Bardon Mill and Plenmeller pits is in the time taken to mine the coal. Both pits seem to have progressed at about the same

Willimontswick Castle from the south. (S Blackburn)

rate; Plenmeller taking about 15 years to cover approximately 450 acres and Bardon Mill taking just over 30 years to work about 900 acres.

The seams were not greatly different, although Bardon Mill used the long-wall mining system more extensively in preference to the bord-and-pillars of earlier pits, therefore the output per acre would be more than at Plenmeller.

The next pit on the list is well sign-posted. It is the Birkshaw Mine which stretched under Barcombe Hill (G.778664), with its monument on top.

Birkshaw is another pit which has been mined at various times from the north-side outcrop; the coal seam, with a maximum thickness of 20 inches, is separated from the Bardon Mill seam by a fault. The Birkshaw seam is about 120 feet higher than the Bardon Mill coal at the fault. Some parts of the coal were worked in 1893 at G.779665; in 1896 at G.785667, and between West Morwood and the Thorngrafton road at G.789668 in 1903; this last drift evidently closing, then reopening again in 1920.

Coal under the monument was worked in 1929, and later, to the south-east at G.782658 in 1933 where the coal was only 14 inches thick. Between West End Town and Birkshaw House some 20-inches-thick coal was worked in 1937 at G.778656. The final date given is 1940 at G.774650, under what was often described as 'the windy corner' overlooking the Chineley Burn gorge; the area of this mine is roughly 200 acres.

To the east and out of sight from our viewing point on the south side of the river, Morwood Colliery, at G.796674, opened about 1941, was driven into the outcrop of an extension of the Birkshaw seam by Robson Brothers of Haltwhistle and had a straightforward layout of a dip, which was extended as the mine developed, until by 1960 it was about 1200 yards in and dipped over 600 feet in that distance. The coal varied between 22 inches and 28 inches; the area of the mine probably covered about 200 acres and closed in 1960.

All that remains of Morwood Colliery: the electrical transformer house and the road embankment on the shore of Grindon Lough. (D Hunter)

About a mile to the south and east of Morwood, and just out of the Haltwhistle Rural District, two mines worked; one at Whitechapel (G.810648) and a smaller pit at Winnetley (G.814658). Whitechapel was the earlier mine. Originally starting as a lead mine was drifted in at water level in a northerly direction from an opening just above the Newcastle-to-Carlisle main road.

Unexpectedly, after a few hundred yards they struck a coal seam, so the miners applied to the land-owner to change the contract wording from lead to coal mining. This was not allowed and they had to abandon the mine, whereupon the landlord started his own colliery from the same drift.

Coal was transported over the road, river and fields to railway sidings near Morralee Farm, in skips taken along by steel ropes on an aerial flight, which was unusual in that the towers were made from timber instead of the usual steel.

The coal skips were sometimes used as unofficial passenger-carrying vehicles if anybody, including the manager, needed to travel between the mine and the railway loading point. One of the drawbacks to

Underground at Morwood Colliery 1958

Top left: Bob Robie. (A Hewitson)
Top right: l-r: Tommy Rogerson, Ronnie Pape, Bob Robie, Willie Roberts. A hydraulic prop in the right foreground keeps the very low roof up; the coal seam can be seen on the left. (A Hewitson)
Bottom right: l-r: Harry Stalker, Frank Barren (with 'batteries' for shot putting), Allen Cowan - in the days before smoking was forbidden underground. (A Hewitson)

this mode of transport was the weather. If a violent rain-storm occurred when riders were on the flight they just had to put up with it; at other times the machinery sometimes stopped or broke down; accidentally and otherwise.

I can just remember seeing rows of silent and empty railway trucks near the main line after Whitechapel Mine closed in the 1930s; golden-coloured iron water continued to flow from the drift and along the roadside ditch for many years until it was piped during road improvements in the late 1980s. The pollution will still be there but out of sight.

Winnetley Mine was situated almost a mile higher up the hill in a north-easterly direction from Whitechapel, and I believe it was started in the late 1930s or early 1940s. I was informed that the main driving to the north-west was about 800 yards long, with workings on either side in good quality coal; in parts the thickness reduced to as low as 12 inches although it was usually nearer 24 inches. As the drift progressed the dip became more pronounced to the north, a reverse inclination to adjacent mines and a similar cant to Plenmeller coal seam.

The dip was abandoned and a new driving started, on the left-hand side nearer the drift mouth and in the direction of the old Whitechapel workings. The coal was up to 24 inches and also good quality.

As Whitechapel was self-draining and lower than Winnetley, it was thought that there would be a great saving in pumping costs if the water could be 'lost' into the old workings. Unfortunately the new driving holed into a large runner of water and the pumps were unable to cope with this flood. To carry on with the new dip would have required new pipes and pumps, a larger electric transformer and many new tram lines. The water was so corrosive that the webs of the tram rails, the pipes and the pumps were quickly eaten away. Also, there were some stepped faults in the seam.

A few more months of driving might have reached the old workings and got rid of this water but it was decided to close the mine about 1963.

Apart from a few small drifts, these last two coal mines appear to have been the last on the east side of the Haltwhistle coalfield. Through a fault east of Winnetley, the lead veins and witherite mines were more evident at one time, Settlingstones being the last to close, in the 1960s.

The above-mentioned coal mines all worked the Little Limestone seam; a few miles to the North the Ventners Hall Colliery worked the Thirlwell Seam, where, according to some notes I have, coal was first raised in October 1938, increasing to about 300 tons per day by the 1940s. In the last year of operation under the NCB, the output was approximately 46,000 tons.

By 1956, the dip had progressed in a southerly direction, over 1000 yards from the surface, to a point almost under the Pont Gallon Burn, near 'the dipper', (G 728698), just short of the later Hilda exploration drift building. This lowest underground position, dipping 300 feet from the drift mouth, was still 600 feet above sea level with 250 feet of cover up to the surface. The fault encountered under the Pont Gallon Burn was penetrated but it was found that the coal seam was not in line with the Ventners seam. When new manager Joe Braidy examined the strata on the other side of the fault, he estimated the coal to be at least 20 feet lower down, but for some reason this work was not carried forward and the place was abandoned.

The sulphur content of the coal at Ventners was not very welcome but it was found that most of the sulphur was in the top part of the seam, so overhead cutters were installed and the top six inches of coal left up. This helped to keep a rather poor roof in place until they won the better coal, leaving behind the high-sulphur coal.

206

After mining to the west to G.720699 up to 1958, the mine closed in February 1959; leaving us with the thought that if they had progressed through the fault, perhaps the coal found there would have been sulphur-free and of better quality; the adjacent Wallshields Mine didn't seem to have the sulphur content, and was it not through that same fault?

Wallshields Mine, further west from Ventners Hall, and in the same seam but through a fault, has had more than one opening and closing but I have mislaid any details of underground workings that I had, which were not complete in any case. ,

In the nearest working underground mine, at Castle Drift, Blenkinsopp (G.666645) a new coal 'god' for this district by the name of 'Shearer' has been working for some time.

It was what we always wanted to see in the pit but never thought it would happen here; a pity it did not come a few years earlier so that at least I could have seen it working.

Although coal and its machinery put me out of action, I had hoped to go back to mining and do a bit more fitting, but health mechanics at the local centre said: 'No', so I'll forgo mining and carry on listening, observing and scribbling.

The shearer is working in a recent development of a mine that was started about 1700 and by the 1830s was one of the reasons for pushing ahead with the building of the railway from Carlisle to Greenhead to move Blenkinsopp coal to western markets more quickly than could be achieved on the poor roads of the time.

It is ironic that the laying of the railway, urged on by Lord Carlisle, lessee of Blenkinsopp Mine, came too late for him to derive much benefit from it; he lost the mine lease to another group in 1835.

Workings in the 1700s at this mine, where the seam dips at one-in-six towards the south-east, appear to

The elegant drift mouth of 1842 with the much later 1990s conveyor belt bringing coal to the surface. (C Parker)

have been managed on the 'water-level system' in the high end of the seam, as at Blackett mine, where the water drained out without resort to pumping. This drainage level seems to have been at the 400 feet above-sea-level mark at Blenkinsopp.

Towards the end of the 1700s, a shaft was sunk near Quarry House (G.667644) to pump the water down to about 300 feet above sea level. This enabled a large area of coal, up to six feet thick, to be worked, perhaps 250 yards wide by almost one mile long, with water self-draining back to the shaft. One engineer advocated the removal of the waterwheel from the nearby cornmill and diversion of the water-race for driving the pump in the Quarry shaft. Steam pumps were used at this shaft and it is doubtful whether the corn-mill wheel was ever moved for pumping. There is now no sign of the mill or machinery which stood very near Wydoncleughside road-end, although there is still a paved channel, which appears to be the tail-race as well as the 1700s water level outflow; this runs under the railway to the Tipalt alongside the old College Farm road.

The block of coal was worked out to the west at water level from the shaft bottom and also via a drift (G.666645), dipping into this coal at an incline suitable for horse-and-pony hauling to the surface.

During Lord Carlisle's 21-year lease of the colliery up to 1834, almost all of the coal appears to have been hauled out of the horse drift from the western area of this tract of coal; the shaft perhaps was used only for pumping and raising its own steam-boiler fuel after the driving at water level was completed in a south-westerly direction.

When the area on the high side of the water level worked out in 1840, a new shaft (G.670643) was sunk near Small Burn, over 300 feet down to coal at 90 feet above sea level. The new shaft pumps drained another mile-long area of a much greater width than previously. At the same time the stone-arched Castle drift, date-stoned 1842, was built down through the older workings to reach the new reserves of coal which the Small Burn shaft would eventually drain out.

A furnace shaft (G.664644) was sunk to the workings near the bottom of the new drift, for ventilation; the top of the shaft with its turreted brick-wall barrier is situated in the grounds in front of the Castle. The 80 feet deep shaft was fitted with ladders inside a scaffolding tower up to the surface and maintained as an emergency escape exit in a later mining period; an air-control door and electric fan were fitted near the shaft-foot.

Coal from the Castle drift was dispatched, in the 1840s, over rails which formed a branch line through Bank Foot from Blenkinsopp Crossings (G.660651) on the recently completed Newcastle-and-Carlisle railway, or was tipped into the nearby coke ovens (G.662647) at Bank Foot.

A lease for the Blenkinsopp Colliery was taken over in 1835 by Messrs. Foster & Dixon, with another firm, Blenkinsopp Coal and Lime Co., involved in

some way. The sinking of the Small Burn shaft and the new Castle drift were carried out after Lord Carlisle's lease expired; the ten horses and ponies used previously would no longer be required to haul coals to the surface: the new, steeper, drift required a mechanical hauler.

Some smaller ponies were still used for the in-bye areas which were worked to the fault and then up the high side towards the Gap Shields district, about one-and-a-half miles from the exit.

The Small Burn shaft was thought by some people to have been a furnace shaft, as at Melkridge, but there was no sign of clinker or ash when the shaft bottom was cleaned out.

A round sump-hole was found to one side of the shaft bottom - so it must have been used as intended, as a pumping shaft and also for raising coal, mined out towards the new drift and in the other direction up to the fault on the east side.

Grassed-over ash-heaps on the surface near the shaft were not from a furnace-shaft fire, but from the boiler that was needed for the winding gear and the pumps.

As the coal round this shaft became exhausted a new driving was made in the side of the shaft about 180 feet from the surface and in a north-easterly direction to tap the coal reserves on the other side of the fault. This was driven through almost at water level, the water running back to a new pumping sump near the side of the shaft.

Foul air from the new driving was extracted up the sealed timber duct, formed by a cord framework up the north side of the shaft; this connected to a divided-off part of the driving to form the return airway. Middle 'brattishing' for a return airway would be needed until the driving broke through rock into the higher section of the seam and joined up with previous workings driven up from the Blenkinsopp seam.

Holes in the shaft side at the new driving height seem to confirm that this was how ventilation was achieved and would explain the almost 180 degree entry to the onset position to avoid the air passage to the cord duct; the return entry also served to divert any runaway sets from plunging straight down the lower part of the shaft from this mid-shaft onset position.

Water was lifted from the new sump at the side of the shaft either by another pump rodding from bank or a branch/bracket fixed to the existing rod. There were some short steep drivings, under G.672646, from Blenkinsopp to this higher seam on the north side between Small Burn shaft and Wrytree Farm, confirming that earlier Blenkinsopp miners had worked up into the higher seam from the shaft-bottom level. When these higher workings joined the new driving, a shorter and easier route was then achieved for the coal to the shaft.

Blenkinsopp Colliery closed about 1889; water built up and overflowed at the shaft near the 400 feet-above-sea-level mark, and remained so for over 45 years except for a short-lived pumping experiment in the 1930s.

A small drift mine (G.678652) at Fell End worked much of the northside coal in the 1930s and 40s and progressed towards the old South Tyne workings. A second drift, (G685657), into the same working, was put down east of Fell End Farm and near the Peatsteel Crags.

The hauler house had the most ingenious 'motor car haulage' system I had ever seen: an old Morris or Austin car engine, gearbox and chassis, minus the rear axle, had been bolted down to four heavy blocks and the prop-shaft connected to the hand-winding axle of a wire-rope hauler which had also been fixed down in line with the drift mouth.

I presumed that this was the first four-speed, petrol-driven hauler of its kind in the district, if not the whole country; another example of Haltwhistle ingenuity.

I was wrong: a year or two later I discovered at Mossy Dryden's drift (G.735604), on Rockhouse Fell, which has since been open-cast mined, a similar petrol hauler which must have been fitted many years before the Fell End model and probably was the prototype.

Evidently the creator of this hauler also had constructed his own locomotive by removing the road wheels from another car, after which he fitted flanged wheels underneath to run on the long tub line to his screens.

Although I never saw this 'patent' I was informed by Jake Johnson that the loco was made from an Overlander car, which was regarded as being much superior to ordinary cars. What a sight it must have been from a distance to see a man, driving through the heather, in what looked like an open-topped car, trailing a set of coal tubs.

What happened to this wonderful machine after Mossy closed the mine is a matter for speculation; had it survived the intervening 60 years since it ran on Rockhouse Fell it would be an historic museum piece. I don't suppose it came to light during open-casting.

Similar motor-car locos of three-feet gauge were used on the line between the aluminium works and the dams at Fort William in Scotland and were capable of speeds over 20mph. Perhaps they copied the idea from the Haltwhistle creation.

If only I had been there to see and take part in the performance. They must have had to drag the old hauler cars across that rough fell land. The haulage machines were in position and used while the drifts were sunk, before tramways were laid over to the roads.

Our gang of young intrepid prospectors went down Peatsteel drift and into the Fell End workings one Sunday in the early 1940s; our only light was from candles. We followed the underground tramway part of the way, but the draught caused by a natural air flow kept blowing out the candles - at least, we thought it was an air flow. Older miners had told us how they judged the state of the air by the brightness of a naked light - 'if the light goes out, get out of the place' was one piece of advice they gave; we decided to come out. It was reassuring to see the square of daylight from down in the mine. Later, we had a lot of explaining to do as to how our school clothes came to be in such a mess…

It was the sight of vapour clouds coming out of Peatsteel crags that attracted us to this drift in the first place; we thought it was caused by wind blowing into the west-facing Fell End drift mouth and through the mine to exit on the hill-top.

A tramway carried coal from Peatsteel drift over the hill and on to screens and hoppers near the Military Road at G.687654.

As schoolboys we were allowed to go potato-picking instead of to lessons during the 1939-45 war; one of the farms visited was Fell End when Alan Maughan farmed there. We often fired rotten spuds into the old pit shaft, never dreaming that someday all the rubbish would be to clear out for an air shaft to Wrytree mine. Work on the potato field finished at 3pm, when we all trooped across the road to help old Joe the banksman for an hour at Fell End Drift.

The electrically driven hauler pulled three tubs of coal up to the surface and then a large wooden stop block was laid across the track behind them. The tubs then were uncoupled singly and allowed to run back to the block where the tub was slewed round 90 degrees on a steel flat sheet in line with a short length of track to the 'cowp'. The loaded tub was tipped on to its side and the coal then spread down the sloping grid to screen out small coal.

There was no machinery other than the hauler but there was a fair supply of hand shovels lying about - although not enough for our gang. Sometimes Joe couldn't get near his tubs because of 'tattie pickers' so he just let us get on with it. Travellers on the road past the pit would think it was a big concern judging by the number of staff attending to the coal tubs at that time of day.

In a very short time the empties were sent back down the pit and a grinning Joe said that if we kept this up we would "stow them off with empties" at the pit-bottom.

Within a minute or so one of the 'tattie pickers' got a fright when a heavy hammer head on the end of an angle bracket, pulled by a long wire from the pit bottom, shot upwards and crashed down on to a steel plate three times. The 'tattie picker' had been standing almost over this hammer when it shot upwards; he thought his end had come but it was only Joe's signal to start hauling another set from the pit.

At a later date, screening operations were moved further east from Fell End to a new position to take coal from Peatsteel drift.

Fell End Mine, which had been run by a group of working miners under the name of Thompson & Partners at one time, closed in the early 1950s.

Over at Angerton Bank Foot, in the late 1950s, GR Wardle & Co. erected screens and hoppers (G.663645) and drifted into the old Blenkinsopp seam outcrop workings. About that time I remember Albany Dodd saying that he hoped the new pit would be a success but he was sure the drift was in the wrong place; he and his brother thought they had taken - officially or otherwise - as much as they could out of the same area many years before but via the old Castle drift.

Fan-house for Wrytree Mine built over old Fell End shaft, also used as an emergency exit. (J Parker, jnr)

As it happened, this first drift was comparatively short-lived and a drift at a much higher level was opened out; it was referred to as 'up the field' (G.660645). A long tramline was needed and this was carried over a deep ravine on Jake Johnson's bridge construction and referred to as 'Tay Bridge No. 3'; a steel tube and girder structure and solidly welded together, it was an improvement on Bouch's design. A large generator, about 140kva powered by a Mirrlees diesel engine, provided power for the mine. This machine had been installed at 'HMS Nuthatch' (Anthorn) Fleet Air Arm Station before installation at Bank Foot.

When the mine worked out, operations were moved over the valley to the Wrytree side, where in 1966 another drift (G.674649) was put down to the seam and worked to the outcrop before mining through older workings from Small Burn shaft.

The Mirrlees generator was moved to Wrytree and worked there until mains electricity was installed, then it was uprooted again and taken to the stone-arched Castle drift to provide power for development work. The new submersible electric pumps in Small Burn shaft lowered the water enough for this work to go ahead.

The old shaft (G.677653) in the Fell End field was again brought into use as an upcast for ventilation with fresh air entering down Wrytree drift.

During the many years that this shaft was out of use, it had been used as a dumping ground and was partly filled with farming debris plus a few rotten potatoes from the 1940s 'tattie pickers'. Many of the animals that expired in the area were thrown down this shaft; it saved digging a hole.

The biggest problem seemed to be all the old fencing wire mixed in with the dead bodies. Clearing that 80 feet-deep shaft was a dreadful job for anyone to have to do, but when it was cleared and a fan fitted, the air circulation was much improved.

Two stalwarts, Sid Smith and Ivan Short, worked for many weeks in the old mine workings at the bottom of the shaft, laboriously digging out and removing the rotting flesh and bones of cattle, sheep and other farm casualties. The only transport possible underground was a wheelbarrow with Sid on the handles and Ivan hauling, with one end of a rope over his shoulder and the other end fixed to the barrow.

The author stands between conveyor facebelt gearhead and the six-feet-thick coal seam at Wrytree Colliery. (J Parker, jnr)

211

Stones fallen from the roof made negotiating the barrow past them a very awkward and dangerous operation, but by far the worst aspect of the job was the terrible smell which clung to their clothes and resulted in the other miners giving them a very wide berth. Sid and Ivan had to put up with some good-natured banter from the others and often had uncomplimentary titles bestowed on them such as 'stinkers,' 'hummers', etc. , but Ivan threatened to come near them if they didn't shut up.

Various methods were tried to empty the shaft before it was finally cleared and a fan fitted; many years later Ivan reckoned he could still remember that awful smell. The shaft was fitted with ladders as an emergency escape route and a hand hauler capable of lifting a stretcher to the surface.

It was said that the old Blenkinsopp mine was sold by auction at one time, possibly in the 1880s; this would not be the actual mine but the closing-down sale of tools, rails, gear. The main buyer, Thompson of Naworth, moved this material nearer to Greenhead and concentrated on the Byron drift (G.660647) to work towards, and join up with, his Roachburn mine under Denton Fell.

Byron mine workings extended over two miles to number seven shaft, beyond the Gap Shields coal area under G.627628 on Denton Fell, just out of the Haltwhistle Rural District and over the county boundary, before joining up with Roachburn pit below G.629624 approx. It was interesting to find that when the two mines joined up the surveying had been miscalculated and the drivings missed one another by 11 yards, the same measurement as the thickness of the adjacent whin dyke which had been holed through below G.625617.

Fortunately, miscalculations seem to be very rare and a more recent survey carried out for the joining up between Castle drift and Wrytree proved just how good surveyors can be with their measurements. Surveying on the surface, say, from Greenhead to Haltwhistle would be straightforward enough but to pinpoint a spot in the bottom of one mine and survey out to bank and over to the other and down to the bottom of that hole and reckon how far apart they are from the starting point - well, to my mind, that is marvellous, especially when they are 'spot on'; the changes of angles and levels over that distance must seem never-ending.

From the in-bye end of Byron drift the mine worked to the south-west and mined through the whin dyke below (G.654622), exploring under the north side field, named Lowdy, on Highside Farm at Kellah; that district was abandoned due to the poor quality coal found there as well as the long haul to the surface.

It was unfortunate in one way that Byron joined into Roachburn. The Byron workings were abandoned because of flooding when the Back Stands Pond burst into Roachburn pit in 1908, resulting in the death of three miners. Conversely, the joining was very fortunate for many of the Roachburn miners who were cut off by the flood and would have been trapped had they not been able to escape via number seven shaft.

After closure, in about 1890, Blenkinsopp pit was left to fill up with water, and as this overflowed at Small Burn shaft it polluted the Tipalt with iron water from there down to the Tyne and beyond. There were complaints from the local estate about the water spoiling their fishing.

What was thought to be the best solution was to pipe this water from the mine shaft down Holme Field to the confluence of the Small Burn and the Tipalt (G.673641), taking the polluted water over the former in an aqueduct and into a specially dug ditch to a second aqueduct over the Hole House Burn (G.678638).

In the 1930s there were two separate pipelines down the Holme Field, coming together at the Small Burn aqueduct; both had water running in them and had

Early view of Byron Mine looking west. Right of the boiler chimneys are Milestone Cottages (once a schoolhouse), demolished to make way for the Greenhead by-pass in the 1980s. Greenhead signal box and crossing are in the middle distance, with the colliery spur from the main Newcastle-to-Carlisle line leading from them. (Haltwhistle Times)

many gratings in concrete covers spaced down the field. Originally, one line was from Small Burn shaft and the other from the Byron pit area.

The late Jack Lattimer knew which drainpipe was from the Small Burn shaft because he did quite a lot of digging round about this pit-head area.

Bill and Albany Dodd mined out many of the coal pillars in the Castle drift but much of the low side coal they had their eyes on was under water. I remember that they were blamed for causing subsidence and breaching Captain Joicy's swimming

pool in the Castle grounds above their underground workings.

It was thought that if the outlet from Small Burn shaft could be lowered, it would drain a large area below 'Dodd's level' as it was known then, and they could mine coal well away from the Castle swimming pool area. That was when Jack Lattimer carried out a mammoth task with his pick, spade and shovel. He dug a ditch, close to 100 yards long, away from the shaft, almost level-bottomed, to the Tipalt river and put a hole through the side of the cast-iron shaft-tubbing lining.

Under the bridges of Spital. The nearest is the newer road bridge of the 1950s replacing the older cast-iron girder bridge; the stone arch is the railway bridge of the 1800s. The little-used 1816 road bridge is furthest upstream and just hidden by overhanging willow trees. The large cast-iron pipes from Small Burn shaft are on the right of the riverbed. The modern cattle passageway is between the pipe and the bridge abutments. (D Hunter)

It was said that this ditch lowered the water to about 17 feet below the top of the shaft and as the shaft collar was at ground level, it must have been an extraordinarily deep ditch. It was the talk of the district while he was digging; I have heard references to it for almost 60 years. Some of this drain was made from wooden planks, probably because there were no pipes to hand. It was successful in that it drained a large area of the mine workings, over 30 yards wide and for almost a mile across the one-in-six slope of the coal seam.

Both of the Holme Field drains had water running in them when I looked through the gratings in the early 1930s, so Jack's howking probably took place after that time; his new drain directed the pit water directly into the Tipalt and by-passed the field drains.

Prior to Jack's excavations, the irony water ran over the Small Burn and Hole House Burn aqueducts into

a long ditch, parallel with the railway, which carried this water close to the Spital Farm, where it entered a large cast-iron pipe in the river to take it under the railway and road bridges, then along the riverside field, in pipes with many inspection chambers, to a point behind the present Haltwhistle cricket pavilion where it flowed out into the Tipalt (G.692634).

It was always assumed that the Coulson or Joicey families arranged for the excavation of this long drain, because they owned both the Blenkinsopp Hall and Castle estates. The offending water issued from the Castle mine which was owned by the landlord and leased to the mining groups in the 1800s, so perhaps they were responsible for any later pollution. The lessees had all departed and probably none of the costs for the drain could be recovered from them in any case.

After flowing on this route for about one-and-a-half miles some of the particles settled, although the pollution was not cured, merely passed on to someone else. Water at the Tipalt foot still was an iron-brown colour.

By the 1930s the aqueducts had collapsed and the length of the Tipalt up to Small Burn returned to the brown colour as before. Were two new aqueducts to be built, water could still run in this ditch to the Spital Farm; this would avoid polluting the Tipalt for over a mile.

Polluted water has run from the mine since the 1880s, so however it is directed, it cannot be any worse but has a chance to be much better.

By what I remember, iron water in the 1930s didn't affect the fish; we always managed a good catch with a long wooden cane and a length of wire.

Iron-water pollution is as nothing compared to pesticides, herbicides, organo-phosphates, and silage-liquid infiltration; the fish we remember are missing from the rivers, although migratory fish

Haltwhistle from the west; the Tipalt flowing into the Tyne on right. (S Blackburn)

reach their spawning grounds when the rivers are in flood.

It was interesting to discover that although some of the metal pipes have gone from under the Spital Bridge, there is now another useful construction under there in the form of a fenced concrete causeway between the field on the Spital side of the railway, under both bridges and into the fields on the cricket field side of the road. This will have ended the hazardous business of trying to move cattle and sheep across the now busier A69 road and deserves recognition for its contribution to road safety.

Almost the same operation as Jack's ditch digging was carried out in the 1960s by Jake Johnson with a Whitlock mechanical digger. However, Jake's work was intended as a temporary measure to carry water from new pump outlets. Instead of using pipes, or wooden planks as Jack had done, he confiscated a load of used oil-drums, removed the tops and bottoms, and laid them end to end in his ditch and covered them over. If Jack Lattimer had seen this drain he would have said, "Tin drains - ay man, whaat next?" but I think he would have approved of

the ease and speed of the digger. Jack dug for weeks; Jake started and finished his drain in little more than a day.

For some unknown reason, the long iron-water ditch over in the wood opposite Redpath road-end (G.682635) was well filled with coke, presumably thrown from the railway, and this helped to keep our Redpath house fire going for years. All we had to do was to shovel it into sacks, carry it over the railway and up the hill. There was no black soot off the coke to block that massive chimney. This good-sized coke was perhaps intended for steel works or blast furnaces and the trucks could have been derailed near Redpath road-end. Whatever happened, the fuel was very welcome at our fireplace.

A great disappointment to me was the fact that while gathering coke, I found a real, full-size locomotive chimney in the ditch and wasn't allowed to take it home; I couldn't budge it but I thought Father might help. It would have made a great garden ornament. 40 years later I searched for this prize but couldn't find it. In the 1930s, a huge Scots pine on the roadside was blown over and stretched over the road and the railway: Father told me that a train from Carlisle had crashed through the top branches of it, which would account for the chimney in the ditch. The large upturned stump of this tree remained sticking up on the side of the road near 'the dirty lonnen' (G.680637) for almost 30 years until the road was widened between Cross Bank, Haltwhistle and Bankfoot.

In recent years, pumping has cleared the water flowing into the Tipalt; it is nothing like the brown water I remember running off the collapsed Small Burn aqueduct in the 1930s; this was about the time the capping was removed from the overflowing Small Burn shaft and it was pumped down to test the rate of flow of the incoming water, which was done by hanging a pump in the shaft and lowering it as the water was pumped out. The pumps were powered by diesel-engined generators standing alongside the railway fence; the iniquitous pump men, so described by some locals, were frowned upon because they actually worked on Sundays.

Schoolteacher Spencer Bell's cottage, originally the old pit offices, was in close proximity to the engines, which roared non-stop for twenty-four hours a day, and for many weeks.

From what I remember, he didn't complain but was interested to see how far they could get the water down, which I believe was 105 feet. This was the depth where the pump output matched the incoming water flow; consequently the water level couldn't be lowered any further with the pumping set they used but this was sufficient to give the rate of flow in the feeder.

I heard at the time of this operation that the pumps were on trial and that the suppliers believed them to be capable of draining the entire pit. The operators realised early on that the pumps were not 'high head' types and weren't capable of draining a 300 feet-deep shaft; it was thought that perhaps the suppliers received no payment out of this venture

and that therefore fuel and labour were the only expenses incurred. I have no details of the company which had this work done but they, no doubt, learned what they wanted to know.

If this figure of 105 feet down is correct, then the water would be lowered to 307 feet above sea level, about the same height as Bardon Mill pit yard surface level.

Cecil Crowe of Haltwhistle was one of the engine-men at Small Burn, and 20 years later, after he retired, he could still remember without any notes the figures involved in the job: gallons per hour, depth pumped to, how long taken and fuel used. Evidently he was very interested in his work, as Mr Teasdale was at the Plenmeller winder. In the 1940s, Cecil looked after the steam boiler at Ventners Hall pit, some years after the Small Burn job.

More pumping was carried out at the shaft in the 1960s to lower the water level in the old Blenkinsopp coal workings. This made it possible to mine out coal pillars which previously had been underwater. Later, much more powerful submersible pumps were installed to lower the water level still further.

All of the old standing water in Blenkinsopp has been pumped out for some years now; the working area in late 1995, about a mile in from the surface, was kept clear of water by stepped pumping back up the dip and via Small Burn shaft to the surface. It was planned that this mine water would flow into lagoons on the surface in an effort to improve the quality of the outflow into the Tipalt.

300 feet below and somewhere under these lagoons and the Tipalt, I recall seeing a long timber barrier, apparently to seal off the area round the Small Burn shaft bottom from the workings towards the College Farm. These heavy, square timber uprights appeared to have been fitted tightly together in a fairly dry state and had expanded later. The joints between these timbers were noticeably swelled out due to expansion.

A messy build-up on the water inlet of one of the submersible pumps suspended down Smallburn shaft. Greystonedale Sumo pump was similar but on a much smaller scale than the Smallburn pumps. (J Parker, jnr)

Another reason for a solid timber wall in this position could have been as a support for the river bed which is almost exactly in line with the timbering. At the high end of this stopping, a large metal pipe about eight inches diameter and valve were fitted through the timber but were very corroded; the remains of the valve and most of the pipe had fallen away; some water flowed through the opening, perhaps the same amount as a two-inch pipe would pass.

Plans show that the bed of the river had been 'clay puddled' above this area about the same time as the stopping, no doubt to try to prevent river water inflow to the workings. This work was done in the 1870s or 80s, although I have no specific details. We can only assume that the barrier below and the puddling above was to contain some flooding.

Circumstances are reversed now regarding the water; because of irony water still issuing from Roachburn and Denton Fell via the Byron drift, suspect water flowing from the borehole (G.663671) near Cairny Croft from the Thirlwall strata and the iron water from Barron House Colliery workings (G.649674) the Tipalt is probably polluting Blenkinsopp pit water.

Pollution in the Tipalt was noticed as long ago as the 1600s when Camden, a contemporary writer, described the Tipalt as 'this ale-coloured stream'.

In the Castle drift an east-west whin-dyke fault crosses below the shearer working area. Many years ago, I recall seeing what I thought was the dyke, on the surface in the Glencune Valley (G.659625), near Maughan's House and what we called Clattering Ford. I later found that this outcropping rock formation lined up with the position of the dyke in Roachburn mine, where it was 11 yards wide, and also with the Wydon Nab/Bellister Castle/Unthank position of the dyke. This dyke separated the Plenmeller and South Tyne workings at Haltwhistle.

I recall Tommy Penrose, who lived at Redpath Cottage in the early 30s and later worked at Ventners Hall pit, saying to farmer Hugh Edgar that if we went to the "rooard end" where Redpath road joined Pinkins Cleugh road (G.670626), we would be

Preparing a pump for reinstalling in the 300-feet-deep shaft. The pump is suspended from the many lengths of steel pipes in the background, the long power cables being clipped to the pipes as they were lowered down. The shaft opening is between the two steel girders on the left, not a very good place to drop a spanner. Working on the pump are: l-r: the author, Alan Mulgrove, Noel Dixon, Jack Wanless. (J Parker, jnr)

standing on a whin dyke. Hugh had always told us young'uns to keep off stone dykes as they were liable to fall on to us, and then he would have to rebuild them, so that statement of Tommy's about standing on a dyke puzzled me for a long time.

Years later I realised he had meant that at the road junction, we would be standing on the surface directly above the vertical seam, or dyke, of whin stone that separates the horizontal coal and other seams, and it looks as if he was right about the position, but we wondered how he had known. Apparently, he had worked for a short time in Byron pit when they mined through the whin dyke into an area to the north of Highside Farm just before the flooding, so he must have calculated the position of the dyke from the plans.

There was little variation between the depth of coal seams either side of the dyke when it was holed through in Roachburn mine; at South Tyne and Plenmeller pits the inclinations of the seams are opposed although they appear to be level with each other in one part, to the north of Plenmeller shaft.

I understand that the coal on the far side of the dyke in Blenkinsopp seems to be out of line in a few places, which may present some problems in the development of new faces. The hungry shearer will not be far behind them; this beast seems to gobble up coal seams at an enormous rate. Developments progress so quickly at Blenkinsopp that I can barely keep up with them. The breaching of the whin dyke has been brought up to date three times up to the present, so the above information about progress could be well out of date by the time this is printed.

In the 1930s we were warned to keep away from old workings in the Fairystairs Wood (G.675635) and the shaft further west on the Redpath Fell/Hole House Fell boundary. I never found the Fairystairs workings but on the fell (G.674633) there seemed to be a small shaft covered over with trunks of trees, near the outcrop of a small seam above the Blenkinsopp coal.

An interesting thing to me is that, at the time of writing this part of the notes, the shearer was working below an area which we regarded as our own personal playground 60 years ago. It would have seemed unbelievable had we been told that some day men would work all those hundreds of feet below us on Redpath Fell. We would have thought they were daft.

Victor Fleming and Louie Scott, South Tyne Colliery workers. (M Henderson)

218

Chapter Eleven

Joe Henderson's delivery van. As well as running a shop on Castle Hill, he was a photographer and took many of the photos in this book. (M Henderson)

Industry still progresses in this part of the world with an ever-greater range of processes.

In the nineteenth and much of the twentieth century, Haltwhistle's traditional small industries included at least three blacksmiths' forges in the town at Market Place, Kiln End behind Wapping, and on Park Road near where the fire station of the 1950s and 60s was situated. This last one was out in the country before the town spread westward. There

were many village forges manned mainly by smiths who worked out of Haltwhistle on one or two set days per week.

Many of the ancestors of old-established builders in the district arrived with the building of the railway eastwards from Carlisle. John Watson of Scotsfield Terrace, who still carries on the monumental work started so long ago and is also our local undertaker, tells us that his forbears came from the West and stayed on. Interestingly, Watsons still have railway connections; their workshop was one of the early waiting rooms on the Haltwhistle railway station and was moved to Scotsfield Terrace when new rooms were built on the station platforms in the early 1900s.

My mother's family also came at that time, but I have no details of events in the 1800s other than that my great grandfather Hunter returned to the West and brought back a bride to Haltwhistle. I don't think he found fault with the local belles, he had had his eye on his intended for many years, waiting for a secure job. He found one at Haltwhistle as the district mason on the Newcastle and Carlisle Railway and stayed on.

I was fortunate in having a very informative Aunt Connie, bless her, with a good memory for most things, or much of our family history would have been lost now. She was a generation out in her reckoning, though, because it must have been her grandfather, not mine as she said, who came with the railway builders and stayed on as the district mason; her father followed in his footsteps and into the same mason's job. He also brought a bride from the West; one of the Milburns from Corby. They must have thought Cumberland brides were special in our family; two of my uncles also married girls from the Carlisle area.

Strangely, none of my five able-bodied uncles on Mother's side took up building work; most of them started at the new pits at South Tyne and Plenmeller, then went into army service during the 1914-18 war. Of uncles, numbers six and seven, one unfortunately died early on from some ailment; the other had an accident with a pair of scissors which always hung on a nail at the end of the wooden mantlepiece. During one of their boisterous games, the scissors were dislodged and young Arthur happened to be in the wrong place; sadly, he lost his sight.

Luckily, and most unusually, for the remaining family of six sons and two daughters, they were all united again after the First World War; most families lost somebody in that war. Some of them returned to mining and worked alongside men who also came from the West when many of the Solway coast mines closed.

Arthur attended the blind school at an early age and learned the usual trade for blind persons then, making wicker baskets, upholstery work, etc. If a safer hook had been fitted in the mantlepiece and not just a plain nail, everything would have been much different for him, but he had a long industrious life and he always amazed us younger ones, when he came visiting us during the wartime, with his ability to guide us through the blacked-out town in the darkness. He only visited the town occasionally but he remembered all the streets and corners he had seen during his few early years before the accident, but he often cursed the Council men who installed new steel tubular signs on the edge of the pavements just where he would walk smack into them; he had a stick but was always wary of tripping up other walkers if he waved it in front of him. He seemed to know where all the gas lamp standards were and if we entered a narrow lane he often warned us to beware of a car, etc. standing nearby; he said he noticed a difference in the echoes between the buildings, on the same lines as a submarine using Sonar equipment. We detected nothing, not even the echoes.

He was a clever card and domino player and any uninformed gamblers who thought he might be easy pickings were welcomed by Arthur's smile but often departed with empty pockets. His large pocket watch on a chain was taken out of his waistcoat pocket if he wanted to know the time, the silver lid opened, the pointers felt with his forefinger, the watch closed and back into his pocket before we got a chance to glance at it, the action was so quick.

On the other side of the family, I was told that my father's grandfather worked on the building of Lambley Viaduct (G.676584), but that is all I know about him. Apart from farming, the family always seems to have worked with stone except for my father's two brothers who became gamekeepers; I have a ten-inch flat sharpening-stone carved: J.P. 1863, whatever that suggests.

I remember many of the names of people who came from Mount Sorrel, Leicestershire, such as Shuttlewood, Underwood, Pougher and Abbotts among others, to work at local quarries, mainly at Walltown. Some, such as Mr Pougher, came and worked in the area as long ago as 1905. Strangely enough, our local quarries now are all closed but Mount Sorrel is still a very large quarrying operation and luckily is clear of any Roman ornaments that might restrict expansion.

People have always moved round the country for work and my father was no exception; before he married, he worked stone in the West Highlands of Scotland and later in Maine, USA , not because of any shortage of work locally, but because of the much higher earnings further afield. Of the USA earnings, he reckoned he could pay a return sea passage, work from spring to autumn, come home when severe frosts stopped all stonework, do nothing through the winter if he chose to, then have plenty of cash to pay another spring passage to the USA and start again. Of course, he worked throughout the winter here and presumably accumulated more money but unfortunately invested it in the railways, which at the time never paid much dividend. He had a saying, "Invest in the Englishman's thirst and you can't go wrong". As youngsters, we thought he must own half a brewery somewhere but he left mainly British Transport Commission shares and we only received what he had put in all those years ago.

Birkett is another name from the West country so they too probably came when the railway was built.

In the early part of the 1900s many Haltwhistle houses were built by contractors from outside the district, such as Strachans from Tyneside who worked on much of East View, Dale Street, Lorne

Park Road houses built by Sweets of Haltwhistle.

Street and possibly built the Council Offices, although C Sweet, a local contractor, put up the Park Road council houses in the 1920s. He must have been a pioneer in building houses with breeze blocks.

I believe these blocks were all made on site, the small coke filling coming from the gasworks and various steam boilers, some sand from the riverside, and a small amount of cement from further afield.

These Park Road house walls were all built of breeze blocks above the damp-course level; the outside half was cement roughcast, the inside plastered, and they have stood the test of time. Unfortunately, some of the ash and unburnt coal content is still active after 70 years and occasionally small bumps appear under the plaster on internal walls.

Watsons built much of the West End housing west of the Metal Bridge, but of stone and brick, not breeze blocks, which, after Sweets contract, do not seem to have been used for outside walls, although they are still used for inside partition walls.

In the late 1940s the local council shared out the building of new council houses in Westlands, and I gather that Birketts, Watsons, Barwick Bros, Johnsons and possibly Murray and Irving all built some of them.

Later schemes seemed to be dominated by Barwick Bros., but Benson and Dixon who had worked for Barwick Bros. started their own business in about 1950 from a small depot behind the Spotted Cow Inn and expanded from there to carry out contracts over a very wide area.

Since the demise of the Rural District Councils and the centralisation of most activities at Hexham, the awarding of any repair works to council properties seemed to go to Hexham workers and nothing much to local building firms. At one time the local council were responsible for water supply, sewerage, refuse collecting and all the property repairs, but now all of these services have been dispersed elsewhere, with the result that everything costs much more because of extra transporting, administration, etc.; even most of the councillors themselves cost so much more, now that they can claim payment. The ratepayers, or whatever fancy description they give everyone now, have to pay.

It always seems to be a strange state of affairs when a councillor from one end of Tynedale can vote on events at the other end and often be unfamiliar with that part of the district. Perhaps some day we will turn full circle and the now mainly ineffectual Parish Councils will run our own local affairs once again.

Of the local builders, Scarths now seem to be the main builder of new houses in the area but I am sure they, like other local firms, will have an uphill struggle trying to win Council work.

JP's sharpening stone of the 1860s.

The longest-serving joiners and contractors who could do cartwrighting were probably Henry Clark & Son in the Tyneside sawmill and later at Park Road. Isaac Hetherington & Son also worked from this Park Road joiner's shop before Clarks moved up there.

Bettons had a workshop almost in the middle of the town behind what was the old off-licence premises, which were demolished to widen Main Street. This joiner's shop stood for many years after the off-licence was removed and the street widened, but it too was pulled down and shops built on the site. Bettons then moved into a building near the old fire-station on Park Road and carried on working from this upstairs workshop.

Not far from there, in about 1950, Hylton Seymour set up in business in joinery and contracting in a large wooden workshop, then later moved to what had been a 1930s fish-and-chip shop off Park Road.

Further west at Smallburn, Walton Brown had a joiner's shop and builder's yard.

This was where a 'Wall of Death' was constructed. Most people thought W Brown and the Ridleys must be mad, of course, but that did not stop them going ahead and building the open-topped circular 'tub', consisting of wooden planks set upright in a circle of some 20-feet diameter and 15 feet high, with inside run-up ramps round the bottom edge.

The motor-bike riders quickly mastered the trick of setting off in the bottom and up the inside of the cylinder, weaving from top to bottom or as they said, from side to side of the track.

They reckoned it was as easy and almost the same as riding along the road...Hmm.

These 'Walls of Death' became popular throughout the country after that time; the Smallburn 'Wall', together with a second model, were moved further afield. The operators thought it was a very profitable

The 'Wall of Death' as built by Walton Brown at Smallburn, Greenhead, with a Ridley and his motorbike speeding around inside the large tub-like structure. This was probably where the term 'flat out' came from; the bikes were almost horizontal and 90 degrees from the vertical when at top speed. (W Treloar)

venture in the early days. It was an extraordinary sideline for a joiner.

Another joiner with an unusual hobby was JG Dixon, who in the 1930s had a workshop behind Norman's butcher's shop in Westgate; the workshop was rather short for working his planing machine so he fitted a large box window at one end and fixed a trap-door at the other. If he wanted to plane very long lengths of timber he opened both trap and window and threaded the timber through the trap into the adjoining yard and fed it into the planer. Then as the timber started going through the wall into the machine we could run down the lane and watch it coming out of the window into the raspberry bushes at the other side.

Whenever Thompsons the Drapers of Westgate needed their car out of the garage behind the shop, they always had to check with John George to be certain of a clear road past his workshop. Because of the noise of the planer, Mr Dixon couldn't hear the car starting up next door and he was liable to push a plank out of the trap-door at any time, into the path of the car, with disastrous results.

John George's hobby was not knocking rasps off or hitting cars in the back yard but was concerned with pipe organs. He built his own.

He fitted this organ into his house at West End and as the longest pipes rose to about 14 feet he removed a large section of the bedroom floor and fitted the pipes up from the sitting room below. I never heard him playing but some said they enjoyed his musical sessions. The organ was removed a long time ago and the bedroom floor reinstated.

Two joiners trained by Hylton Seymour have both started their own businesses; John Wilson in the Park Road workshop previously used by Hylton, and Brian Todd in a building at the West End which was originally a lemonade works, then a dairy and a warehouse and now his joiner's shop.

Early plumbers seem to have been J Keen & Sons on Wapping; J Kitchin & Sons, who came from the Carlisle area and had a workshop down the Black Bull Lane, and Harry Irving who went into business with a plumber's workshop on Edens Lawn, almost back-to-back with Kitchin's workshop.

J Kitchin & Sons designed and patented a cattle drinking vessel in the 1920s, made of cast iron with separate ball-valve chamber, before these were in general use in cowsheds countrywide. This was well engineered but slightly bulky for the confines of the cowstalls, so the spring press valve bowl was preferred when it became available and the Kitchin patent went out of favour. Some of Kitchin's models at Wool House Farm near Bardon Mill were still working in 1950 but were about to be replaced for smaller press-valve bowls.

About that time, a well-known company brought out a pressed steel drinking bowl with ball valve which was smaller than Kitchin's but with the same layout; evidently the Haltwhistle patent had lapsed. I helped to remove the Kitchin water bowls from the Wool House byre while I was working for Oliver & Snowdon Ltd. in the early 1950s, then fitted new Fordham spring-push water bowls and service pipes. I started working for O&S in January 1950 after moving back to Haltwhistle from the Bimingham area and one of my first jobs was fitting a free-standing boiler in a new farm building at Muggleswick, Co Durham in extremely cold weather.

Just across the valley was the Consett Iron Works, now demolished, from which periodically would be tipped a load of yellow-hot slag over the foundry tip; I could have utilised some of that heat. Here I was up at this cold exposed place, half-frozen, and there was all that heat going to waste.

Most of the work at O&S was done at the workshops in Westgate, Haltwhistle and at farms within a few miles, but the Hexham office, manned on Tuesdays within the mart, sometimes took on work over a much wider area; they seemed to refuse nothing, even if it meant a long journey to the job.

One job I remember came up when a farmer at Ardley in Hexhamshire phoned for a fitter to come as his old Fordson tractor had expired in the middle of a field. When I got the message I was repairing mowing machines in the workshop and as Ardley was about 20 miles distant, and with no transport other than the shop bike, I thought I would have to refuse, but the farmer agreed to collect me, he was so desperate to get his tractor going. Some time later we set off in his car with what I thought his tractor needed and enjoyed a good 'crack' until at Haydon Spa when we noticed a sinking feeling - a flat tyre.

After I changed the wheel we set off again towards Hexham, where he insisted on taking the wheel to a garage at the other side of the town. Although it was getting late, I didn't mind the extra ride but I thought, 'I bet he does when he gets the bill from O&S for my time.' Eventually, we arrived at the farm and he gave me instructions where to find the tractor, then went off for his tea, while I set off, carrying spanners and a magneto, to the ailing tractor which I spotted in the distance over what looked like half the shire.

J Kitchin's workshop on Black Bull Lane; further down the lane is Church Street which was on the site of what is now Edens Lawn Park. (P Bell)

After a long walk to the machine, a turn of the starting handle told me want I wanted to know, so after fitting the new magneto, the engine started and I drove the old thing back to the farm. The farmer said he would take me to Hexham; he could not go further as he had an appointment; I would have to go home by bus - in my state, half his clay field on my overalls with spanners sticking out and carrying an old oily magneto in black oily hands...well - why not?

I dreaded what the conductress would say but as this was an old rear door bus, I went right to the front as far from other passengers as possible and stood facing the back with the magneto rolling about the floor between my feet. I dared not sit down in my oily state. The conductress took my grubby half-crown and said nothing about black marks. I was glad to get off that bus; it is a long way to stand from Hexham and I felt like an exhibition in front of the other passengers. To cap it all, the workshops were closed and everybody had gone, so I dropped the old magneto in the bin and also went home. Hunger always lured me home.

The next magneto job was much nearer, just at the end of the Haltwhistle Tyne Bridge and the same again: no men, no vehicles, but I just walked down and changed the magneto and walked back again. Costs often caused some amusement, like the time when a milking machine with its many pipelines was installed at one farm and one of the long pipe runs was to be fitted under the yard in a trench. As work proceeded JWJ, the foreman, asked the farmer when the trench was going to be dug as we were almost ready to fit the pipe. Farmer replied that he had no time to dig it and for us lazy 'so and sos' to get on with it.

JWJ thought for a few seconds then said that if we dug it, the cost would be six shillings per hour for each man and the same for any time we were held up waiting for the trench to be dug. I had never seen such a transformation in a man. He marched off, returning with pick, spade and shovel; cobble stones flew in all directions followed by earth and soil and the trench was dug in a very short time. A day or two later JWJ came up to the workshops from the office grinning and chortled: "I've been checking figures and found that after all, the milking machine job had been priced for us to do the trench digging - mebbe that'll teach him not to call us lazy."

On one water-line job I remember saying that some part of the job should be done a different way but JWJ said that was the way it was planned and we had to carry on with it, so I thought: "I bet they find

THE TRENCH WAS DUG IN NO TIME

The flying cobbles.

out some day how wrong it is." Sure enough, some years afterwards, when I had started my own business, I was called to that same installation to renew the long pipeline and the farmers remembered my previous complaint. They laughed, remembering how they had said to JWJ at the time that perhaps I was right, and JWJ had replied: "Yes, I think he's right - but I don't want him to hear me admit that!" and the farmers had another laugh. "Now," I said, "who should be laughing - you're having to pay twice for this job where once would have done." The grins disappeared and I had no more interruptions from them.

What was wrong about the first installation was the fact that we were laying a galvanised steel pipeline through soil with a high content of peat moss, and I knew a similar pipe had been eaten through in six years across a moss in Shropshire. Now it had happened here and had to be renewed with plastic tubing, just as before.

I had always looked forward to the time when I could start my own business. However, a job was advertised in June 1950 for a millwright for British Paints Ltd., as it was called then, at Greystonedale works. I supposed they meant a fitter so I called at the firm's engineering office at Newcastle, where, unbelievably, they had four draughtsmen working at drawing boards in the outer office. 'What can they find mechanical to draw in a paint factory?' I wondered. I told the engineer what kind of jobs I had done and he thought that was fine, so it was arranged that I should start at the factory as soon as possible, although I had always intended to keep clear of full-time factory and mining work.

I soon found out what they meant by millwright: I had to do everything that was needed to keep the factory, or mill, in production. There were still many agitating gear-sets to be made up and fitted in a renewal programme; these consisted of a bevel crown wheel and pinion reduction drive with brakes, fitted to the top of each of the 3000-gallon vats and driven by flat belt from a line-shafting. Most of the electrical installation renewals had been completed.

In this job I could do the work more or less in the way I thought was best and I can't remember any great problems cropping up. In my spare time after work, I rebuilt in the workshop what I thought was an unusual four-seater 1932 MG sports car fitted with a six-cylinder engine. After a bit of racing round the countryside with it, I then sold it and bought a 1937 Singer van. This was in readiness for a future business if I could manage it.

The factory work was interesting and varied and I carried out some work there that I had never been called on to do previously, such as on the steam boiler, the retubing and testing etc., which were on a big scale. The large-flour mill type of grinder had stones fitted that must have weighed almost a ton each and needed dressing at one time; much lighter grinders with metal grinding plates were the only kind I had repaired beforehand.

After two years at BPL, the renewals were completed and I did some of the production work in between repair jobs for another year before I took the plunge and became self-employed.

I made an agreement with BPL to carry out any repairs or renewals as a contractor, and surprisingly a machine broke down on the first Monday after I left BPL's employment. This looked promising, and even if there was about the same number of repair jobs as when I had worked there full-time, together with other work that was building up, I reckoned it would keep me going, and like O&S I took everything that came along. A great help had been the offer from the Edgars at Redpath of free accommodation until I got established and a workshop in part of the old farmhouse and plenty of farm jobs if I ran short of work.

The workshop had been the large dairy in the old house and I well remember in the 1930s, Mrs Edgar asking me to turn the end-over-end churn while they

A butter churn.

were making butter. Until that time, I knew not what went on in the dairy and I hadn't seen this machine that looked like a rain barrel with a steel axle fitted through the sides and fixed-in bearings on a big wooden frame and with a much larger handle than the ones we found on the road and took to West End Garage.

The churn was loaded with cream and it turned all right so they left me to it, but not for long: Mrs Edgar and her help, Jenny, came into the dairy and said I wasn't turning quick enough, so I increased the push and pull on the handle until it suited them. It was very hard work trying to turn the churn and I was informed that the butter would be forming a solid lump.

I was sure of that and soon found out why it was called an end-over-end churn. When I turned the churn until it was just past level, the lump must have slipped from one end to the other and suddenly it pushed the churn round and lifted me off the ground with the handle, then with a struggle, I had to turn the churn from its vertical position, with the lump at one end, until it was just past level once more, when away went the butter with a swish but with me off the handle this time.

I got hold of the churn barrel and pushed it round instead of fighting with the handle, it was easier that way, if slower. After this initiation I dodged the dairy and left Jenny, the little servant girl, to the struggle.

In a special place near the byre, cream separating was done with a hand-turned machine, made by Mellotte in Belgium, and I could manage, even enjoy, that job; the only heavy turning was at the beginning until the spinners were up to speed, which caused a small bell to tinkle; if all went quiet, the men milking in the byre were not long in shouting for more speed.

Cream was stored from each milking until the once-a-week butter-making day; the separated milk was fed to calves and pigs; they gulped it down in a very short time.

The butter churn was installed in the new house dairy when I moved into the old one, with a workbench, welder and tools. Electricity was yet to come to Redpath so I couldn't use the lathe or drilling machine until I found another workshop, which I did in 1954, behind Norman's butcher's shop in Westgate, Haltwhistle; a building always known as Toddy's Stable, which was big enough for four horses.

Toddy was one of the old cartmen, among other things, of Haltwhistle and had a similar business to Ned Keen's, Wallace Laidlow's and the Town Foot Kennedy's. These were some of the first horse-and-cart haulage contractors in the town and continued after motor lorries appeared.

My mother's eldest brother, JW Hunter or Jack, used Toddy's Stable in connection with a business he started in Westgate which failed during the 1926 general strike. Prior to this venture, Jack had worked in Oliver & Snowdon's shop when Matt Coulson, described by Uncle Jack as head and chief, ran the business. Jack worked with Eddy Laidlow, also a shop and warehouse assistant.

One of the dodges these two shop-lads got up to when they fancied a sly smoke was to go upstairs

A separator.

and start mixing various seeds ready for the farm sowings. These were normally mixed in a big tin bath on the wooden floor and dragged round to the various sacks to have the right varieties and quantities added. Jack and Eddy had a different system; they each sat on a sackful of seeds, on opposite sides of the room, lit up the Woodbines then kicked the bath along the floor and thumped a part-filled sack on the floor. After a short time, the other smoker kicked the bath back along the floor and thumped his sack.

Downstairs, Matt carried on serving his customers, evidently quite pleased to hear the industrious lads working so hard upstairs, although he did shout up on occasions asking if there was something burning up there; Jack said this usually happened when they forgot to open the windows but years later he wondered if Matt knew what went on anyway.

Jack left O&S to start a similar business in the Westgate shop, previously known as Askew's Stores, in the 1920s, with Mother as the travelling saleswoman - on a bike. It was not easy, starting in opposition to O&S and John Liddell & Son, so I was surprised when Uncle Jack said that he had fitted

a number of farm cream separators; O&S always thought they had the monopoly in supplying these machines. Unfortunately for Jack, he started just before the 1926 strike and during that time he supplied foodstuffs to friends and acquaintances on a promise; they had no money at the time, but the bank didn't work on promises, so he went 'bust'. Another drawback was the late payment of accounts by farming customers; they never paid until they sold their lambs in the autumn or cattle in the spring; usually six months after the bill was presented.

The shop and house were taken over by Thompsons the drapers and Toddy's Stable was used by JG Dixon for his joiner's shop, where we watched the timber moving into one end of the building and out the other as it went through the planer machine. When JG gave up the stables, they were unused for a time until they were required by the Ministry of Food, who laid a new concrete floor, fitted a new door and adapted the building for meat distribution.

After Ministry of Food days the stable was unused until I rented it in 1954 from Normans' the butchers;

JW (Jack) Hunter.
(M Hunter)

A 1920s view of Westgate, Haltwhistle; JW Hunter shop on left; Oliver & Snowdon shop further down street on right where JWH previously worked.
(C Keen)

I fitted corner stairs to replace the small trap-door and ladder from the stable hayloft and fitted two lengths of Cascalite sheeting in the roof to admit daylight to the loft. A doorway high up in the wall which had been used to fork hay into the loft for the horses was ideal for admitting long lengths of steel pipes and timber for storage.

At that time there was plenty of work in the plumbing and building industries and I did a lot of work for JV Little, who had taken over Harry Irving's plumbing business and couldn't cope with the amount of work. Government grants on installing new bathrooms boosted this work, but a great deal of renewal work was required in those houses which didn't qualify for grants; nevertheless, householders were anxious to have their homes modernised.

Some West End houses had bathrooms fitted when built in the early 1900s and were ready for renewing. Kitchins', the old established plumbers, installed most of the lead-piped plumbing in the Crossfield Streets when bathrooms were more of a curio than anything else. The pipes were on the surface, it was hinted, to show visitors that the householders had 'real' plumbing.

Those were the days of wiped solder joints on lead pipes and as I remember, the joints made by Kitchins' were watertight but without the smooth finish of those made many years later by Mattie Reay or Charlie Makepeace at J Keen & Sons'; the work of Harry Irving and his trainees appeared to be polished.

Harry Irving, during his training, worked on housing schemes in the Newcastle area and as he liked soldering lead joints, he got most of them to do, so he would get plenty of practice.

The longest wiped solder joints that I heard of in the district were done by Harry at the local paint factory, when the lead linings of some large storage tanks ruptured and he ended up redoing most of the original jointing, in addition to the repairs. They were yards long and to make matters worse, the fumes caused by the heat of soldering near oil made breathing difficult, so fresh air had to be blown into the tanks. Nowadays they would use plastic linings.

I once heard about Harry joining a large lead pipe at Gilsland and, as often happened, a few onlookers gathered to watch the performance. I suspect he was a bit of a showman and made an elegant job of blow-lamping and wiping the almost molten solder round the joint, and when he considered the joint to be complete, he whipped out his handkerchief with a great flourish and holding it taut between his hands, deftly removed the very slight ridge left where he had stopped wiping. Apprentice Robbie said he was proud to have been associated with that pipe job, which was talked about for a long time after.

I still have some solder wiping cloths but very rarely use them; the steel parts of the blow lamps have long since gone rusty.

Most builders seem to have their own plumbing departments nowadays but there are still local plumbing businesses such as John Sweet's, Jim Todd's, and others I don't know about.

After using Toddy's Stable for two years, I noticed a 'For Sale' sign on a shop known as Hunter's Tea Store, with a substantial cellar and which had been rented by Broughs Ltd. for their grocer's shop until they bought another shop further up Westgate. A Mr Thompson from Haydon Bridge bought it from Hunters intending to start a drapery business but the firm he worked for made him a director so the shop came back on to the market. I thought if I could repair a few floor-boards and some of the plaster I could start a shop and have the huge cellar below as a workshop.

As usual, there is always much more work than anticipated to be done on old buildings and the Westgate shop was no exception; everything in the shop was removed: floors, ceilings, wall coverings and the shop front with windows and door.

Hunter's Tea Store on left of photo, later to become John Parker's shop. (S Blackburn)

Improvements took about nine months, working in my spare time, just to make the shop area presentable for opening; the rest of the building took much longer.

Before buying the shop, I worked on bathroom renewals for JV Little and then for many local builders. As the rush for new bathrooms and kitchens slackened off, I took on more building work which merged with the shop repairs; buckets of mixed cement left over from contracts during the day were used in the shop repairs in the evenings, which saved a lot of waste. This went on for some years until I had renewed everything and extended the property until it was almost twice the original size; only the original stone wall above the shop front and the two gable ends remained unaltered.

I doubt if I would have gone near the place if I had known it needed so much work done, until I realised it was for my own benefit when I ended up with a good workshop in the basement, a modern shop and two more levels above.

The two shops next door on the east side had a few changes before and while I was doing my alterations. Broughs, having bought the shop two doors away, had the former cafe altered, including the fitting of a much wider shop window; unfortunately, while this work was being carried out, the supports gave way and all the stonework above crashed down on to the pavement. Fortunately nobody was hurt, the walls were built up again and the work finished, enabling Broughs to move into their new shop.

Meanwhile, I married and we moved into the same house that our family had flitted to all those years ago from Redpath. After a few years, and with two young children, we thought it would be more convenient to construct a flat above the shop instead of the second showroom that had been planned, and as this work progressed, the shop between ours and Brough's new shop came on to the market when Oakland Nurseries decided to relinquish their fruit and vegetable shop and concentrate on the Melkridge Nurseries.

Broughs bought the Oaklands shop to join on to their new one and moved out into what had been Dryden's shoe shop; this enabled the two shops to be demolished and a new steel-framed building erected on the site.

After the builders had set all the foundation bolts, this steel structure was quickly erected with the aid of a crane and a few spider-like experts bolting the girders together. When it was finished and ready for the builders to fill in the walls, I could quite easily rock the whole structure by hand from our roof, but after the bricks were built in, everything was then firm enough. We moved into our new flat just after Broughs moved into their new shop.

Our alterations were never completed; we hankered after being back in the country and bought Slaggyford Station House and yard with outline planning for two houses, the intention being to build the two houses, one to live in and the other to sell to pay for the building work involved. Before we even started on detailed plans, a house with some land became available with vacant possession, so we sold the shop with many improvements still undone and moved out.

Plans for improvements don't always turn out as intended and we were certainly not the first to change our minds.

About 1920, Murrays planned on expanding their West End lemonade works at Tyne View, with a view to sending their products over a much wider area - by rail. Behind the works where their property adjoined railway land, concrete was used to form a loading point but it is doubtful if railway sidings were ever extended this far. Murrays evidently thought it better to move to a new factory on Main Street and continue to deliver their products by road; which they did until Mr Murray retired and the firm closed down in the 1980s. The West End property was used as Keen's Dairy or Creamery, Nichol Elliott's warehouse, Holden's Oil Registers and is now Brian Todd's joiner's shop.

Changes in trading have resulted in the disappearance of many of the older craftsmen such as tailors, cobblers and saddlers. At one time, Foster & Robison, which is now Clive Brown's, employed tailors in the rear workrooms of their Market Place shop and Dent the tailor was kept busy up the steps in Crown Court. Hastewells also employed tailors but for the many years I have known of him, Jackie Maughan was always self-employed at Town Hall Crescent and carried out high quality tailoring.

In the saddlery trade there were Greggs and Richardson, both on the Market Place, south side, but of course most of their trade disappeared when tractors took over from farm horses.

Cobblers continued slightly longer but most shoe repairs, if people bother with them, are sent further afield nowadays. In the 1930s and 40s, clog and shoemakers Hudspith, Dickinson, Co-op, Waugh, Drydon and Leighton and possibly others, worked as cobblers and all were kept busy.

Another trade that seems to be much reduced in numbers is that of printing, possibly because the machines used now are so much more efficient. Modern computers and machines are worlds apart from the old printing machines. At one time, machines at Mansfields, Saints and Grahams thumped away all day, as well as the machines of spare-time printers with their Adanas, etc. Present day printers are Blakes at the West End Industrial Estate.

Left: Bobby Robison stands outside his shop in Haltwhistle Market Place. (S Blackburn)
Below: WE Pape's clogmaker's shop east of Market Place (now Archway Cottage). (I Hunter)

Quite an important industry was built up in the district by the bakery trades, which I thought had all disappeared, but apparently not quite all.

Elliotts of Haltwhistle always spring to mind when I think of bakers in the town in earlier days but there were Birketts at Park View and the Co-op up Park Road in a very unhygenic-looking corrugated iron shed.

Many smaller 'home' bakers flourished and one of them, Tommy Hannah, with his ever-spotless white apron, waxed moustache and flattened hair-style, could be described as such. He baked in the kitchen of the house part and carried his wares straight into the shop which is now Greggs, Sports Outfitters.

Elliotts on the other hand employed many men and women at their extensive bakery on Aesica Road. Three large ovens were in use plus a steam-heated proving oven. These were coke-fired at one time, then converted to gas, then finally to oil-firing. A speciality in the 1930s was chocolate eclairs. The plain eclairs, after baking, were put through a long machine on a conveyor belt where they came under a curtain of molten chocolate and were cooled off in readiness for packing by the time they reached the far end. Many a time we paused on our way to school and enviously watched this operation, through the window facing on to Banks Terrace.

20 years later I was there when this machine or a similar one was dismantled on the first floor, together with the steam-heated chocolate-melter, for shipment to Ireland. A bread-slicer and wrapping machine stood in the bakery for a time but I never saw it working and I was never asked to fit it up. It also went to Ireland eventually.

When bread and cakes production ceased, the bakery produced dog rusks for some time and part of the building was used as a storage depot. About that time I had some fun altering a bread-slicer to cut thicker slices for these rusks.

Some time later the firm decided to install an elevator from the ground floor up to the middle floor where the rusk oven and slicers were situated and on to the top floor.

This long elevator, very much like a hay-bale elevator, was to be used for moving sacks of raw materials up to the top floor and finished rusks down to the ground-floor loading point; it had to be capable of forward and reverse push-button control from any one of the three floors.

After the machinery was fitted, wired up and switched on, only a disappointing buzz came from the driving motor. The fitter most probably felt as Norman Renwick did with Isaac Hetherington's sawmill motor in the 1930s, but was certain, just as Norman had been, that all the wiring was fitted exactly to the maker's diagram. All terminal blocks and wiring were rechecked but still the motor refused to start.

One man took the diagram home with him to study in the evening and arrived the next day to say he was sure that one particular cable was in the wrong terminals. These were changed over and away it went. It transpired that a missing small part of the diagram showed where the change-over occurred in the harness wiring, but whatever the fault was, the elevator did the job satisfactorily for some years.

Bread and cake delivery vans loaded up from ever-changing stocks, supplied by Graves bakery at Chester-le-Street. Bread left unsold on the van was mixed into the dog rusk dough the next day, slapped into loaf tins, half-cooked, the loaves sliced double thickness and laid on drying trays in a large gas-fired oven until crisp, then bagged up and sent to various greyhound kennels throughout the country.

Elliotts were very fortunate in having an ingenious mechanic to keep their delivery vans on the road. Jimmy Pratt must have rebuilt many of the Bedford vans, most of which were 1930s vintage, as well as fitting them out with sliding trays and framework for carrying bread and cakes. He carried out most of this work in a large garage/workshop on the Pinfold, near the bottom of the Comb Hill, and kept the vehicles mobile until he retired. The firm then gradually replaced Jimmy's vans with larger models. Jimmy bored out the cylinders in a few of our van engines when they became worn and fitted new pistons for us, usually in his spare time in the evenings - and I never found any fault with his work.

After a time the dog-rusk making ceased and the bakery closed to be opened by another firm, who moved their pressure washer assembly factory from the old South Tyne Colliery buildings.

The Co-op Bakery on Park Road also closed and was converted to lock-up garages in the 1950s; the Co-op later took over the Gilsland bakery from N Elliott about 1960 and ran it for some years before closing down what had been the original Wardle's of Gilsland Bakery.

Fortunately, all is not lost; although Birketts closed their bakery business, the present owners, G & ME

Reed of Park View, again produce a wide variety of home baking, carrying on a tradition of many years standing at this shop. The presentation of the products in clean and smart surroundings is nice to see and reassuring. As a bonus, the enticing smell of new baking often wafts along the street in this end of Haltwhistle.

Birketts' bakery business first started in Haltwhistle and I believe that by 1996, from their headquarters at Penrith, they ran 200 shops and three bakeries, so if Mr and Mrs Reed are modelling themselves on Birketts they still have a few more shops to go.

Two other firms, Oliver & Snowdon and John Liddell & Son, were originally millers and corn merchants and also agricultural suppliers.

One of these firms supplied the first horse-drawn grass-mowing machine in the district, which I think was a McCormick. At that time hay meadows were mown by gangs of men with scythes, so a fair gathering of farmers came to see this machine perform in a field which was later the football field and is now built over by the houses of Westlands. A cut of about three feet wide was taken at horse-walking speed, which amazed the onlookers, but it was quickly condemned because they said that the machine blades 'chattered' the grass stalks and this would prevent the latermath or the 'fog' from growing properly. The farmers were converted later. McCormick had developed the mowing machine in about 1834 in the USA but it was near half a century later before Haltwhistle saw it. Those farmers would have been confounded by today's high speed-mowers, which make more of a scything cut and don't 'chatter' the grass. As we all know 'fog' grows whatever kind of mowing machine is used and so farmers bought the machines in any case. These were followed by rakers, turners, strewers, etc. but like metal ploughs and stitchers, were manufactured by firms a distance from Haltwhistle, unlike the now collectable wooden harrow sets, carts, hay bogies, sledge/clod crushers and the like

Wooden harrows made by Haltwhistle blacksmiths and joiners. The pull being offset from the centre, the harrows dragged at an angle enabling the spikes to cover all the area under them so did not need to be made like the modern 'zig-zag' type. (D Hunter)

which were made by the above two firms and local joiners; ironwork came from local blacksmiths.

Later Oliver & Snowdon and Liddells supplied and repaired farm tractors and implements. Fitters were employed for repairing farm machinery and installing the early cream separators, water bowls, milking machines and parlours.

Another sideline was the supplying of wind-powered water pumps made by Goodwin, the nearest to Haltwhistle that I know of being at Fell House Farm. This pump unfortunately was allowed to grind itself to a standstill after mains water was installed. These high windmills were erected by Goodwins' own fitters and the last time I saw them performing was at Wardoughan Farm, Gilsland when they fitted a windmill for Joe Jackson in 1945.

I remember working on the top of this mill in the middle of that bleak 1963 winter replacing a broken pump lift-rod. It could not have happened at a colder time but Joe promised - from ground level - to try and arrange any future breakdowns for the middle of the summer. I threw my gloves down at him, I couldn't work with them on anyway.

Oliver & Snowdon and Liddells fitted the pipelines from these wind-pumps to the farm buildings but later they also fitted electrically-driven pumps. Now wind-power seems to be making a comeback but sadly both of these firms have been absorbed by larger companies and the Haltwhistle premises changed to other businesses.

Another long-gone small industry was worked by Haltwhistle people, although the 'factory' was situated in a yard behind Railway Terrace, Greenhead and near the old locomotive shed. Good quality stockings were produced there and I believe Mrs Elliott from Fair Hill West and Thompsons the drapers were some of the people involved. Most of the older miners wore very strong knee stockings for their work and many of them would be made at Greenhead.

Windmill at the Centre for Alternative Technology, Machynlleth, Powys.

A 1920s photograph of a young George Wardle standing with the family bakery van near Gilsland shows him wearing an example of the type of stockings manufactured at the Greenhead factory.

Incidentally, readers might be interested to know that the Greenhead loco shed of 1836, used for some years by Alf Surtees for his coal business, is the oldest intact loco shed in the country. Although it is many years since I first went into it, the lines were still set in the floor and there was a long filled-in inspection pit for locos.

According to railway historians, this shed was used for the two years that the railway from Carlisle terminated at Greenhead; when the Newcastle and Carlisle Railway was completed, the shed was closed and no locos were stabled there after that time, about 160 ago. With coal trucks to shunt at Bank Foot for Blenkinsopp Mine, for the pit yard at Barron House for Thirlwall Colliery just west of Greenhead, and for the later whinstone quarry aerial flight terminal in the station, it would have made sense to stable the shunting-engine in the shed. Truck-hauling could be done by horses in the pit yards, but locos normally would be used near the running lines.

Many traditional industries have gone, to be replaced by less labour-intensive concerns; it is doubtful if local firms could employ as many as they did in, say, the 1920s, considering that the Plenmeller Colliery work-force varied from three up to five hundred men and boys and South Tyne Colliery about the same, plus the many workers involved in other industries large and small.

A great deal is owed to those enterprising businesses which over the years have contributed so much to this ' town of all sorts' and have kept Haltwhistle and its people industrious.

Above: A young George Wardle with what appears to be a Chevrolet bakery van near Gilsland Spa Hotel about 1922.
Right: Aerial photo of Greenhead: old Greenhead bank on left, Glenwelt bank centre; the loco shed is the large building north of the railway, towards the left of the photo. (S Blackburn)

P.S. for JP

Sadly, my very dear husband died of lung cancer before his book was published. J.P. was blessed with a phenomenal memory, enjoyed a wide range of interests and had a talent for innovation: he was part of that all-but-lost Britain described by Robert Stephenson as: "A nation of mechanical engineers." I was privileged to share the life of this truly remarkable man; not given to shows of emotion, he wanted to be remembered not with a tear but with a smile as that engendered by that particularly Haltwhistle brand of dry humour, illustrated by his response to an anxiously hovering colliery-manager worried by an ocean of rapidly rising water, caused by a power-cut. J.P.: "Wey - what di yi want me ti dee - drink eet?"

'I wish you the deep peace of the quiet earth.' D.P.

JP at Blenkinsopp Collieries taking a break to do a spot of 'fishing'. J Parker (jnr)